Handmade
for Profit!

OTHER BOOKS BY BARBARA BRABEC

Homemade Money

Creative Cash

Handmade for Profit!

Hundreds of Secrets to Success in Selling Arts & Crafts

Barbara Brabec

M. Evans and Company, Inc.
NEW YORK

Illustrations on pages 4, 7, 14, 23, 25, 31, 48, 70, 74, 75, 91, 111, 124, 130, 145, 162, 173, 201, 205, 245, 252, 253, and 255 courtesy of *Crafts Magazine*. Used with permission of PJS Publications Inc., a K-III Communications Company. Copyright © 1987 to 1996 *Crafts Magazine*.

M. Evans and Company, Inc.
216 East 49th Street
New York, New York 10017

Library of Congress Cataloging-in-Publication Data

Brabec, Barbara
    Handmade for profit : hundreds of secrets to success in selling arts & crafts / Barbara Brabec
        p.   cm.
    Includes index.
    ISBN 0-87131-800-8 (cloth). — ISBN 0-87131-812-1 (pbk.)
    1. Handicraft industries—Management.   2. Selling—Handicraft.
I. Title.
HD2341.B713   1996
745.5'068—dc20   96-22960
                                                                                    CIP

Design and composition by John Reinhardt Book Design

Manufactured in the United States of America

9   8   7   6   5   4   3   2   1

For my husband, Harry,
who has patiently tolerated me and my craft activities
for more than thirty-five years.

Acknowledgments

I want to thank Judith Brossart, editor of *Crafts Magazine*, for the help and encouragement she has always given me and my writing. By publishing my monthly crafts marketing column, she has enabled me to regularly communicate with hundreds of thousands of crafters throughout North America for nearly twenty years. As a result, I've been able to gather and pass along a unique collection of information and ideas helpful to others.

My special thanks to everyone who has ever taken the time to write to me. By generously sharing their experiences and creative marketing ideas, these individuals have shown concern for and love of their fellow crafters.

Contents

Foreword

For more than seventeen years, Barbara Brabec has been advising readers of *Crafts Magazine* how to "Sell What You Make." If you had purchased each of the more than 200 issues for which she has written a column, you would have spent more than $500 for just some of the advice Barbara has included in *Handmade for Profit!* The book you're holding is a real bargain! In it, you'll find invaluable advice that can help you turn your crafting activities into the proverbial gold mine.

In 1979 when Barbara wrote her first column for *Crafts Magazine*, women were just starting to use their creativity to sell crafts they made around their kitchen tables in order to make "pin money" to supplement their family incomes. In the seventeen years they've been following Barbara's advice, they've grown in number and have become more savvy at buying their supplies wholesale and pricing their wares at profit-making retail prices. She has encouraged them to promote themselves with flyers, catalogs, and things as simple as business cards and stationery. She has taught them how to build a display for a crafts fair, how to find out-of-state customers and, more importantly, how to make more money.

Over the years, selling handmade crafts for extra money has evolved into a full-time business for many families. As business has grown too large for the kitchen table, scores of husbands have joined their wives in their endeavors and that "hobby" is now the mainstay of many a family's income. Currently 42 percent, or 168,000 *Crafts* readers, sell what they make. Of these 168,000 readers, 30,000 consider selling their crafts, a homebased business. And many of them have eagerly read and followed every word Barbara has written.

Now in the 90s, as corporate America is downsizing and laying off thousands of people, we're seeing a shift in business in America. Forced by circumstances beyond their control, many of those displaced workers who are leisure-time crafters are going to turn to their crafts to build a small, profitable business. I firmly believe that *Handmade for Profit!* will be the textbook of choice for those who desire to control their own financial destiny.

—Judith Brossart,
Editor, *Crafts Magazine*

CHAPTER ONE

The "Creative Cash" Market

Throughout North America, thousands of people are experiencing "craft encounters of the closest kind" as they suddenly discover they have a creative streak or artistic talent.

Thanks to the many books and magazines that now offer how-to projects and patterns, the average person can easily learn any art or craft technique of interest. And people everywhere do have a great desire to practice an art or craft themselves. This trend was first documented in a 1975 survey conducted by the National Research Center of the Arts, which also revealed that 75 percent of the public thought it was important to have a community center where one could learn arts and crafts.

Crafts and hobbies have become big business in the past decade. Today, 90 percent of American households have at least one person participating in crafts, and these consumers are spending over ten million dollars a year on craft supplies and related products. "Crafts have exploded in the 90s," says Pat Koziol, executive director of the Hobby Industry Association (HIA). "The leisure market, of which crafting is the most creative part, represents a significant amount in consumer sales yearly. We can safely say that crafts and crafting have arrived."

In an article for *USA Today*, Anita Manning reported on the growing number of people under pressure in their jobs who have turned to crafts for stress relief in the 90s. "They do it not only to express creativity but to work off anxieties," she said. "Craft work fits enjoyably into their stressed-out schedules and budgets."

A crafts hobby can bring much more than fun and stress relief, however. When properly developed, your art or craft skills can help you earn what I call "creative cash," a phrase I coined in 1979 when I wrote a best-selling book by that title. Like that book, this one explains how to earn a share of today's "creative cash market" simply by doing things you enjoy most and may already do best. The primary goal of this book is to help you start making money from your art or craft hobby *right now* or, if you're already selling what you make, to help you increase sales and annual profits.

Crafts' Importance to the Economy

No one knows for sure how many homebased businesses there are in the United States and Canada, or how many of them might be craft-oriented. We know only that the numbers are significant and rising. Estimates on the size of the U.S. home business industry range from seven to twenty-four million part- and full-time businesses, depending on whose statistics you read. While some market research experts have placed the dollar size of this industry as high as $383 billion annually, this is merely an educated guess. Based on research done by some states, however, it is reasonable to believe that the annual economic impact of homebased *craft* businesses is $3 billion or more.

In Canada, similar research shows that one in four homes has a homebased business, and many of them are craft businesses. A mid-90s survey found that homebased businesses were then contributing $1.2 billion to the economy—almost as much as Canada's fishing and mining industries. At the same time, a study in England revealed that crafts were contributing about $130 million to that country's gross national product, not counting "under the table" craft businesses.

"The crafts industry is growing at a rate exceeding the expectations of market analysts," says crafts publisher Bill Ronay, "and it's enjoying an equal if not greater exploitation by the consuming public. Arts and crafts have become a vital part of everyday life and they are spawning new industries in the process. Craft malls are but one example."

Arts and crafts are popular in many other countries, too. My readers have reported on the increasing craft activity in South Africa, New Zealand, and Australia. Puerto Rico has a huge community of professional artisans, and in Mexico the production of such crafts as ceramics, weavings, and woodcarvings has made many rural Mexicans prosperous. In 1988, to draw attention to crafts and the benefits derived from craft activities, two of the major craft industry trade associations designated March as National Craft Month. Now this American celebration is spreading around the world as various national associations plan events reflecting cultural differences and crafting preferences.

Who's Crafting and Why

Except in the area of woodworking, where about two-thirds of the participants are male, hobbycrafters are far more likely to be female than male, reports HIA. Many males also work in leather crafts, art and drawing, glass crafts and do-it-yourself framing. Among women, needlecraft remains the most popular craft activity in 80 percent of households. Other craft activities of high interest include wreath and wall decor, cross-stitch embroidery, ceramics, weaving, beading/beadcrafts and jewelry making. I believe most of America's crafters fall into one of four categories:

1. Hobbyists who craft just for the fun of it
2. Those who sell occasionally (or want to)
3. Part-time crafters who earn a substantial amount of money from their crafts, yet may not feel they are really "in business"
4. Craft professionals (called "professional crafters" or PCs by some) whose primary goal in selling is to earn a part- or full-time living.

Because there are hundreds of different arts and crafts, individuals who work with their hands tend to think of themselves in specific terms, such as stitcher, quilter, painter, woodworker, stained glass artist, jeweler, potter, folk artist, weaver, spinner, basketmaker, dollmaker and so on. Some of these people are "craftsmen" and some are "craftswomen," but because of the sensitivity many people have expressed about sexist language, it is now common for writers to refer to groups of creative people as "artists," "craftspeople," "artisans," "crafters," and so on. If you are a needleworker or home sewer, or someone who practices an unusual craft, please don't feel left out when I use these broad terms. If you make anything by hand, you are part of the huge and steadily growing arts and crafts industry. [NOTE: In their zeal to make sure no one is offended, some editors ask writers not to use the word "craftsmanship," but I think it would be a shame to let such a beautiful word fall from our language. Whether politically correct or not, this word cannot easily be replaced. Fine craftsmanship is, and always will be, the hallmark of a successful craft producer.]

Since more women than men craft, it follows that more women than men start homebased craft businesses. Supporting this statement are figures I got from a spokesperson for Coomers craft malls. Some eight thousand crafters sell through these stores, but only 20 percent or so are male. In the past twenty-five years, I figure I've received at least two hundred thousand letters from people who were interested or involved in arts and crafts, and I'd guess that about 95 percent of this mail has been from women. For some reason, men don't search out or share information the way women do. (Humorously speaking, I think this has something to do with the fact that a man, when lost, will drive for hours before he will ask anyone for directions, while a woman's first instinct is to pull into the nearest gas station for help.) It should not be surprising, then, that most of the tips and ideas in this book have come from women.

What This Book Will Do for You

This book contains all the information you need to get started selling at the retail level and keep growing. It is a collection of the best crafts marketing tips and ideas gleaned from twenty years of publishing a periodical and writing craft magazine columns. One of those columns, "Selling What You Make," has been running in *Crafts Magazine* since 1978. Through the years, thousands of readers have shared their experiences and success tips with me, and many of them are quoted by name in this book. Although I'm no longer in touch with all of these individuals, I am nonetheless grateful to them for originally sharing information with me so I could pass it along to others. It is their real-life experiences that give this book its authenticity and excitement. If you will read it carefully and *apply the information it offers,* I guarantee it will

- Show you how to start making money *right now* from something you love to do
- Increase your sales and profits if you're already selling
- Encourage you to get more serious about the business side of crafts
- Prompt you to set exciting new life goals.

Notice the emphasis on "apply the information"? You know that old saying about leading a horse to water. While I can give you all the information you need to successfully sell handmade items of any kind, I can't force you to get out and do this. I can only try to prompt you to action with words and encouraging examples of how others have done this. With all the crafts writing I've done in the past twenty-five years, I figure I've helped launch more craft businesses than

Helen of Troy launched ships. With this new book, I hope to help launch thousands more.

Your "GET READY" Recipe for Success

To start making money from your arts and crafts talents, follow the steps in my "GET READY Recipe for Success":

G et it together! As soon as your home begins to share space with a moneymaking venture, everything changes. You will save time and stress by getting your home and personal life organized before you begin to sell your handmade creations.

E ducate yourself to your possibilities for financial profit from selling handcrafts and related products and services. Attend craft conferences, small business workshops, join art or craft organizations, and read, read, *read*!

T alk to other creative people who share your enthusiasm for crafts. Browse craft fairs and write letters to interesting people you've read about. Take every available opportunity to network.

R esolve to give your new endeavor your best effort. Remember these four *P*s of accomplishment: Plan purposefully, Prepare prayerfully, Proceed positively, and Pursue persistently.

E mulate but do not copy the products, designs, and selling methods used by others. You are unique, and God has given you special gifts or abilities that no other person has. Your challenge in life is to discover and develop them. (Tip: Generally, these are things that come easy for you, things you seem to have a natural "bent" for.)

A nticipate that you will have problems. *Everyone* has problems. Fortunately, this book offers solutions to the most common problems you're likely to encounter in starting a business at home.

D evelop a written plan of everything you need to do to get started selling. As a wise man once said, "If you don't know where you're going, you might miss it when you get there."

Y OU are the most special ingredient in this recipe, so begin by remembering that you can do anything you set your heart on doing. If there is no one else around to do it, it's okay to pat yourself on the back each time you achieve a new goal or do something you didn't know you could do.

There has been a well-established professional arts and crafts community since the mid-60s, and dozens of periodicals and organizations now serve the small business needs of North America's professional artists and crafters. Hundreds more cater to the interests of hobbyists in this field. Of the ten million dollars now spent annually on craft supplies, professional crafters are spending approximately two million, says Maria Nerius, editor of *Craft Supply Magazine*.

At this time you still may be learning or working to perfect a particular art or craft. As you make one new handmade creation after another, you may find yourself thinking, "This is great! I didn't know I could do this!" Your friends and family may be showing signs of amazement, if not outright envy, and you can hardly wait to try that new idea you got this morning.

As exciting as it can be to just make things, it's doubly exciting when you begin to sell what you make and get positive feedback from appreciative buyers. As soon as you take this step, I guarantee all kinds of interesting things will happen. You will gain self-confidence and poise. You will get ideas you could not have envisioned before getting out in the public as a seller. While selling at fairs and shows, you will meet people you never would have met otherwise. Shop owners may approach you, asking if you could sell to them at wholesale prices, and someone from your local paper may want to interview you. If you are featured in the paper, your spouse will be amazed, your family will be proud, your friends and neighbors will be impressed, and you will be so excited you can't sleep.

You will never know where your talents and ideas might take you if you don't give them a chance to grow and develop. Where arts and crafts are concerned, ordinary people often accomplish the most extraordinary things. Don't you agree the possibilities ought to be explored?

So Many Crafts, So Many Possibilities!

Have you ever thought about the many things that people do
   in their homes for fun and profit? Well, I have, and so should you.
Today a living room is apt to share its time and space
   with equipment used to make things for the busy marketplace.

Here yarns are spun and weavings done for sale to stores or shops,
   and with work like this in progress, all normal housework stops!
In cozy little offices in rooms once used for dining,
   more than one ambitious person will be writing or designing.

Creative people don't just sleep in rooms that hold a bed;
   they may be doing needlepoint and quilting there instead.
The bathroom also doubles as a workroom now and then,
   where people go to dye their yarn or dip batik again.

These days the rec room isn't used for pool or cards or darts;
   it's now a little factory where the craft production starts.
Dad and Mom and all the kids may go there after dinner
   to manufacture something that is sure to be a winner.

And think of all the cars without a roof above their hoods,
   'cause garages aren't for parking, they're for crafting arty goods.
Like wooden toys, ceramic work or things made out of glass,
   or metal sculpture, furniture or objets d'art en masse.

And the kitchen? Ah, the kitchen, it is such a busy place,
   but the things that are a cookin' won't end up inside your face.
Take bread dough for example, it's not what you bake and eat,
   it's something that you bake, then paint, in colors nice 'n' neat.

Do you begin to see the point poetically I'm making—
   that "arts and crafts" (now household words) are sometimes overtaking
entire households, stem to stern, disrupting normal living . . .
   yet sometimes satisfaction is the only thing they're giving.

If this is true with you, my friend, you ought to do some thinking.
   Perhaps it's time to sell the crafts you spend so much time making.
Because you give your arts and crafts their very sustenance,
   don't you agree it would be nice if they helped pay the rent?

More Help on Library Shelves

Thousands of new books are published every year, some of which are bound to be on your favorite art, craft or hobby. To learn about them, get acquainted with *Books in Print*. This annual directory is supplemented with periodic editions of *Guide to Forthcoming Books*. Look under subject categories of interest to turn up new book titles and pertinent information regarding each book's publisher, publication date, price, etc. When you've listed

In a survey of its readers in 1993, *Craft Supply Magazine* found that its average reader was:

". . . a woman, age 38, who decided to turn her passion for crafts into a business. After five years of struggling at the kitchen table, handling everything from manufacturing and marketing to accounting and sales, she obtained the financing necessary to make the business grow. She now owns and operates a business that either solely supports or supplements the family income."

all the books that sound exciting to you, check the card index or computerized information system in your library to see if they are on library shelves. To get you started, I've included a short recommended reading list below and at the end of most chapters in this book. If you can't locate a particular book in a bookstore, and it's not on library shelves either, remember that most libraries can obtain hard-to-find books through their Inter-Library Loan program.

While browsing in the library, take a look at these problem-solving reference directories:

■ *The Standard Periodical Directory* and *Ulrich's International Periodicals Directory*. These directories are helpful if you know the name of a magazine or newsletter but lack its address. These two annuals describe thousands of consumer magazines, trade journals, newsletters, government publications, directories, yearbooks and other periodicals in both the United States and Canada. Listings are arranged alphabetically as well as by subject matter.

■ *Encyclopedia of Associations*. There are organizations for just about every art and craft you can name, and many publish periodicals or sponsor conferences and trade shows to help members get ahead. This directory will help you connect with them. Membership in an art or craft organization may enable you to buy more affordable health insurance and obtain merchant status for your business. Many organizations also offer discounts on office supplies and raw materials and publish a member newsletter or directory.

■ The *Thomas Register of American Manufacturers*. Its twenty-three volumes profile more than 150,000 companies with a description of over 50,000 individual product and service headings and 112,000 trade and brand names. Very helpful when you're trying to locate raw material suppliers, wholesale supply sources, or the owners of brand names and trademarks. Companies are listed alphabetically and by type of product.

Recommended Reading

- *The Basic Guide to Selling Arts & Crafts* by James Dillehay (Warm Snow Publishers).
- *Crafting as a Business—The Do-it-Yourself Guide to a Successful Crafts Business* by Wendy Rosen (Chilton Book Co).
- *Crafting for Dollars—How to Establish & Profit from a Career in Crafts* by Sylvia Landman (Prima).
- *Creative Cash: How to Sell Your Crafts, Needlework, Designs & Know-How*, 5th edition, by Barbara Brabec (Barbara Brabec Productions).
- *How to Start Making Money with Your Crafts* by Kathryn Caputo (Betterway Books).
- *Selling What You Make: Profit from Your Handcrafts* by James E. Seitz, Ph.D. (TAB Books.)
- *You Can Make Money from Your Arts and Crafts* by Steve and Cindy Long (Mark Publishing).

NOTE: In addition to books available in bookstores and libraries, there are dozens of self-published craft business manuals, how-to guides, reports, marketing directories, newsletters and magazines available only by mail from individual homebased publishers. Often, such publications contain inside information unavailable from any other source. Because such resources come and go with constant address and price changes, I keep such information up-to-date on computer and publish it in the form of laser-printed resource lists. For more information, write to Barbara Brabec Productions, Dept. HFP, P.O. Box 2137, Naperville, IL 60567.

CHAPTER TWO

Building Confidence and Setting Goals

If you feel fearful and insecure, it's not because you lack cour-age or self-confidence, only that you've locked them inside you for so long they can't get out. What you have to do is find the key that unlocks the door.

If you have not yet begun to sell the things you make, look around your home and tell me what you see. By any chance, have you reached what I call the "crafts saturation point?" That is, are you now making so many things you can't give all of them away? I went through this phase myself back in the 60s, and my real motivation to sell came the day my husband walked into my hobby room and said, "Your crafts are nice . . . but what are you going to *do* with all of this stuff?"

I knew then that I had to do one of two things: stop producing or start selling. Every serious crafter eventually reaches this point and almost has to start selling if only to pay for supplies and make room for new creations yet to come. In time, even those who only craft for fun will begin to entertain the idea of selling when friends begin to comment, "Your work is lovely! Have you ever thought about selling it?"

Although many people will never find the courage to plunge into the mar-ketplace, the idea of selling may lurk in their minds like a cat waiting for a mouse to make its move. Once a person has been bitten by the "selling bug," many questions automatically arise. Where are the markets? What selling methods are best? Where do I get the information needed to turn a hobby into a business? Once a few things have sold, a crafter may begin to look for ways to improve sales and ask, "How do I get into big time selling?"

Although I will occasionally touch on the topic of wholesaling, "big time selling" is not what this book is about. It's about how to get started selling directly to consumers at the retail level in ways that beginners find most comfortable. It's about developing talents and skills, exploring new territory, branching out and moving on. It's also about *business*.

Why do I keep talking about *business* when all you're interested in is making money? Ah, there's the rub! *You can't have one without the other.* You may sell your crafts and say you're not "in business," but in the eyes of the law, you are in business the minute you start to sell anything. When you do this, you are also subject to a variety of local, state and federal laws, rules, regulations and taxes. (You'll learn more about this in chapter four.)

If you do not have a business background or a job that has encouraged your entrepreneurial instincts in the past, you may be resistant to the idea of starting a homebased crafts business. If this scares you now, don't worry about it. Just slip this idea into your subconscious mind and let it rest there awhile. The more of this book you read, the more you'll learn about the personal and financial advantages of turning your hobby into a genuine homebased business. By the time you've finished this book, the idea of a real crafts business may feel as comfortable as an old pair of shoes.

An "Analyze Your Excuses" Exercise

No matter what we attempt to do in life, the hardest part is just getting started. Here are some of the excuses I've heard from people who said they wanted to sell their crafts but just couldn't seem to get started. Which of these "roadblocks" are preventing you from following your dream?

- ❑ It's hard to decide what to sell.
- ❑ I'm not good at selling.
- ❑ I don't know how to find buyers.
- ❑ I have no business experience.
- ❑ I don't know how to price my products.
- ❑ I'm too old (or too young).
- ❑ I don't have enough time.
- ❑ I have no start-up money.
- ❑ My family might complain if I got too involved.
- ❑ I'd look like a fool if I tried and failed.
- ❑ I don't know anything about taxes, laws or bookkeeping.

With a list of excuses like this, it's no wonder so many craft businesses never get born! If you see yourself in the above list and wish you knew how to get past the hurdles in your path, try the following exercise. It will help you expose your fears, decide what you do best, and set some new goals. You'll need three sheets of paper.

1. *Expose Your Fears.* On the first sheet, complete this sentence: "I have not gotten serious about a craft business because. . . ." Be honest with yourself—identify what scares you most. Once identified, fears can be killed, one by one, through self-study and experience. Above all, don't fear failure itself. Successful businesses, like successful lives, are built not only on one small success after another, but on one small failure after another. Each small failure is a new learning experience that illuminates for us the things that won't work and teaches us to avoid larger failures of a similar kind. Thus, each small failure automatically leads to a small success somewhere along the line.

2. *Identify Yourself.* On the second sheet, write a description of who you are and what you do best. Examples: "I am a needleworker who creates patterns for other stitchers," or "I am a folk artist who paints on weathered wood," or "I make contemporary furniture and accessories." Giving yourself this kind of formal identity will do wonders for your ego and help you target customer prospects.

3. *Set Some Short-Term Goals.* On the third sheet, list three things you will do this month to get moving on your craft business. For example, you might start checking the kind of handcrafted merchandise being sold in local shops or craft malls. You might list six things you've made that buyers might view as a coordinated product line. Another goal might be to get together with a creative friend who will listen to your ideas and give you practical reactions to them. It doesn't matter what three things you do— pick anything that makes you feel comfortable. The important thing is *just to get started.* Once you do, I predict your enthusiasm and moneymaking ideas will grow like a snowball rolling downhill.

Crafting a Success Plan

By now, you see the advantage of putting your plans in writing. A computer makes writing easier, but if you don't have a computer, a notebook will do. Instead of a spiral-bound pad, try a loose-leaf notebook that allows you to set up categories and add and remove pages. Give your notebook an exciting title that reflects your secret dreams and hopes for the future. After it's begun, reread it often to remind yourself of where you want to go and how you plan to get there. Following are some suggested categories to start with. Add others as they come to mind, and jot down your thoughts about each of them:

- My Dreams and Goals (immediate and long-term)
- Moneytalk (your reasons for working, your income goals, an estimate of how much money you'll need to get started and where you'll get this start-up money)
- Time (number of hours you plan to work each week, where you will find them and how you plan to fit everything into your daily schedule)
- Business Brainstorming (business names you like, ideas for products you might make, where you will set up a business management corner in your home, what office supplies and equipment you'll need to manage your moneymaking endeavor, how family and friends might help you achieve your goal, etc.)
- Production Plan (supplies and materials needed, supply sources you need to locate, how you or others will produce goods for sale, what outside help you might need)
- Marketing Plan (how and where you plan to sell everything you make)
- Start-up Plan (follow the specific steps given in this chapter)

If you are not doing it already, I suggest you grab a highlighter pen and start marking any part of this book that rings a bell in your mind or gives you a great idea (providing, of course, that the book you're reading hasn't been borrowed from the library). If it has, I believe you will want your own copy for future reference.

Tip

As you read, jot notes in the margin the minute you get a good idea because ideas don't keep. If ideas aren't captured the minute we get them, they may be lost forever, like dreams briefly recalled in the morning. Or, as someone once said, "To err is human; to forget, routine."

After you've finished this book and have set up your notebook, go back and pick up on the highlighted portions and transfer your "idea notes" to the appropriate pages of your notebook. Periodically, when you feel you're ready for a change or a new challenge, reread this book and your entire notebook again. As time passes, your vision will change and things you cannot relate to now will have new meaning. It's like rereading the Bible or seeing a great classic film once again. Because of how we change with each passing year, the way we respond either at the age of forty or sixty will be totally different from the way we responded at the age of twenty. Leafing through your notebook will also motivate you and help plant ideas and goals more firmly in your subconscious mind. Make a promise to yourself to follow your dream, and don't let others discourage you.

People who don't have dreams and goals of their own are often quick to put down other people's ideas. Cindi, a beginning dollmaker, told me that as a child she had only two dreams: to create living dolls (a family) and to be Madame Alexander. "It was as I began to get older," she wrote, "that adults taught me to think more 'sensibly.' Now, at forty, I've realized something important: my dreams were the reality, and others' dreams for me were the fantasy."

Karen, a teddy bear maker, told me that when her craft business wasn't going the way she wanted it to, she began to lose interest in it. "I finally figured out what the problem was," she said. "I was listening to what others said I should do instead of listening to myself."

What these letter-writers didn't realize at the time was that in telling me about their dreams, they were putting their goals in writing and strengthening their beliefs in the process. When they believed their goals were possible, magical things began to happen.

A Time Management Exercise

One of your goals might be to find more time for crafting and selling. "Time is what we want the most and what we use the worst," someone has said. Anyone who is currently in the dreaming-about-a-business-stage needs to take a good look at how their time is presently being spent (or wasted). Before we can capture time that is slipping through our fingers, we need to study how we're spending it.

Every day for a month, keep track of how you spend your waking hours. Before long you'll be able to identify time-wasting patterns you can change. You may be surprised to learn how much time you spend reading the paper over a cup of coffee, chatting with neighbors, visiting with friends on the phone, running errands, watching television, working around the house, doing community projects and so on.

Time Management Tips

To save time, get organized. Reorganize or rearrange your workspace so you can be more productive in the coming year. A small investment in new storage shelves, boxes, organizers or wall decor can do wonders for your morale. If you don't have a whole room to yourself, make room for what you want to do by changing the way you live. Claim extra drawers and one of the closets in your home. Consider the use of a room divider to turn one large room into two, and take a closer look at the space in your basement, garage, or back porch. You have space somewhere—the trick is to use it efficiently. Decorator magazines offer many ideas. Here are other tips from my readers:

◆ "To avoid interruptions while I'm working, I turn on the telephone answering machine. To make better use of my time, I make a list each day of the things I plan to do the next day, such as call customers from 9:30 to 10:30 A.M., write letters from 10:30 till noon, and do artwork from 12:30 to 3 P.M."

— Barbara Schaffer, *calligrapher*

◆ "I've found it best to dedicate a work area or table that is exclusively mine. Experience taught me I was sacrificing a lot of progress and ultimately profit by spending valuable time dragging out boxes of supplies and getting set up, so I commandeered what used to be ESK (eating space in kitchen)."

— Susan Young, *decorative painter*

◆ "The calendar is the law by which most of us operate. It divides our years into months, days or even hours that we spend or waste. To be in control of your calendar, always write on it in pencil. Crossing out ink on the calendar, then trying to fit a new scribble into that small space makes a mess on the page. You look at the mess, then feel disorganized and frustrated."

— Barbara Massie,
crafts business teacher and author

We all have extra time. The challenge is simply to find it. Generally, this means we must stop doing one thing to make time for another, or at least rearrange our time so we have special blocks of time for other activities, such as developing a profitable little business at home.

Set Goals, Make Gains

Here are four goals Jeanne Swartz set when she made the decision to get serious about selling her Gifts from the Heart:

1. Expand variety of items. (She expanded her mop and broom doll line by adding different types of dolls and a wider variety of designs.)
2. Improve craft display. (She added handmade display racks, new table skirting, a business sign and lighting to brighten dark corners.)
3. Reanalyze pricing. (Her goal was to keep prices low enough to please her customers and high enough to please her.)
4. Concentrate on quality. (Because she looks for attractiveness and quality in a product, she figures her customers shop the same way.)

Setting New Goals

Do you want to be a carefree crafter, a hobby seller, or a real crafts business owner? Do you have ambitions of success, money or fame? Many people fail to achieve goals because they have not been clearly expressed. Instead of speaking in vague terms about having "a really successful home shop" or "a craft business that is profitable," establish a specific money goal, an annual dollar amount that would make you feel your business was a success.

The trick to achieving any goal is to first picture it in your mind, so put all your goals in writing and reread them periodically to reinforce your mental success pictures. You're halfway to achieving a goal when you believe it's possible. "You are everything you choose to be. You are as unlimited as the endless universe," says Shad Helmstetter in his motivational book, *What to Say When You Talk to Yourself.* Look in the mirror each morning and repeat this message until you believe it!

In setting goals and writing your plan, include your own definitions for "profitable" and "success." To many, these words have little connection with money. "Profitable" might mean experience, acquired knowledge, valuable personal contacts or a new understanding of your capabilities or limitations. "Success" can mean being in control of your own life, making new friends or discovering a new world of possibilities. To one middle-aged woman in North Dakota, success was expressed simply and poignantly like this: "I want to make my own way so I won't have to depend on someone else."

A reader once told me that her greatest ambition was to become rich and famous for her art. Another said she wanted "to create something all her own that she could sell for hundreds of dollars at an art show." While such goals are possible, they are not realistic financial goals for beginners. It is always wise to temper dreams of riches with thoughts of reality, lest you become discouraged when big profits aren't realized. It's also better to seek recognition than fame. In expressing this ambition, a beginning crafter said, "I want to be recognized as a professional craftsperson and designer, to be able to make a living as a craftsperson." This is a worthy and achievable goal.

Craft Networking

Have you ever heard about "craft networking?" Back in 1981, these words were unknown in the crafts community. Until my friend Joyce Bennett uttered them the day we were discussing a talk I was to give for the Society of Craft Designers, I never thought of them as a pair. They carried quite a punch because I suddenly realized this was what I had been doing for years.

After presenting my craft networking speech, I turned it into a special report and slowly began to educate the crafts community to the idea of networking as a way to get ahead in a crafts business at home. I explained that one of the greatest satisfactions from craft networking is the emotional reinforcement you gain. We all need networks of friends to survive and, as one of my readers put it, "It's nice to know there is someone out there you can turn to for moral support." Through networking, individual confidence builds and grows, and through communication with one another we learn that our problems are not unique. How reassuring it is to know that the same things that have happened to us have happened to others.

Generally, I find women to be better networkers than men. Maybe this is because women have always networked under the guise of *kaffeeklatsching*, chatting at the beauty parlor or lunching with friends. In earlier years, quilting bees and threshing events drew women together, enabling them to be more helpful and supportive of one another. While many craftspeople are networking today, others remain secretive about their craft ideas and marketing outlets. Some fear that a sharing of confidential information or "trade secrets" will hurt their business or chances for future sales, but this is unlikely to happen. My homebased business has never been hurt or held back because I shared hard-to-get information with a business friend or even a competitor. I have always operated in the belief that we only have what we give away, and everything we give comes back double. What goes for love and friendship also goes for information and ideas. As someone once said, "We make a living by what we get, and we make a life by what we give."

Inspired by one of my articles, a dollmaker wrote to tell me she had started networking and asking questions. "The price of all those long-distance phone calls was worth it," she said. "I was amazed at how generous other craftswomen were with their help, advice, praise and encouragement."

If you're dreaming about starting a crafts business, or interested in expanding one already begun, networking with people who share your interests and ambitions may be the single most important thing you can do now and throughout the life of your crafts business. There is an old saying that "knowledge is power," so the more you have, the greater your chances for success in any new endeavor. Too few craftspeople take advantage of their networking opportunities, however. The excuse I've heard most often for not joining an organization or subscribing to periodicals that will connect them to other craftspeople is, "Oh, I'm much too busy producing crafts . . . or designing them . . . or selling them . . . to read periodicals or join an organization."

Starting your own supportive network is as easy as inviting a few craft friends to lunch and arranging to meet regularly in the future to discuss mutual problems and concerns. To expand the size of any support group, set up a meeting at the library or other public building and ask your newspaper to announce it. You may be surprised by the turnout, especially in rural areas where crafters may feel particularly isolated.

Barbara's Success Story

The most important thing I've learned from my many years of self-employment— and the most encouraging thing I can tell you now—is that one thing always leads to another. Perhaps my story will give you added encouragement to pursue your secret dream.

When I developed a passionate interest in arts and crafts in the mid-60s, I never imagined that my crafts hobby would lead me to a full-time homebased writing and publishing business. I often think back to the day when three little words changed my life and put me on an exciting new road of discovery.

On graduating from high school, I went to work as a secretary in Chicago. Five years later I met and married Harry Brabec, my knight in shining armor. I kept working for the first five years of marriage, after which time Harry suggested I stay home and just be Mrs. Brabec for a while. "But I'd be bored to tears with nothing to do all day," I said, and he said, "Get a hobby." Those three little words changed not only my life, but his. *I discovered crafts.*

First there was my "Glitter All Over the Place" period, which Harry put an immediate end to the first time he found glitter in his soup.

Then came my "Ceramic Chips in the Shag Rug" era, which ruined more than one of my husband's sly barefoot runs to the refrigerator after I'd gone to

Motivated to Succeed

Nothing motivates one to success like a genuine need for money. When doctors told Joyce, a self-taught artist and designer, that her husband had multiple sclerosis, she found the motivation she needed to become the family breadwinner. With a husband in a wheelchair and three small children depending on her, she stopped marketing her wood products at craft shows and launched a home party business featuring her custom-designed furniture and folk art. She got free information and assistance from the U.S. Small Business Administration (SBA), which also gave her a small business loan to get started. Before long, Joyce was employing up to fifty people during peak production periods, and more than a hundred women across the country were hosting home parties featuring her products.

bed. The jig was up each time he stepped on a sliver and yelped with pain. Harry often said that entering the living room in the days when I was cutting mosaic tiles was like walking into a war zone since he never knew when a flying chip would hit him in the eye.

I dabbled in oil painting for a while, but that didn't last long. In a one-bedroom apartment, the smell of turpentine at dinnertime was too much even for me to bear. Harry was relieved when I switched to acrylics but alarmed when I told him I'd found a supplier who had dozens of unfinished basswood items I could paint and sell. By now, we were living in a two-bedroom apartment, and one bedroom had been turned into a crafts studio for me. I was getting serious about selling, and before long, I had diversified into driftwood and weathered wood and was turning out decorative accessories, pictures and plaques by the dozen. I discovered a whole new world of possibilities the day I bought a book titled *You, Too, Can Whittle and Carve*.

I recall the evening I retired to one corner of the living room with my how-to book, a small piece of balsa wood and my new X-Acto knife. "What are you doing?" Harry asked. "Carving a donkey's head," I replied. We hadn't been married long at that point, so he naturally found this amusing. (Until that moment, the only thing I'd ever carved was a Thanksgiving turkey, yet I had not the slightest doubt I could do what I said I was going to do.) A couple of hours later when I astonished my husband with a finished carving, I was off and running on another new road of discovery. For many evenings thereafter, Harry would sit in the living room to read and I'd join him with my whittling. Just to let him know I loved him, every so often I'd zonk him on the nose with a flying wood chip.

When we purchased our first house, the extra space spurred my creativity. My purchase of a Moto Tool to speed my woodcarving soon led to my "Saw-

Why Dreams Are Delayed

In just four sentences, one of my readers perfectly described the roadblock so many women encounter when they consider a small business at home. "I delayed my business first of all because my children were small and needed all the love, attention and help I could give them," writes Diane in Illinois. "Second, I lacked knowledge about my favorite craft and the business world in general. Third, as a young, struggling family, our finances were limited. Fourth, doing something scary—like starting my own business—also made me wait so long before taking the plunge."

But there is still another stumbling block, and it's bigger than all the rest, Diane said. "In all the excuses I have mentioned, I have found one thing in common of which I was totally unaware: Time. I now realize that time managed me instead of me managing it. And now that I look back, I can see there was much I could have done if only I had managed my time better."

Diane's business is now a reality. She has learned more about time management, business basics and her favorite craft of needlepoint. Money is still a consideration, but she is no longer afraid to fail. Best of all, she has learned something special about her family. When she finally told her children and husband of her dreams and desires, she was stunned by the support and encouragement she got from them. "How I wish I had called upon them sooner," she said.

If you haven't done so already, take time now to have a talk with your family. Give them a chance to help you realize your special dream.

dust in the Basement" period. The fine sawdust from this tool seemed to drift throughout the house, which annoyed Harry because he likes both a clean house and workshop area. It was about this time in my life that I starting shirking my homemaking duties. I was much too busy making crafts to clean house, you see, and when I started my present business in 1981, things only got worse.

In addition to putting up with my craft antics and loss of interest in housework, Harry also found his patience sorely tried every time we went somewhere because I'd insist on visiting that "cute little craft shop down the street." Of course, I was trying to figure out what was selling, and for how much, and could I sell my stuff there, too.

Does any of this sound familiar?

For the next three years, I created a variety of products that I offered for sale through several local shops and fairs. I'm so grateful now that some of my best one-of-a-kind music boxes, sculpture and carvings never sold because I

have so enjoyed owning and looking at these pieces all these years. I now realize that if they had been sold, I never would have replaced them. That is why I urge you never to sell a piece of craftwork that means a great deal to you unless you are sure you can make a replacement item for yourself. Some crafts are made to be given away, some are made to be sold, and some should be made to keep. Money is a poor substitute for a beautiful item that speaks to your heart and can't be replaced once gone.

In 1971, after three years of selling my crafts, I stopped making things for sale when Harry suggested that what the world needed now was a crafts magazine that would help other crafters sell their work. Almost overnight, we found ourselves involved full-time in the publication of a magazine we named *Artisan Crafts.* This quarterly survived five years before quietly dying during the 1975 recession. For a long time afterward, Harry joked that the magazine was a literary success and a financial flop. It's true this venture was not *financially* profitable, but in time it proved to be one of my most profitable life experiences.

If I had not had the courage to try something new and totally foreign to me (magazine publishing), I never would have met the person who referred me to the book publisher who asked me to write my first book. That book, *Creative Cash,* dramatically changed my life because it led me to start the full-time writing and publishing business I still operate from home today. It was at this point that I launched a newsletter that led to my first speaking job, which led to the writing and publishing of other books and more speaking engagements in both the United States and Canada.

My crafts hobby dramatically changed my husband's life as well. Because of my involvement in crafts, he was drawn into the industry in the 1970s. Among other things, his work as a crafts festival producer for Busch Gardens got us two six-week trips-of-a-lifetime traveling first-class throughout Europe on a company expense account.

In 1989, because of the popularity of another of my books, I was invited to Hollywood for a week-long appearance on ABC-TV's *Home Show.* Their home-business segment, titled "Homemade Money" after my best-selling book, prompted thousands of people to rush to bookstores to purchase a copy. This led to other television appearances.

By telling you this, I hope to illustrate how one thing always leads to another and why it's so important to *just get moving!* In the three decades since I first began to develop my artistic and creative talents, I've never had a boring day, and I owe it all to my husband for uttering those three little words ("get a hobby") in 1965. Throughout my writing and publishing career, crafting has remained my most enjoyable pastime and favorite business stress reliever. I still love to whittle, sculpt with hobby clay and do cross-stitch embroidery, but these crafts were moved to the back burner in 1995 when I got interested

---

Motivational Tips

◆ "Create what gives you joy, both in the making and in the final product."

— Linda Crocco

◆ "Listen to all the advice people give you, but realize that all the advice people give you is not going to be good advice."

— Stewart Madsen

◆ "Be persistent. If you have a good product, don't give up if your first few attempts to sell are unsuccessful."

— Beverly Ciesielski

◆ "Look at future trends and specialize in just a few things."

— Jami Schneider

◆ "Provide a place for yourself in your home that is your private corner to work on crafts. Be prepared to devote a lot of time if you want to be a successful full-time selling crafter."

— Patricia Hall

◆ "Plan, plan, plan! It's a lot of work to get started and get your items on the market."

— Donna Wagoner

---

in making teddy bears. After discovering (to my surprise) that I had some ability as a teddy bear designer, I decided to launch a sideline mail-order pattern and kit business. By the time this book is published, my first products will be ready for sale. Harry has named this period of my life "Fur All Over the Place" and he helps me by running the vacuum cleaner more often. "At least fur bits are better than glitter," he sighs.

P.S. By trying something new, I got the idea for another book. It will show readers how to turn original designs and creative ideas into profitable how-to articles, books, patterns, kits and related products and publications.

It's Okay to Be Scared

Selling is a natural step in looking for a response to your creative efforts, but the desire to sell is usually accompanied by feelings of fear. So the first hurdle you will have to overcome is likely to be lack of self-confidence. Perhaps you can identify with Holly in Massachusetts, who told me she had always wanted a craft business. "For a long time I lacked the confidence to take the first big step," she said. "I finally checked out the items being sold in country stores and compared them with what I could accomplish. I'm still in the early stages, but it was your words of encouragement about getting started and taking risks that tipped the scales in favor of trying. I hope to someday reach the point where my work is a significant supplement to our income and that it always remains exciting."

The more you learn, the more confident you will become. Before you know it, you'll have the courage to sneak up on fear and give it a good whack!

We are always most comfortable when we're operating within our personal "comfort zone," doing things we know how to do, in places we've already been, around people we know. I like what quilt designer and author Jean Ray Laury once said on this topic: "If you are being pulled out of your comfort zone, out of your area of competence, you are being challenged. Anything that challenges tends to push us to the extremes of our abilities . . . and that is when we discover things about ourselves."

Lacking experience, I was scared the first time I tried to sell my crafts at a show. And I was scared when I began to publish a magazine because I wasn't a writer then, and I knew nothing about the publishing industry. (As an ex-secretary, my greatest business skill was typing 120 words a minute.) It took me more than a week to write one article for the premier issue, but after a while I got the hang of stringing words together. When a publisher asked me to write my first book, I confidently replied, "Sure," and then began to worry about making a fool of myself. Even after five years of producing a magazine, I knew nothing about the *craft* of writing. I quickly realized this was something I would have to learn the hard way.

As a beginning speaker, I was nervous and uncomfortable although I knew my topic well. I'm no longer scared of speaking in public or being on radio or television because I've done it so often before, but the next time I'm asked to do something I've never done before, I'll have to fight the old fear demons again, just like everybody else. So begin this book with the idea that it's okay to be scared. The more you learn about the unknown territory you're entering, the less fearful you will be.

 *Recommended Reading*

- *The Creative Woman's Getting-It-All-Together (At Home) Handbook* by Jean Ray Laury (Hot Fudge Press).
- *Get It All Done and Still Be Human* by Robbie and Tony Fanning (Open Chain Publishing).
- *What Are Your Goals: Powerful Questions to Discover What You Want Out of Life* by Gary R. Blair (Wharton Publishing).
- *What to Say When You Talk to Yourself* by Shad Helmstetter (Grindle Press).

CHAPTER THREE

Developing Your Product Line

The real secret to selling more of what you make is to make more of what people want to buy.

Before entering the crafts marketplace, and as long as you remain in it, you need to do market research to find out what other artists and crafters are selling. Think of this as interesting detective work. Visit craft fairs, craft malls, handcraft shops and gift shops that carry handmade items. Pay particular attention to prices, sizes and the kind of raw materials used in products. Observe how the price increases on items that use better materials. Watch how colors change each year, reflecting hot new trends. When you see the same colors or shades of color everywhere you look, that suggests a color trend for that particular year. If you try to sell flashy colors in a year when earth tones are hot, your sales may suffer.

As you do your Sherlock Holmes bit, ask yourself how your crafts compare to what's available locally, regionally or nationally. If you plan to make and sell what everyone else is trying to sell, it will be hard to compete. However, if you can come up with even a few unusual items, and will make an effort to find the right marketing outlet for them, you may find yourself smiling all the way to the bank.

"Make something different and consumable that others are not doing in your area," advises Jeri Fry. "To satisfy your repeat customers, always have some new item to offer each year," says Debbie Stansfield. Tole painter Barbara Dunn once shared these secrets to her success: "Doing extensive, constant

Personalize It!

Being different is an important key to success in selling crafts. I'm reminded of Ruth in Arkansas, who makes a different kind of applehead doll. Each doll is a unique character and each does something different. For instance, a farmer may be "slopping his hog," a lady in a cook's hat may be holding a roasted turkey on a tray, a man may be sitting on a stump eating watermelon, and an old woman may be sitting in a rocking chair working on a quilt. Ruth takes orders for special requests, and she says some are a real challenge.

Ruth has learned that personalizing a craft adds to its salability. In addition to making apple dolls, Ruth also paints. After she filled a custom order for a sixtieth wedding anniversary present, she began to get requests from other people for the same kind of item. What was it? A picture of the couple walking to the little country church they regularly attend. Now we suddenly have *nostalgia*—something that always sells at a good price.

Perhaps you're a decorative painter. If so, don't always paint only the kind of pictures you want to paint. Instead, think about what nostalgic buyers are willing to spend money on. If you can't paint people, perhaps you can do nostalgic paintings of homes, places of business, that little church where a couple was married or a favorite pet. I wouldn't give you a dollar for a painting of just any old dog, but while we had our beloved dog, Ginger, I would have paid plenty for a great portrait of her. The difference is the sales power of nostalgia.

research has helped me more than anything else. I pay close attention all the time to what other tole painters are selling. Then I offer something different. I think crafters ought to try to produce work that falls into one of these general categories: so cute it can't be resisted; functional with fair price (giving buyers further reason to buy); original and totally different from anything they've seen (keeping the market new); and, above all, quality work."

In other chapters of this book you will learn how to price your products for maximum sales success and find the right marketing outlet for your wares. This chapter offers perspective on what buyers want in a handmade product and what you can do to make your products more appealing to them. Because there are literally thousands of products you could make for sale, I have not attempted to give you ideas on exactly what to make. Instead, I hope to stimulate your imagination so you can come up with good ideas based on your own market research.

Getting It Together

A mistake commonly made by beginners is to produce items in several craft mediums that are not related to one another. For maximum success, you need to diversify and have a variety of products in different sizes and price ranges, but don't offer a hodgepodge of crafts made from many different kinds of materials. Specialize in one or two major craft areas and be creative by combining popular craft materials that aren't normally used together, such as stitchery with ceramics or sewn items with wood.

What's important here is that you give buyers the impression that you've "got it all together" and are not just a hobbyist who can't decide what to sell. In her book, *How to Start Making Money with Your Crafts*, Kathryn Caputo includes a good chapter on how to define a product line. "You can't do everything and do it well," she emphasizes. "Explore one craft to the fullest. Find new products to make from it. Find new ways to improve upon old ideas. Be original. Be creative. Your focus on one craft will bring you very positive results."

"Concentrate on one or two items so you can mass produce and avoid the tendency to try too many projects at one time," seconds Suzi Fox. Jami Schneider suggests that you consider trends and specialize in just a few things. Carol Ann Ogorzalek's tip is to keep changing your craft line and bring back items from earlier years that haven't been seen for a while. "I think seasoned craft sellers get in a rut and keep selling the same things year after year when they should be broadening their crafting horizons by trying some new items," adds Barbara McCoy.

Tip

In trying to develop a line, learn to think in product categories. Examples: home decor, toys, clothing, gifts for men, collectibles, dolls, Christmas ornaments, etc. Or, concentrate on one or two crafts, such as woodwork, quilting, stained glass, dough art, sewing, etc., and create separate product lines within those categories.

Products That Always Sell Well

Below, I've identified seven main categories of products that seem to sell consistently in both good and bad economic times. Make a list of the individual
craft items you've thought about selling and see if they fit into one or more of
the following categories:

1. Functional items people can use in their daily lives
2. Gift items that answer specific needs
3. Decorative accessories and furnishings
4. Collectibles and other nostalgic items
5. Garments, jewelry and other fashion accessories
6. Custom-designed products
7. Leisure interests

Not every product that falls into one of these categories is going to sell, of
course. One reason is that consumers do not merely buy things—they buy
products (and services) that offer *benefits*. Thus, the more benefits you can
include in a product, the easier it will be to sell. To identify the benefits of your
products, consider that:

*Buyers appreciate and will always be interested in purchasing functional
items they can use in their daily lives*, but when money is tight, such items
may have to offer something more than practicality. If a useful product also
offers a timesaving or organizational benefit, makes a dreary job more fun,
elicits feelings of nostalgia, or merely makes one smile, it has a greater chance
of selling. "Make things that are useful and practical," says Joanne Ford. "If
things fall apart, people will remember you. Word-of-mouth will either make
you or break you."

Even when there is little money for luxuries, people need gift items, and they
will buy crafts that solve specific gift-giving needs. "There is no barometer for
what will sell," says Shelley Yockelson," but necessity always makes people
buy more (for example, the Christmas rush coming)." The Christmas season
is always a big bonanza for crafters, but don't overlook all the other times
during the year when people need special gifts for such occasions as birthdays, anniversaries, a job promotion, graduation, housewarming, baby shower,
Valentine's Day, Easter, Thanksgiving, Mother's Day, Father's Day, and so on.
When such products can also be personalized in some way, their value
increases.

Name It!

If you offer a variety of products, divide them into product lines of six items or more, then give each product line a special name. Ann Schroedl, owner of Hanndy Hints, offers a variety of specialty gift items for the sewing enthusiast, quilter or crafter. Some of her product lines are "Americana Note Cards," "Quilt Square Stickers," "Magnetic Notekeepers," and "Bumper Stickers." To create a line, think in terms of what goes together. Examples:

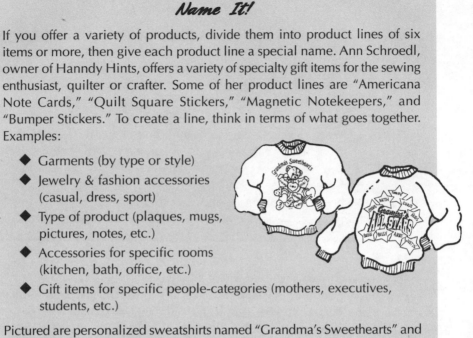

◆ Garments (by type or style)

◆ Jewelry & fashion accessories (casual, dress, sport)

◆ Type of product (plaques, mugs, pictures, notes, etc.)

◆ Accessories for specific rooms (kitchen, bath, office, etc.)

◆ Gift items for specific people-categories (mothers, executives, students, etc.)

Pictured are personalized sweatshirts named "Grandma's Sweethearts" and "Grandpa's All Stars"

People buy decorative crafts and accessories because such products satisfy particular decorating needs or an individual's desire to own something beautiful. Some people derive great satisfaction from buying something special for themselves when they don't have money for larger purchases. Many years ago when the country was in a recession, my husband and I were sad because we didn't have enough money to buy a house or new car. So, when we could least afford it, we rewarded ourselves with our first piece of expensive artwork. Benefit? It did wonders for our morale.

Craft items that always seem to find a market are those that appeal to collectors, a group of buyers who are less concerned with price than the average consumer. They tend to buy on impulse whenever they find something that strikes a nostalgic chord or satisfies a longing of the heart. And make no mistake about it, *these are marketable benefits.* You may already produce collectible items that can be easily marketed to such collectors as animal lovers, sporting enthusiasts, musicians, circus fans, carousel buffs, people who love dolls, teddy bears, miniatures, stained glass, woodcarvings, toys . . . the list goes on and on.

Gifts for Babies

If you don't already have products for babies, maybe you should consider adding some. Try to think beyond crocheted or knitted items, which rarely can be sold for prices that justify the time spent in creating them. Think instead of novelty items suitable for baby showers, custom-made items that can be personalized with a child's name and higher-priced decorative items for a nursery or child's room.

Theresa Norton developed a line of birth announcements, then went on to offer a selection of baby books and handmade baby afghans. One mother I met at a conference used her art talents to design "fantasy rooms" envisioned by new mothers—painting the walls with scenes from fairy tales. She lived in an affluent neighborhood and could charge a pretty penny for this service. It wasn't long before she had all the work she wanted.

Everyone needs clothing, even when money is tight. Sellers who offer handmade garments, designer jewelry and related accessories need to emphasize how their products will make people *feel*. Remember that people naturally want to feel more attractive, and they enjoy wearing clothing and accessories that make them stand out in a crowd (*the benefit*). Even people who work at home may buy designer jeans, humorous sweatshirts and handmade sandals to get the benefit of sheer comfort and the satisfaction of looking good in their private environment.

When you offer custom-design services, you are offering buyers a very special benefit: a product made especially for them and one that is truly unique. Products can be customized by giving buyers a choice of colors, sizes, styles, designs or personalization with initials or a name. Never hesitate to charge extra for custom-design services because they simply can't be found in any store, and the kind of person who wants such items for personal use or gifts is not likely to haggle about price.

If you can offer a product that will help people fill their leisure hours, you will have no trouble selling it. Many craft professionals successfully sell handcrafted musical instruments, games, puzzles, and humorous playthings for adults. Patterns or kits for toys, dolls, teddy bears and other things that people enjoy making for themselves or as gifts will always be good sellers. Anyone who does stitchery is always looking for yet another new needlepoint canvas or cross-stitch chart. (For more information on this topic, see "Ten Other Ways to Profit from Your Creativity" in Chapter Fourteen.)

Find a Niche and Fill It!

A market niche is a place where product and buyer fit like a hand in a glove. There are large market niches, small market niches and niches within niches. (See nearby "Niche Market Checklist" to identify general niche markets for your products.) As you plan your product line, keep asking yourself who's likely to be most interested in each product.

It's always difficult to sell something to a mass market, so anytime you can narrow your market by targeting a specific niche, your sales are likely to improve. To do this, think in terms of how your products *benefit* specific buyers or solve a particular problem. Sometimes a product benefit will automatically trigger a niche market idea. Here are fifteen examples of special niches some crafters have found:

- Mother-and-daughter team Liz and Maryn targeted pet owners with a sense of humor for their line of amusing cat and dog costumes that include devil horns and capes, Santa hats, and angel wings.

- After Jerry invented a pet-grooming comb for dogs and cats, he found two special niche markets: people who keep angora rabbits, and spinners who need to comb locks before spinning.

- Judy from South Dakota and Marie from Missouri each found a niche when they began to offer gift baskets that feature special products made in their own state, thus catering to buyers who are proud to live in these states or yearn to return.

- Sharon found a terrific niche market for her hand-painted, Christmas-ornament eggs when she began to paint Santa Claus in his sled flying over the skyline of particular cities, such as Chicago, San Francisco, and New York.

- Faye found a new market when she began to do "Grandma" and "Grandpa" sweatshirts embroidered with the names of her grandchildren.

- Joy, who raises sheep and sells wool, found a large niche audience of buyers who appreciate wool products. After identifying this niche, she went on to develop a line of over a hundred sheep-related products she now markets by mail.

- Norma glazes photos onto ceramic plates, cups and picture frames. She has found all kinds of niche markets by focusing on items that make great gifts for such people as graduates, nurses, new moms,

Profits from Mother Nature

Many beautiful items can be made from raw materials that cost you nothing. Rocks, driftwood, flowers and seashells immediately come to mind.

Marcia McDonough and Jill Jefferies established a successful crafts partnership built on Mother Nature's bounty that keeps a dozen people working part-time in their homes. They manufacture a varied line of character doll ornaments with heads hand-carved from the burrs of teasel plants, a weed that grows plentifully along West Virginia's country roads. One secret to their sales success is locating specialty stores that appreciate Appalachian crafts, finding them in such unlikely places as California. Working through a sales rep, they have also found an international market for their products in several far-eastern countries.

grandparents and newlyweds or anniversary couples. She also glazes snapshots that simply remind people of special times in their life.

Susan, who sells teddy bears and other toys made from recycled fur coats and other products, caters to ecologically minded people.

Roz targeted brides as her niche market when she began to do beadwork on wedding gowns and veils.

Katie found an interesting niche market for her hand-painted saws when she realized that many widows wanted paintings on saws their husbands had used all their lives.

Shirley targeted the handicapped elderly as her niche market when she began to manufacture knit garments that closed with Velcro and snaps.

Sidney's niche market is huge: women who stitch items as gifts. She will create a custom-designed needlework chart from a photo of a house, car, boat, or business logo. (Other designers offer similar services doing pet pictures or people portraits.)

Judith found an unusual niche for one of her product lines. She has been selling matted and framed quotations at art shows for several years. Among her specialties is a line of T-shirts focusing on quotations about left-handedness. Since a significant percentage of the population is "lefties," this has become a hot-selling item.

Myra found a sizable "military niche" for the needlework charts she creates of ship emblems and "patches" of all divisions of the U.S. military service.

Niche Market Checklist

Consumer Markets

❑ **Women**

> Homemakers
> Brides-to-be
> New moms
> Grandmothers

❑ **Men**

> Sports enthusiasts (baseball, golf, hunting, boating, etc.)
> Grandfathers
> Fellows who need gifts for wife or secretary

❑ **Business professionals/men and women**

> Doctors, lawyers, accountants, teachers, office workers, nurses, home-business owners, etc. (literally hundreds of categories here)

❑ **Farmers or farm families** (with special interest in horses, sheep, pigs, cows, steam engines, special crops, etc.)

❑ **People who live in a specific city, state or region**

❑ **Disabled elderly**

❑ **Ecologically minded consumers**

❑ **Craft enthusiasts** (List all the individual crafts and look for niche interests within each craft category)

❑ **Collectors and nostalgia buffs** (Hundreds of categories here—circus, carousel, trains, dolls, music boxes, toys, miniatures, etc.)

❑ **Pet lovers** (identify specific pet groups)

Wholesale Markets

❑ **Gift shops**

> Handcraft shops
> Commercial gift shops (general)
> Gift shops in tourist areas or hospitals
> Christian gift shops
> Shops featuring collectibles and novelties
> Year-round Christmas shops

❑ **Mail-order catalog houses**

> General consumer gift catalogs
> Special-interest consumer catalogs (books, tools, supplies, kits, kitchenware, jewelry, etc.)
> Special-interest craft and hobby catalogs

❑ **Specialty shops, stores or departments in stores**

> Cookware, Baby, Sewing, Toys & Dolls, Christmas, Sports, Woodenware, etc.

■ Bente expanded her knitting and weaving business by identifying a problem she had always had: finding the right buttons and clasps to put the finishing touch on her creations. Her niche market was knitters, but because her product line was pewter buttons and accessories of Nordic design made by a company in Norway, she also targeted Norwegians as a group who might use buttons in their sewing and other craft work.

Using Commercial Patterns and Designs

Some crafters tend to "lift" designs used by others. This is both impolite and unethical, not to mention illegal when a crafter has protected an original design by copyright (which most professional crafters are now doing). Since you could be sued for wrongly using someone else's pattern or design, it's important to learn a little about copyrights and the copyright law.

All commercial patterns are protected by copyright and sold to consumers with the understanding that they are to be used *for personal use only.* The fact that you have purchased a pattern or design does not give you a right to sell products made from that pattern or design, any more than your purchase of a piece of artwork gives you the right to recreate it for sale in some other form, such as notepaper or calendars. Only the original creator has such rights. You have simply purchased the physical property for private use.

In spite of this "legality," crafters have been using commercial patterns and designs for years to make products for sale at craft fairs. When sales are limited to this market, problems are not likely to occur. Legal problems may arise, however, if such patterns are used to make finished items offered for sale in consignment shops, rent-a-space gift shops and other retail outlets. Although I am not qualified to give legal advice on copyright law, I have made a thorough study of this topic and have checked with a copyright attorney to verify the accuracy of the information that follows. It will help you avoid legal problems when using commercial patterns and designs to make products for sale.

Projects in Craft Magazines

Generally, it is okay to use the patterns and designs you find in craft and needlework magazines *provided such publications own the copyrights to those designs and authorize readers to use them for profit.* One magazine that does this is *Crafts,* where my "Selling What You Make" column has appeared monthly since 1978. In an editorial, Judith Brossart explained this magazine's policy: "PJS Publications Inc. copyrights the entire magazine, but you, our readers can still use the projects to make for resale. The rule is *you must make the entire*

Dry It and Sell It

Glenn Stark diversified his farm operation by creating a unique gift item, a miniature version of the old-style corn drying rack featuring colorful miniature corn. It was a big job to harvest this corn by hand, sort it and place the ears on dryers, but the first winter Glenn and his family made and sold 250 of the miniature dryers at craft fairs and nearby shops.

Two things that rarely fail to find a market are miniature food items and dried gift products such as herbal mixes, flower arrangements or applehead dolls. Think about a special crop you might grow to diversify your farm income, but don't think miniature only. Also consider products you might grow for sale as supplies to crafters, such as corn husks for dolls and related items, wheat for wheat weavings or dried items for making wreaths, pictures, flower arrangements or potpourris.

project(s) yourself and be the only person who profits from it! You may not set up an assembly line, have someone else do part of the work, or sell your finished items through a consignment shop."

Other magazines may have a similar policy, but the only way to know for sure its to write to each of them and find out. The big question is whether the magazine or the designer owns the copyright. Some designers sell their how-to projects on an all-rights basis, while others sell only "first rights" (meaning they have retained the exclusive right to sell finished products or kits made from their own patterns and designs). If you learn that a copyright is owned by a designer, you could write to him or her in care of the magazine, requesting permission to make and sell the item. Some designers may give permission to make a limited number of items for sale at the retail level, and most would be receptive to the idea of being paid a royalty on a product that might reach a large wholesale market.

Quilting and Sewing Patterns

Contemporary quilt designers will find eager buyers among people who appreciate fine art, and they may be able to copyright their original creations. Many buyers, however, prefer to buy quilts made from traditional patterns they recognize. Because the old quilt patterns are not protected by copyrights, they can be freely used for commercial purposes.

Patterns that you buy in your local fabric store can be used to make custom-made clothing and other items for individual buyers, but you cannot wholesale a line of products made from such patterns. In some cases, it is legally dangerous even to sell a few products at a crafts fair or home boutique. For example, the fact that you can buy a pattern to make a Raggedy Ann doll does not mean you can legally make that product for sale. Crafters are walking on dangerous ground whenever they offer for sale any product that bears a reproduction of famous characters such as Snoopy, the Sesame Street Gang or the cartoon characters of Warner Brothers and the Walt Disney Company.

Famous Copyrighted Characters

While browsing a sidewalk craft fair in my town, I noticed that several crafters were selling originally designed clothing made from fabric with Walt Disney characters on it. Trying to be helpful, I explained to one seller that unless she had a licensing arrangement with Disney, she was violating their copyright and could get into trouble. She didn't take kindly to my advice, saying, "Everyone else is selling things with Disney characters on them, so why shouldn't I?"

The fact that everybody is doing something doesn't make it right, and in this case, it was not only illegal but financially dangerous for the crafters in question. (This problem was compounded by the fact that a quantity of fabric with Disney characters on it had accidentally slipped into retail sewing stores in 1995. Disney later recalled this fabric and reportedly sued some retailers for selling Disney-related merchandise without a license.) Because the Walt Disney Company is aggressive in protecting its rights, you should never, *never* sell a product with one of their designs on it.

Changing Patterns for Your Own Use

I'll bet some of you are thinking you don't have anything to worry about because when you use a pattern, you always make changes to it. Unfortunately, changing a pattern does not entitle you to claim the revised pattern as your own. You can't just lift something here, add it to something there, change this and rearrange that.

Imagine this scenario: A consumer has purchased a pattern to get ideas for items she can make to sell at retail. She decides she can improve the pattern by making changes here and there. In time she comes up with what she actually believes is an "original pattern," and she justifies the originality of this pattern by the fact that her finished item does not look *exactly* like the one that inspired her design. But if it only looks "similar," that would be sufficient grounds for a lawsuit, provided the copyright holder wanted to go that far. (Generally, if you're found to be innocently infringing on someone else's copyright, you'll get a polite but stern letter from the designer's attorney telling you to cease selling that item at once.)

Reevaluate Your Product Line

After you've been selling for a while, take time to reevaluate your product line and consider new buyer groups you might target. Do you have an interesting variety of things in different sizes, shapes, colors and designs? What could you do to spice up your line? Could you change certain products in your line to make them appeal to different people, for example:

◆ Men instead of women (or vice versa)

◆ Boys instead of girls

◆ Corporate buyers instead of consumers

◆ College students instead of younger children

◆ Sportswomen instead of sportsmen

◆ Career women instead of homemakers

If your "similar creation" is sold in finished form at the retail level only (fairs, holiday boutiques, bazaars, or by mail), chances are good that no one will ever notice (or care) that, technically, you've violated the copyright law and a designer's rights. But let's take this a step further. What if our imaginary consumer now decides to print her "original pattern" for sale to other crafters. Whoops! Now she's really asking for trouble. You see, if any *portion* of her pattern is identical to the pattern she originally bought, or if she has merely rearranged the order of the printed instructions or changed a few words here and there, she has violated the original designer's copyright.

Never assume that such copyright infringement will go unnoticed by the original designer. The crafts community has an excellent word-of-mouth network that carries such news. Moreover, designers commonly purchase copies of all patterns for items similar to those they've designed just to be sure no one is profiting from their copyrighted work. They lay the patterns out side by side to determine if their patterns have "inspired" copies. If so, they will be quick to put an end to the matter with a letter from an attorney. If pattern sales do not cease, the copyright infringer may be forced to refund all money customers send in the future or give all profits to the original creator.

The Designer's Viewpoint

Most designers realize that craft consumers are using their patterns to make a few items for sale in local fairs, boutiques and shops. While they rarely encourage this practice, most do nothing to curtail it unless an individual abuses this privilege. What concerns them are individuals who try to build a business

Analyze Sales and Costs

Barbara Tauber operates Barbara's Creations, selling a variety of fabric items priced between $9.95 and $51.95. Her line includes seasonal crafts, pillows and stitched verses for special occasions and people. "Quality is very important," she says. "I add up to twenty new items every year, bring back last year's best items and drop the rest. As long as an item sells well, I keep making it. I have a witch that is a classic and has been around for the fifteen years that I have been in business."

When an old item begins to drop in sales, Barbara weeds it out and moves on. Unlike most craft sellers, she annually reviews sales and items and has inventory sheets and notebooks with information going back ten years. "You have to keep a tight rein on expenses and know down to the penny what every item costs," she emphasizes.

around their copyrighted patterns and designs. It is at this point that "commercialization" raises its ugly head and begins to threaten the profits of the original designer or publisher.

For example, let's say that a designer sells an original doll pattern to a magazine on a first-rights basis. This means the magazine can publish the how-to pattern once for the benefit of its readers with the idea that they will probably make one or two for their personal use, as gifts, or maybe for sale at a local fair.

Now imagine that the designer sees a market for her doll in kit form, or a major manufacturer wants to buy the rights to produce it *en masse*, offering royalties on each sale. If craft consumers across the country are selling finished versions of her original design in the same marketplace, this will obviously hurt her potential for profit. At this point, a professional designer may be forced to take legal action. I recall the story of one doll designer who sold her patterns by mail for years. Then a woman used one of her patterns to create a variation of the doll, claiming it as her own. When the original designer learned that a rip-off of her doll had been offered to a manufacturer for mass production, she had to sue the craftsperson to protect her copyright.

To reiterate, some people believe it's okay to take bits and pieces from several copyrighted patterns, a head here, a leg and arm there, facial features from another source. But this does not constitute "originality," and since the original designers of any feature that has been copied can come after the infringer, the possibilities for a legal confrontation have only been multiplied.

Developing Your Own Designs

Today's more discerning buyers are tired of seeing the same handmade items everywhere they go. Thus, if you offer the same things everyone else is selling, your sales will suffer. In trying to get ideas for what will sell at a crafts fair, do some serious market research by browsing many different craft fairs. Study all the exhibits, the individual product lines, the way merchandise is displayed, and how it is priced. Walk in the customer's shoes and ask yourself what you'd be willing to buy at each fair. Make notes about things that turn you off. Notice which booths are attracting the most lookers and which ones seem to be making the most sales. What is there about these particular exhibits that stands out in your mind? This kind of market research will often trigger profitable ideas and provide answers to your own selling problems.

Tip

"Walk the shows and fairs to see what's there and what's not," advises a crafter who specializes in scarecrows. "Then, using your own creativity and imagination, make what's not there. I did, and I went from $67 at my first show to a gross income of $25,000 for four months of shows."

"Anything that appears in a national crafts magazine is guaranteed to be for sale at later craft fairs," says Joyce Roark, who has learned the importance of using only her own designs. "If something is fast and inexpensive to make, chances are hundreds of other crafters in your area are making the same thing. Such products are harder to sell because the customer has many crafters to choose from."

Joyce subscribes to a variety of craft magazines to stay knowledgeable about what other crafters are making, but she does not use commercially available patterns for things she sells. "If I can make it, so can millions of other people," she says. Each year, Joyce introduces all-new designs of items in her Loving Thoughts line, which includes jewelry, pillow covers, angels, dolls and tree ornaments. "I never sell the same thing two years in a row," she says, "and I try constantly to improve on my designs. Originally designed products with reasonable prices are one secret to successfully outselling other crafters."

I think I just heard someone moan, "But I'm not an artist! I can't even draw a straight line." True, you may not be an artist, but there is a natural streak of creativity and artistry in each of us. Some people design by making sketches.

Concentrate on Quality

Custom-made dolls were the staple of Stewart Madsen's crafts business until he accidentally discovered a great demand for his custom-made Halloween costumes. One thing Stewart has learned from selling both dolls and costumes is that word-of-mouth referrals are the most valuable form of advertising. "If you give customers quality, they will return and bring their friends, but if you give them junk, they will forget you quicker than yesterday's meatloaf," he warns.

Stewart's dolls are made generally of felt with embroidered or painted faces, but sometimes a face may be of paper mache or clay. "Customers may want a doll that looks like someone in particular, or one with a particular baby outfit in a display setting," he says. "Many of my customers have some fabric they value, probably for sentimental reasons, and they want it used rather than just sitting in a drawer. Because each of my dolls are handmade and unique, I have no standard price."

In building a successful crafts business, Stewart emphasizes the importance of ignoring minor setbacks, learning from your mistakes and listening to all the advice people give you, even if it's not necessarily good advice. "Let your customers know you care about them and want them to buy the best, then sell only the best to them," he concludes.

Others design by feel and intuition, trying first one idea or technique, then another. My most creative ideas generally come in the form of a "brilliant brainstorm" when I'm in the middle of a project. This creative design process can be speeded up simply by getting in the habit of constantly feeding your mind with fresh images and ideas. Then you'll have a reservoir from which to draw when you want to express a new level of creativity.

I've always believed that creativity is merely the discovery of something that's been there all along. The trouble with most people is that they begin with a negative attitude, dismissing the possibility that they may really have creative abilities. Instead, why don't you look in the mirror and say to yourself, "I've got a lot of undiscovered talent somewhere, and I intend to find it!"

How? Begin by sharpening your sense of creativity and design by developing a "seeing eye." Don't just *look* at something, really try to *see* it. Designs are everywhere for the taking. You need only train your eyes to see them. When you look at clouds, haven't you sometimes seen something interesting in their formations—an animal, perhaps, or a face? Have you ever noticed the interesting design on your window as the setting sun casts a shadow of bare branches or looked at an object silhouetted against the sun? When looking at such

Three Quick "What-to-Make" Tips

What else can you make for sale? "Things that grandparents can buy that their young grandchildren can play with and not destroy are always good sellers," advises Eleanor Holt.

"Try to appeal more to children, offering gifts they can buy for relatives and friends," says Theresa Jackson. "Small items, low prices."

"Make nothing you cannot give as a present, so lack of sales is not a total loss," adds Linda Throckmorton.

common things as spider webs, leaves, and seashells, look for the patterns (sometimes it helps to squint a little), then try to draw what you've seen.

Now don't tell me you can't draw. You did it as a child, right? So what makes you think you can no longer do this? Even childlike drawings can form the foundation for usable designs. (What you call "crude" may be perceived by others as "primitive folk art," which commands high prices.) You won't see anything unless you really look, and ideas won't come to you unless you work to get them.

Tip

After you have filled your mind with ideas and impressions, ask "How can I combine these ideas in a way that is different from what everyone else is doing?"

Randall Barr knows what I'm talking about. In 1995, he sold nearly 6,000 of his "Time Flies" Birdhouse Clocks, and he would have sold 10,000 if he could have figured out how to make that many. So how did he get such a clever product idea? "Most of my ideas come to me either when I'm just going to sleep or just waking up," he said. "I kind of program myself to be aware of ideas, and the Birdhouse Clock was just one of those 'Ah-ha!' ideas we all get from time to time. After having bypass surgery in 1993, I had to get out of the oil business, but I still needed something to do. I had been making music boxes for sale at craft fairs, and then I got the idea of making a music box clock. As I was programming my subconscious mind to the idea that I needed to come up with something more unusual than this, my younger daughter came home one weekend with a handmade gift for her mother. It was a little birdhouse she had made with a mushroom bird on it. I had never seen a mushroom bird before, but after finding a supply source for the item, I remembered George Washington Carver and how he had asked God what he could do with a peanut. So I asked what I could do with a mushroom bird, and Birdhouse Clocks were the answer."

This is a perfect example of how creativity and serendipity work hand in hand (with a little help from the Divine Creator), a topic I've discussed at greater length in the last chapter of this book.

CHAPTER FOUR

Getting Serious about Business

The first step to building a profitable crafts enterprise at home is to think of it as a business, not a hobby. It doesn't matter whether your annual income goal is $500 or $50,000 a year— what's important is that you treat your new endeavor as a real business.

"Can a person really make enough money in the crafts business to support a family?" asks a crafter named Sharon. "If so, how? Everyone I talk to simply does it for extra money."

It's natural for beginning sellers to consider money from crafts as "pin money" or hobby income hardly worth mentioning, let alone reporting to the Internal Revenue Service. In time, however, the dollars begin to multiply with something left over after expenses. At the point when this money becomes regular supplemental income, it takes on new significance. Although many creative people could go on to build a business that would generate enough money to support themselves or a family, most back off at this point and settle for extra income. As I explained in Chapter Two, the reasons for this are many, but often they boil down to being afraid of the unknown.

There is nothing wrong in selling crafts for fun and extra money. Everything in this book is designed to help you do exactly that. An involvement in art or crafts is a life-enriching experience and, in these hard economic times, even an extra thousand dollars a year from a hobby activity can make a big difference to an individual or family. *But so many people settle for making just a little money when, with extra effort and a change of attitude, they could earn a lot more.* If you want to sell mostly for the fun of it, that's fine. But if you really need supplemental income or want to turn your art or craft into a full-time homebased business, this chapter contains the nitty-gritty information you need to get started on the right foot.

While it's true that a well-managed homebased crafts business can become a wonderful little money machine that regularly contributes much-needed income, this money isn't going to pour from heaven. You're going to have to *work* to earn it, and the amount of money you can expect to make from your crafts activity will be directly related to

1. The kind of products you are selling and the quality of materials being used
2. The quality of your designs and how well your products are crafted
3. Whether there is a need in the marketplace for the type of products you make
4. How much competition you have
5. How well your prices are matched to your targeted buying audience
6. How professionally your products are packaged and presented for sale
7. How efficiently you manage the business details of your moneymaking activity
8. How diligently you work to improve your marketing strategies
9. How willing you are to keep trying to improve everything you do
10. Your attitude about what you are doing

Most of today's successful crafters began as hobbyists who knew how to do one thing exceptionally well, and they achieved financial success because they paid attention to the ten points above. Whether your financial goals are large or small, you will find yourself way ahead of the competition if you begin your new crafts endeavor as a real business and not just a moneymaking hobby. Once you believe you are really "in business" and not just fooling around, your whole attitude will change and your opportunities for profit will begin to multiply.

Tip

The more professional you become in your approach to selling, the more money you are likely to earn. The more you earn, the more serious you will become about your small business endeavor.

Ten Craft Business Start-Up Steps

Because this is a crafts marketing book and not a home-business guide, my discussion of business basics must be limited to a brief discussion of what I believe to be the ten most important things you should do when starting a small crafts business at home. If you are already selling your crafts and have neglected to take care of some of the legal and financial matters discussed below, do them now. It is never too late to do things right. For detailed information on all of the following topics and many others related to starting and managing a business, see my recommended reading list at the end of this chapter.

STEP 1:   Find Out about Zoning Regulations, Licenses and Permits

Zoning. Call your city hall or the library for a copy of your community's zoning regulations. Find out what zone you're in and read the section that pertains to home occupations. Depending on where you live, and when your community last updated its zoning laws, you may or may not have a zoning problem. Generally, artists, craftspeople, writers, designers and mail order businesses have few worries about zoning laws because such businesses cause no noise, customer traffic or parking problems. In fact, unless a neighbor complains, zoning officials have no way of knowing what people are doing in the privacy of their homes. If someone does complain, and you are investigated by zoning officials, you may be asked to cease your home-business activities. Although there have been exceptions, people are rarely fined for a zoning violation unless they persist in the operation of a business after they have been warned to stop.

Tip

If you rent or live in a condominium, your lease or title papers may specifically restrict any kind of business, thus the operation of one could invalidate your tenant's or homeowner's insurance policy.

If zoning conditions in your community are not favorable, be particularly careful about attracting attention to yourself through publicity in your local paper, and avoid customer traffic to your home shop or studio. This kind of activity in a quiet residential neighborhood is likely to trigger complaints and an investigation by zoning officials.

Licenses and Permits. When you start to sell arts and crafts, you automatically become a "homebased business owner" in the eyes of city officials, although you may think of yourself as only a hobbyist. In their zeal to collect additional tax money, many communities are now requiring all homebased businesses to get special licenses or permits. Check with your city or county clerk to see if you need any kind of permit or license to legally produce items in your home for sale at fairs and shows.

STEP 2: Acquaint Yourself with IRS Regulations

You may sell what you make and call it "extra money," but the IRS will call it "profit or loss from business" and expect you to report all your income from crafts, along with related expenses, on a Schedule C (Form 1040).

The IRS says you are in business if you (1) are sincerely trying to make a profit, (2) are making regular business transactions, and (3) have made a profit at least three years out of five. If you make sales, but do not meet the above criteria, your business will be ruled a "hobby," but this income must still be reported on Schedule C. With both types of business, you deduct expenses against the income, but in the case of a hobby business you may deduct expenses only up to the amount of hobby income.

Many crafters sell at fairs, take cash only, and do not report their earnings to the IRS. You can usually spot such people at a crafts fair because they are the ones who ask for cash instead of checks or credit cards, and they never charge sales tax on purchases. I hope you will not be one of these people, because the risk isn't worth it. This practice can only lead to worries about getting caught, and it does nothing to help a small crafts business grow. There are severe penalties for intentional tax evasion or falsification of tax returns.

Actually, there are many personal and financial advantages to declaring your extra crafts income to the IRS. Besides having peace of mind as a legal taxpayer, you may find that your small business profits will give you extra power when applying for a loan or a new credit card. Currently, home-business owners are also entitled to many special home-related tax deductions not enjoyed by the average taxpayer, and taxes can be completely avoided on a portion of net profits through such strategies as hiring one's spouse or children or placing funds in an Individual Retirement Account (IRA) or other retirement fund.

NOTE: This book assumes that the legal form of business most readers will be using is a Sole Proprietorship. If you wish to form as a Sub-Chapter S,

C Corporation, Partnership or Limited Liability Company, it would be wise to consult an attorney or other professional for information on the tax consequences of each of these legal forms of business.

STEP 3: *Register the Name of Your Crafts Business with Local Officials*

When you operate under any name other than your own, you are using a fictitious or assumed business or trade name that must be registered with local authorities. Thus, if you are Mary Smith, and you call your crafts endeavor "Knotty But Nice," you would be using an assumed name. On legal documents and at your bank, it would read, "Mary Smith, dba Knotty But Nice." (The "dba" means "doing business as.")

The registration procedure may vary from state to state, but you will probably have to complete a form given to you by the county clerk and pay a small registration fee. In most states, you must also place a legal ad in a general-circulation newspaper in the county and run it three times. (The appropriate ad copy will be provided to you on request either by the county clerk or the newspaper.) After the ad has run, you will receive a certificate that will be forwarded to the county clerk, who will file it with your registration form. This will make your business completely legitimate. (If you don't want your neighbors to know you're running a business at home—perhaps because you're violating local zoning laws—the newspaper ad can be run in any nearby town or city in your county.)

Tip

If you have not registered your business name to date, *do so now*. Since the form you will complete does not ask when you started your business, the county clerk will assume you're just starting and there should be no problem. *Don't ignore this small legal detail*. If you fail to protect your crafts business name through local registration, anyone who wants to steal it from you can do so simply by filing the form you failed to file with the county clerk.

Optional: To give your business name wider protection and prevent any corporate entity from using it, register it with your state. Call the office of your secretary of state to obtain the necessary form. Expect to pay a small registration fee. National protection for a business name and logo may be obtained with a trademark. Information on how to do this will be found in booklets available from the Patent & Trademark Office. (See Step 7 for address.)

Picking a Good Business Name

The name you give to your crafts business says a lot about who you are and what you do. More important, your business name, coupled with the kind of printed materials you use, gives prospective customers an immediate impression that will ultimately affect their buying decision.

If a name sounds more like a hobby than a business, buyers may be dubious about the quality of products offered or be unwilling to pay the price you need to make a profit. For example, consider the different mental pictures you form when you compare "Kathy's Krafts" to "Katherine's Keepsakes." The latter name not only sounds more professional but suggests a higher-priced line of products.

Many crafters use their first name as part of their business name, such as "Candy's Country Baskets" or "Lou's Stained Glass Art." Other sellers cleverly incorporate their first or last names into a business name appropriate to what they do. Shelley Davies named her business "The Silver Shell Boutique." Donna Dunnigan uses "Dunnigan Designs."

Cleverness is always to be congratulated, but be careful to pick a business name that accurately describes your business and will not become obsolete when you expand your product line. When Holly Button told me she had named her new business "Button & Bows," I thought this was a great name for a sewing business. When Holly said she was planning to sell floral crafts, however, I wondered if she was incorporating buttons and bows in her products. If so, her work is likely to stand apart from the crowd; if not, this name could confuse prospective customers who may be expecting a different kind of product line.

Common phrases often inspire great business names that customers are unlikely to forget. For example, designer Ellen Goldberg turned the phrase "whether or not" into "Leather or Knot," a perfect name for her line of "art to wear" accessories. And do you remember that old movie with Natalie Wood and Robert Wagner called *Splendor in the Grass*? It inspired Lorraine Kallman to name her folk art and decorative painting business "Splendor in the Crafts." Later, at a crafts fair, Lorraine discovered a business named "Splendor in the Glass," suggesting that other craftspeople have also played around with the words in this old movie title. "Creative minds are all on the same plane," explains Carol Hendrix, "Sooner or later different minds are bound to have the same ideas."

STEP 4: Call Your Telephone Company

Many crafters print their home telephone number on their craft business card not realizing that this may be a violation of local telephone regulations. Generally, a personal phone number may not legally be advertised on your business card, letterhead, promotional printed materials or in advertisements. If you use your telephone only to make outgoing calls and not to directly solicit business, you may be able to operate for some time without the expense of a separate business line. If you plan to invite business by phone, however, or are trying to build relationships with wholesale buyers, you'd better bite the bullet and have a separate business line installed, along with an answering machine or voice mail system. Because so many people now work at home, telephone companies are devising new second-line options that may be more affordable than you think. Do explore them because it's hard to grow a business if you can't advertise your phone number.

STEP 5: Open a Checking Account for Your Business

The IRS frowns on taxpayers who try to operate a business out of their personal checkbook because this is not a clear separation of personal and business income and expenses. Call the financial institutions in your area (savings and loans as well as banks) to get comparative costs of a small business checking account. Ask about charges for checks deposited, deposits made, bounced-check charges, cost of checks, etc. If you have a mail order business, pay particular attention to what a bank will charge to process out-of-state checks. To avoid these high fees, I run all my checks through an account I have with a savings and loan association, which charges no service fees and pays interest besides. Savings and loan associations do not give business line-of-credit loans or offer merchant credit card status, however, so take this into consideration when opening an account.

There are different types of business checking accounts, so emphasize that you want to begin with the least expensive account available. (One big difference is the amount you will be charged for printed checks.) If you feel you cannot afford a standard business account, and don't plan to write many business checks, open a separate personal checking account in your name. Don't put your business name on the checks, however, or your bank may insist that you open a standard business account instead. By depositing all your business income to this account and paying all your business expenses from it, you will be creating the necessary separation of personal and business income and expenses the IRS requires.

When talking to the various financial institutions in your area, also get comparative prices for a safety deposit box. I think of my business safety deposit box as another form of insurance because it contains valuable and irreplaceable business papers, computer software and backup tapes, copyrights, master sets of published material, a photographic record of insured property and much more.

STEP 6: *Obtain a Retailer's Occupation Tax Registration Number*

With few exceptions, all states have sales taxes, and in most states there are county and city taxes as well. If you make anything for sale, or if you buy goods for resale, you are required to register your crafts business (even a hobby business) with the Department of Revenue (Sales Tax Division) in your state. This is a simple and painless procedure. You complete a form to receive a special document from the state that will bear a tax exemption number that is sometimes called a "Retailer's Occupation Tax Registration Number" or, more generally, a "resale tax number." The registration fee varies from state to state.

This tax number will enable you to buy materials at wholesale prices without paying sales tax. You cannot, however, run down to the corner crafts store, buy a few dollars' worth of supplies and avoid sales tax. Once you have a tax number, you must start to collect sales tax on everything you sell to consumers, sending the appropriate reports and payments to the state. (It is illegal to collect sales tax and retain it as income).

Many crafters believe that if they sell "just for the fun of it," they are not considered to be in business and thus do not need to be concerned with the collection of sales tax. This is not true. It doesn't matter to your state's Department of Revenue whether you are "in business" in the eyes of the Internal Revenue Service or not. All this agency is concerned with is *whether you are selling directly to consumers on the retail level*. If so, you must collect sales tax and file regular reports with the state. Hobby sellers are not exempt from this law, regardless of how few sales they make.

Tip

You do not have to collect sales tax when you sell crafts through a consignment shop, craft mall or rent-a-shelf-store. It is a shop's responsibility to collect this tax and forward it to the state.

Although craftspeople who sell only at wholesale do not need to collect sales tax on their sales to shops and stores, they do need a tax exemption certification from the state if they want to avoid paying sales tax on purchases of raw materials. Further, they must obtain for their own files the resale tax number of any retail shop or store with whom they do business.

Wingspan.com

Steve

Handy Checklist
of Telephone Calls to Make

☑ **City or County Hall.** Ask for information about:
- Zoning regulations in your area *Michael Crescenzo*
- How to register your crafts business name *537-6171*
- Licenses or permits needed for a homebased business *Lois Chenault 537-6131*

None *None* *Karen Malcom* *Admin. Staff 537-6005*

USE 730 instead of 537
365-6174 · 6171

365
6464

365-6129
6131

☑ **Local IRS office.** Ask for these free tax booklets:
- Publication #334, "Tax Guide for Small Business" *#510*
- Publication #587, "Business Use of Your Home"

On Web http://www.irs.ustreas.gov/prod/forms_pubs/index.html

❏ **Local telephone company**. Ask about the cost of a second line for business and any special services offered to people who work at home.

❏ **Local financial institutions (banks and savings and loans)**. Get information on the cost of a business checking account and safety deposit box.

☑ **Your state's Department of Revenue, Sales Tax Division**. Ask what you need to do to get a sales tax number or tax exemption certificate. *R1 →* *①*

❏ **The insurance agent who handles your homeowner's or renter's policy**. Check on adding an inexpensive rider to your policy that will cover all the supplies and materials in your homebased office, crafts studio or workshop. Also ask about "umbrella policies" that offer extra liability coverage.

❏ **Your auto insurance agent**. Explain that you will occasionally use your vehicle for business.

☑ **Your secretary of state, state capital**. Ask for information on how to register your business name on the state level.

❏ **The U.S. Small Business Administration (SBA)**. Call 1-800-827-5722 to reach the SBA's "Small Business Answer Desk" and access a variety of prerecorded messages. A wealth of free information and publications are available to you on request.

Sba.gov: Print forms

STEP 7: *Learn about Federal Regulations Applicable
                  to Your Crafts Business.*

There are several laws and regulations that have significance for artists and craftspeople, and the different government agencies listed below will send free information on request:

■ Bureau of Consumer Protection, Division of Special Statutes, 6th & Pennsylvania Ave. NW, Washington, DC 20580. Information on labels or tags required by law for items made of wool or textiles. ("Textiles" includes garments, quilts, stuffed toys, knitting, rugs, yarn, piece goods, etc.) Ask specifically for these booklets: *Textile Fiber Products Identification Act* and the *Wool Products Labeling Act of 1939.*

■ Consumer Products Safety Commission, Bureau of Compliance, 5401 Westbard Avenue, Bethesda, MD 20207. Information on safety standards for toys and other products designed for children. Ask for booklets on the *Consumer Product Safety Act of 1972, The Flammable Fabrics Act.*

■ The Copyright Office, Register of Copyrights, Library of Congress, Washington DC 20559. Information on how to register and protect your original designs and patterns. Request all free publications, particularly those on how to file a copyright claim, protect your rights under current copyright law and investigate the copyright status of a work.

■ Federal Trade Commission (FTC), Div. of Legal & Public Records, 6th St. & Pennsylvania Ave. NW, Washington, DC 20580. For information on trade practice and labeling rules. The FTC requires a label for wool and textile products indicating when imported ingredients are used, even when the product is made in the United States. It also requires a permanently affixed "care label" (how to wash or clean) on all textile wearing apparel and household furnishings. Ask specifically for booklets on *The Fabric Care Labeling Rule* and *The Wool Products Labeling Act of 1939.* The FTC also enforces trade practice rules and labeling requirements applicable to specific industries. You may need to read one of these FTC booklets as well: *Guide for the Jewelry Industry; The Hand Knitting Yarn Industry* and *The Catalog Jewelry and Giftware Industry.* If you plan to sell crafts by mail, also request the FTC booklets that explain truth in advertising laws and the 30-day mail order rule.

■ Patent & Trademark Office, U.S. Department of Commerce, Washington, DC 20231. Information about patents and trademarks.

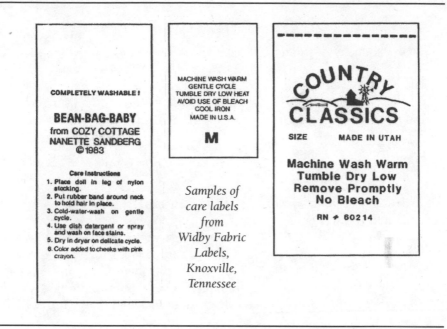

COMPLETELY WASHABLE!

BEAN-BAG-BABY
from COZY COTTAGE
NANETTE SANDBERG
©1983

Care Instructions

1. Place doll in leg of nylon stocking.
2. Put rubber band around neck to hold hair in place.
3. Cold-water-wash on gentle cycle.
4. Use dish detergent or spray and wash on face stains.
5. Dry in dryer on delicate cycle.
6. Color added to cheeks with pink crayon.

MACHINE WASH WARM
GENTLE CYCLE
TUMBLE DRY LOW HEAT
AVOID USE OF BLEACH
COOL IRON
MADE IN U.S.A.

M

Samples of care labels from Widby Fabric Labels, Knoxville, Tennessee

COUNTRY CLASSICS

SIZE   MADE IN UTAH

**Machine Wash Warm
Tumble Dry Low
Remove Promptly
No Bleach**

RN # 60214

STEP 8: Set Up a Good Record-Keeping System.

People who lack business experience often worry need-lessly about keeping records and tax information. I have no great love for the Internal Revenue Service, but one nice thing about the IRS is that it does not require any special kind of bookkeeping system for businesses. It simply requires one to keep accurate records on all money that comes in and goes out.

That means you can start with a simple journal and ledger book from an office supply store. (Check out the *Dome Simplified Monthly* record-keeping book.) As you begin to sell, you will quickly learn what kind of records you need to keep to monitor sales and figure profits. Devise any system that feels comfortable to you and gives you the necessary figures needed for your an-nual Schedule C Form. Your bookkeeping will automatically improve as you learn more about business and the kind of information you want to record for your own use. If you keep accurate records during the year, it will be easy at year's end to work with a tax advisor or accountant to prepare your annual tax return. Specific record-keeping tips have been included in other chapters of this book—check the index to find all of them.

Record-Keeping Tips

◆ "So many of us are so thrilled to sell our wares that we forget we have expenses. I have a book with the various categories of expenses related to my business, from porcelain and supplies to office expenses, freight charges, education (books, seminars, etc.) and taxes. I do a listing every month of all my sales and expenses, and at the end of the year I have a clear and verifiable picture of my net profit. This makes it easy to get all the paperwork together for my tax man."
— Gaby Olson

◆ "Every year after Christmas, review all your records. Make a list of what sold and what didn't, including details about style, size, colors and so on. Remake only the things that sold, paying particular attention to colors, styles and sizes that sold best. If you are selling through a shop and can't mark down items that didn't sell, remove them to make room for new items. I add new items every three or four months during the year. That way people will keep coming back to see what new items you have."
— Jerry Deidrich

◆ "You have to know what every item costs in order to make a profit. I keep notebooks with sales information. Every year, I carefully monitor my inventory records and review sales to learn which items are selling best. When an item starts dropping in sales, I weed it out and move on."
— Barbara Tauber

For help in setting up a professional bookkeeping system on paper, see the book, *Small Time Operator* in the Resources section. If you have a computer, there are several simple bookkeeping and tax accounting software programs that will make this job easy. Any computer software store can tell you about them.

STEP 9: Make Sure You're Properly Insured.

Homeowner's or Renter's Policy. You may have quite a bit of money invested in tools, equipment, raw materials and finished handcrafts, so be sure to tell your insurance agent that you are running a business at home. Anything you use to generate income would be exempt from coverage on a personal policy. To protect such items, you can add a special rider (very inexpensive) to your homeowner's or renter's policy to cover business equipment, supplies, inventory, goods made for sale but not yet shipped, etc. Or, check out the special home-business policies now being offered by various insurance companies.

Many art and craft organizations also offer insurance programs to their members. For example, the American Craft Association offers a studio policy that protects against loss to both unfinished and finished works, at home or away, including craft fairs, malls and rent-a-space shops. (Their toll-free number is 1-800-724-0859.) The National Association of Fine Artists offers health, life, disability, dental, property and casualty insurance to artists and crafters. (Their toll-free number is 1-800-996-NAFA.) To find other organizations with insurance programs, check your library for a national directory of associations and organizations.

Computer Insurance. If you use a home computer in your business, do not insure your computer system on the same business rider that protects your office or workshop. Such coverage is usually limited to fire or theft, and losses may be calculated on a depreciated basis instead of replacement cost. The best coverage will be obtained from a company that specializes in computer insurance and offers broad, all-risk coverage on a replacement cost basis. One such company is Safeware, The Insurance Agency, Inc., in Columbus, Ohio. Check computer magazines for ads from other companies.

Personal Liability Insurance. The average homeowner's policy includes some personal liability insurance but does not cover business activities on the premises. Be sure to find out how much personal liability insurance you have. This is especially important if customers regularly come into your home to buy crafts. (Why people are on your property may determine the amount of liability coverage your policy provides.) Discuss this matter with your insurance agent and ask if an umbrella policy might extend your personal liability coverage on homebased business activities. A million dollars' worth of coverage may cost less than a hundred dollars a year.

Car Insurance. Be sure to tell your insurance agent if you occasionally use your car for business purposes. Make sure you have coverage for an accident that might occur when you are driving to or from a crafts fair or delivering merchandise to buyers. Also, if you plan to let an employee drive your personal vehicle, ask your insurance agent about "nonownership contingent liability protection," which would protect you in the event your employee had an accident while driving your car. Where insurance is concerned, the more questions you ask, the safer you'll be.

Product Liability Insurance. Few craft sellers purchase product liability insurance because craft products are considered relatively safe. Much depends on what is being offered for sale and whether the average buyer could conceivably suffer any kind of injury from such a product. If you have a growing wholesale business, however, you may one day discover that some buyers will not purchase your merchandise unless you carry product liability insurance. The cost of a policy varies from one area to another but is generally based on one's annual gross sales, the number of products sold, and the possible risks associated with each of them. Agencies that sell business or commercial insurance can provide more specific information.

STEP 10:   Decide Which Printed Materials You Need to Do an Effective Promotional and Selling Job.

This topic is so important that I've given it a separate chapter of its own. (In Chapter Thirteen, you will find tips on the specific printed materials you can use to increase sales, improve your professional image and get higher prices for everything you sell.)

You may have noticed that "call a lawyer" is not on my list of the ten most important things to do. Contrary to popular belief, there is no need to consult a lawyer when starting a homebased business as a sole proprietorship. Sure, a lawyer will be happy to charge you a big fee for answering a lot of small business questions, but you can get the same information and more from any of the small business books I've recommended at the end of this chapter.

You would be wise, however, to consult a lawyer if you are forming a partnership or corporation, entering into a long-term agreement, making a licensing or franchise arrangement, buying property, negotiating or enforcing any kind of contract or trying to stop someone's infringement of your registered trademark or copyright. You do not need a lawyer, however, to file a copyright form.

Recommended Reading

It is beyond the scope of this book to provide detailed information on all the tax, legal and financial topics relevant to people who sell arts and crafts. However, such information is readily available to you in these and other books in your library or bookstore.

● *Business Forms and Contracts for Craftspeople* by Leonard D. DuBoff (Interweave Press).

● *Homemade Money—How to Select, Start, Manage, Market and Multiply the Profits of a Business at Home* by Barbara Brabec (Betterway Books).

● *The Law (in Plain English) for Craftspeople* by Leonard D. DuBoff (Interweave Press).

● *Make It Legal* by Lee Wilson (Allworth Press/North Light Books).

● *Patent, Copyright & Trademark: A Desk Reference to Intellectual Property Law* by attorney Stephen Elias (Nolo Press).

● *Small Time Operator—How to Start Your Own Business, Keep Your Books, Pay Your Taxes, and Stay Out of Trouble* by Bernard Kamoroff, CPA (Bell Springs Publishing).

● *Turning Your Great Idea Into a Great Success* by Judy Ryder (Peterson's).

CHAPTER FIVE

Pricing Problems and Solutions

"Price" is the figure something sells for. "Value" is what that item is worth to a buyer. Quite often the two have nothing to do with one another.

Do successful sellers use formulas to set prices on their products and services, or do they just charge what they think people will pay? Yes, to both questions. Smart craftspeople do use pricing formulas, but they also weigh their formulated prices against the marketplace itself, and either raise or lower them according to their instinct about what the market will bear. Formulas are fun, but they are often impractical. Here is a simple one you can play around with:

Materials + Labor + Overhead + Profit = Wholesale price × 2 = Retail

Athough pricing formulas appear in all the craft business books, few crafters use them with success, so let's put formulas aside and explore common pricing problems and solutions that have worked for others. To give you an idea of how insecure others are on this topic, consider the following questions posed in one of my pricing workshops for members of a professional arts and crafts organization (most of whom had been selling at arts and crafts fairs for years):

■ How do you get the price you are worth?
■ Why do I feel guilty asking the price I think I'm worth?
■ How do we convince a customer that the price on our items is fair?

Why do we always feel that we need to underprice our items in order for them to sell?

Is it best to price your items at even or uneven figures?

How do you figure overhead costs?

Does pricing too low make your product appear inferior?

Should I charge more than I am now getting for a product that is absolutely unique? I sell out nearly every show.

How can I sell at wholesale when I have trouble getting people to pay my retail price?

How do you set a price and stick with it? If someone says "Oh, I can't afford that," I feel sorry for them and lower my price. Then I'm mad because I lose."

Once I have established a price, is it okay to change it, depending on where my show will be?

In working with this group of professional crafters, I conducted a little experiment. I asked everyone to write two figures on a slip of paper: What they thought their time was worth an hour, and what they figured they were actually getting per hour for the time they were putting into their art or craft. Here is how 107 individuals responded to that question. (The slash mark between crafts indicates different craftspeople):

My Time is Worth:	I'm Actually Getting:
$1	$8 (wood items)
$4	$4 (painting and needlework)
$4.50	$1.50 (paper products)
$5	$7.50 (fabric); $3.50 (fabrics and needlework/ soapmaking); $2.50 (woodcrafts); $2 (quilting and stitchery/floral and wood/wire trees); $1.50 (knitting/eggcraft); $1 (tole painting)
$5.50	$1.75 (folk art)
$6	$4 (ceramics); $3.50 (weaving/wood and fabric crafts); $3 (mixed media); $2 (fabric); $1 (mixed media)
$6.50	$10.75 (tole painting)
$7	$4 (wood and fiber); $3 (cloth dolls/fabrics); $2 woodworking/woodturnings)

continued on next page

My Time is Worth:	I'm Actually Getting:
$8	$4 (sewing); $3 (pottery); $2 (fiber artist/dried flowers)
$9	$4 (wooden furniture, toys); $1.20 (fiber)
$10	$10 (stoneware pottery/paper/fabric lampshades); $8 (stained glass) $7 (cut and pierced and fabric lampshades); $6 (bread dough art/hand-painted crocks/glass/wood and decorative painting/ wreaths/dried flowers/dried arrangements/fabric sculpture); $5 (wood crafts/ceramics/folk art and basketry/floral work, fibercrafts/baskets/weaving/ wood products/stained glass/wood and decorative painting/silk flowers and lap quilts/soft sculpture toys/floral design/metals/wood cuts and folk painting/tole painting/stained glass); $4 (quilting); $3 (mixed media/stained glass/dried florals/wood/ lace); $2.50 (cloth dolls/silver jewelry); $2 (pine cones/painting/cross stitch/needlework);$1 (fabric); $.50 (cross stitch in handmade frames)
$12	$6 (wood items); $5 (wood and folk art painting); $4 (baskets); $1 (pierced lampshades)
$13	$5 (baskets)
$14	$5 (fabric crafts)
$15	$10 (fiber arts); $9 (wood and fabric);$7.50 (decorative painting); $7 (wheat weaving); $6 (fibercrafts/ clothing); $5.50 (Victorian painted wood); $5 (woodcarving/macrame and wreaths/ woodcrafts); 1 (dried flowers)
$18	$10 (porcelain repair); $4 (teacher)
$20	$10 (fiber/dried flowers/goldsmith/lampshades); $7 (wood signs);$5 (needlework/oil painting/ basketry/fabric sculpture)
$25	$12 (silhouette pictures); $10 (doll design patterns);$2 (photographer)

As you can see, the greatest area of response was in the $10 per hour category, and within this category, most crafters reported earning just $5 per hour. Only in a couple of instances did people report earning more per hour than they actually thought they were worth. Notice the different values craftspeople working in the same medium place on the worth of their time and what they are actually receiving per hour. For example, people working in wood reported receiving as little as $2.50 and as much as $10 per hour. Notice that only a dozen people out of 107 (11 percent) thought they were worth $20 an hour, but *none* of them were making this much. In fact, on average, these 107 crafters thought their time was worth $10.87 an hour, but on average, they were making only $2.82 an hour.

Rather than discourage you with such figures, I'm hoping to shock some of you awake, to make you realize that your prices and craft profits are never going to climb higher until you learn to take pricing seriously. First, you need to study the marketplace to see what's selling and what you might offer that no one else is selling. Then you need to "psych out" your buyers.

The Psychology of Pricing

Have you ever noticed that people with limited funds will often pay more for a product or service than they originally intended, simply because they need to buy a little confidence or prestige along with their purchase? Paying more for something gives some people a feeling of importance or something to brag about to friends.

When you realize that people will also pay a great deal more for certain things nostalgic, whimsical or collectible, you will have discovered yet another important pricing secret related to human nature. People do not buy products or services per se, they buy *benefits*. And that is exactly what you provide each time you satisfy a buyer's secret urge or inner longing. You also provide benefits when you save buyers time, money or aggravation, solve some difficult gift-giving problems, allay certain fears or add to their general peace of mind.

Knowledge about pricing comes with time, experience and confidence in your own worth as a producer of quality handcrafted merchandise. As a creative person who appreciates handmade things, it may be hard for you to accept that most buyers do not care how long it takes you to make something or how much it costs to make. Their only concern is whether your price matches their pocketbook and their estimation of the worth of your product.

If your prices are on the high side, buyers will naturally weigh their desire for your craftwork against the money they have to spend. Some of them will mentally compare your beautiful creations to the price of machine-made imitations and walk away feeling that your prices are unrealistic. On the other hand, if your prices are too low for the high-quality work you are offering, some people may feel you do not place a high enough value on your work, so they do not care to own it.

Because you are dealing with human nature when you sell handcrafts, it helps to develop an invisible shell to protect you from less appreciative people.

Getting a Grip on Expenses

All businesses deal with three sets of expense figures: production costs, selling expenses, and overhead. Production costs include all the raw materials that go into your products, while selling expenses include such things as show fees, display costs, photography, packaging materials, samples and sales commissions. Overhead expenses include telephone, fax and computer expenses, equipment purchases, maintenance and depreciation, office supplies, stationery, postage and postal fees, bank charges, legal and professional expenses, travel and auto expenses, subscriptions, memberships and conference fees, advertising, bank fees and cost of accepting credit card charges, employee or independent contractor or employee expense, and "home office expenses" (a percentage of your rent or mortgage expense, taxes, insurance and utilities).

For simplicity's sake, most crafters include selling costs in with their regular overhead figures. Once you know what your average overhead is each year, you can use this figure and divide by the number of hours you work each year to arrive at an hourly overhead figure. For example, if your overhead is $3,000 and you work 1,000 hours a year, your hourly overhead would be $3. You could either add this to your hourly labor wage or apply it proportionally to each of your products on a percentage basis. Thus, if you can make three of something in an hour, and you've calculated your hourly overhead to be $3, you would then add $1 to the price of each item you make to cover your overhead. Or, if it takes two hours to make a product, you would add $6 to the product's cost to cover your overhead.

Keep in mind that other consumers and wholesale buyers are currently spending millions of dollars each year at fine craft shows across the country, proving that many people do appreciate the value of handcrafts and are willing to pay a good price to obtain them. Your constant challenge as a crafts seller will be to find these buyers.

Underpricing Crafts

After giving a series of crafts marketing workshops in Michigan at the height of the 1982 recession, I finally understood that the biggest problem of beginning sellers is not just pricing but underpricing of their products. Many people I spoke with in Michigan felt their handcrafted products could not sell at higher prices, yet most had never *tried* to sell them at a higher price. They

were instead basing their "pricing logic" on their own limited knowledge of
what the local market would bear, and they had no conception of what tourists or buyers in larger cities might pay.

If the rest of the country was then in a recession, Michigan was in a depres-
sion, according to the home economists I talked with. Yet, in Midland, Michigan, a craft shop owner told me that price was not the object when items were
well made and in keeping with what buyers wanted to buy at that time. And a
craftswoman who was then selling lifesize cloth sculptures at $350–$400 told
me, "The economy has had no adverse effect on my sales. If anything, the
recession has helped sales because people need something to make them laugh,
and my sculptures do just that."

In the years since I did those workshops in Michigan, recessions have come
and gone and crafters are still underpricing their work. From a survey of thirty
professional craftspeople who attended one of my all-day seminars in Missouri in 1995, I learned that

38% were earning less than $5 per hour, with two reporting 20 to 30 cents
    per hour
44% (nearly half) said they figured they were earning between $5 and $10
    per hour
 1% reported between $12 and $15 per hour
17% between $20 and $50 per hour

In gross dollars annually,

57% were earning under $5,000
28% were earning between $6,000 and $20,000
 2% were earning $21,000 to $50,000
13% were earning more than $50,000 (with one business reporting nearly
    $500,000 a year)

As a hobby seller, you may be content to take what you can get from local
residents, but if you are striving to be more successful and you can't sell something at a profit in your area, *go somewhere else.* Enter craft fairs of a higher
caliber outside your usual market area. Sell through craft malls or rent-a-space
shops in more affluent areas, or test an ad in one of the consumer magazines
that now showcase American handcrafts. (See Chapter Twelve for more information on these "catalog-magazines.") Consider creating a few products you can
wholesale and present them to buyers in other cities. As one bright craftswoman
pointed out in one of my workshops, "I don't see a brick wall around our town."

Why You Shouldn't Lower Prices at a Fair

Some crafters say they negotiate prices at craft fairs or lower them toward the end of the day, but this is an unprofitable strategy used mostly by hobby sellers. If lack of sales convinces you that your prices are too high, change them before trying to sell them at another fair, but don't mark them down at day's end just to get rid of them.

"I have been going to craft fairs for four years now," says a crafter from El Paso. "In my opinion, no crafter should lower prices at the end of the day at a fair. Customers do watch everything that goes on. If customers notice you lowering your prices at the end of the day, they will wait to see how low the prices will go, and they may even ask you to lower your prices more. Also, customers may come to you and ask you to lower your prices in the morning because they have something else to do, and because they recall that you lowered your prices at the last fair. What would you tell such a customer when new customers are listening?

"You always have the few who try to get you to lower your prices by belittling your craftsmanship. You can have a fair on one side of town and crafts you felt would sell, don't. Then across town you attend another fair and everything sells. What has worked for me is not to lower prices but to pack up my crafts and say I did well and will do better at the next fair because peoples' tastes are different everywhere I go."

Anticipate questions you're likely to get from customers and be ready with answers. In the *Crafting for Profit* newsletter published by *Better Homes and Gardens,* retailer Bruce Baker, a veteran of hundreds of crafts shows, shared some of the stock phrases he uses. He calls them his "Don't Go Away Mad (Just Go Away)" comments. For example, if someone whines, "$75 for *that*?" he just smiles and says, "They're not for everyone." Or if someone is quibbling about the price of everything, he might say, "Does this look like a garage sale to you?" or, "I'd love to be able to sell it for that, but I can't. If you check around, I think you'll find my prices quite competitive."

The important thing, Baker emphasizes, is to always deliver your don't-go-away-mad messages in a good-natured manner. "Aggressiveness is harmful; assertiveness gains respect."

The next time your fellow crafters start lowering prices at the end of a day, refuse to lower yours on the grounds that your beautiful creations are worth as much at the end of the day as they were at the beginning. If you hold fast and refuse to mark down your prices—and tell customers why—I believe you will make as many sales as anyone. And you will certainly stand out in the crowd! If someone really likes your work, they will buy it at full price and respect you for not lowering your standards.

¢ Price Endings: Even or Uneven?

If you pay close attention to price tags on all kinds of merchandise, you will begin to notice that each industry uses a certain pricing structure. Books, for example, have prices that end in "95" or "99." Fine art is always priced in even dollars and no cents. Gift shops seem to like merchandise that ends in "50." Some people think $9.98 sounds less expensive than $10, but to me it sounds like the price you expect to pay for something in a discount store. For that reason, I do not recomend using prices that end in "98" or "99." There are no hard and fast rules, but I think you also should avoid using the following prices, which I have rarely seen used by professional sellers:

$8, $9, $11, $13, $14, $17, $18, $19, $28, $29, $31 and so on.

Using a price that ends with "25" seems foolish to me since a quarter means nothing to most people. In moving up to "50," the most popular prices for crafts seem to be $2.50, $3.50, $7.50 and $12.50. Instead of using $5.50, however, I suggest you move the price up to $6; instead of using $8.50 or $9.50, go to $10; instead of $13.50 or $14.50, go to $15 and so on. My logic has always been that if I were willing to pay $4.50 for something, I would just as easily pay $5. In transferring this logic to buyers, I believe that anyone who is willing to pay $16.50 will probably pay $20 without question. If they're willing to pay $32.75, they will pay $35, and so on. Remember that people often buy crafts because their heart has dictated the purchase, so they are not likely to quibble over a quarter or a couple of dollars.

The Value of Your Time

One of the most important elements in any pricing formula is value of one's time. Many factors come into play when you try to figure out the value of your time, including your age, previous salaried job experience, where you live, your need for money and so on. If you are selling with the thought of eventually making crafts a part-time profession, you will naturally want to receive as much per hour as possible. But if you are retired or involved in crafts strictly for pleasure, your entire outlook on selling will be different. You may be selling only to get rid of all the things you're making that you no longer have room to keep. When I began to craft, I used to joke that my mother's home

Don't Carry "Quality" Too Far

A crafter named Judi once complained that people didn't appreciate the Christmas ornaments she made, each of which took up to fifteen hours to make. "I mold my ornaments myself with a combination of plaster and stone, painstakingly paint the tiniest details on them, then give them three or four coats of clear varnish," she wrote. "Yet I have found that people are unwilling to pay more than a few dollars for them. I would rather give them away than sell them for such a low price."

Judi said her husband suggested she put less detail in her work, change to a cheaper plaster mix and give the ornaments only one coat of varnish, but Judi felt she couldn't do this. "I take pride in what I make and I can't bring myself to peddle something I have no pride in," she said.

Although such an attitude about quality in crafts is admirable, it is also impractical from a marketing standpoint. You can't put fifteen hours into an object as ordinary as a Christmas ornament and expect the average person to pay you for your time in making it. Like so many others before her, Judy soon learned that she had to make a decision: Did she want to be "an artist," or did she want to be a professional crafter? "Artists" tend to make what they want to make, not what people want to buy. One-of-a-kind creations are their specialty, and they are often hard to sell at a profit.

"Professional crafters," on the other hand, create for the markeplace, making multiples of each of several items in a line. Sure, it's boring to make the same items over and over again, often in assembly-line fashion, but if making money is the object, then this is what you must do. In the end, all creative people who offer their wares to the public have to decide whether their ultimate goal is going to be money or personal satisfaction.

was decorated in "Early Barbara." Once all my family and friends had received my crafts as gifts, I felt I either had to start selling or stop producing.

I once knew an amazing woman who began a successful crafts career at the age of seventy. She said, "I figure my time does not have much market value at this point in my life, and labor costs definitely do not enter into the picture. For one who has been familiar with time and cost studies in my business years, I'm ashamed to admit to such unbusinesslike methods of pricing, but I'm sure about one thing: the people who buy my work appreciate handwork and pay my asking price without question. I'm sure if I figured materials and labor accurately, the prices would have to be much higher, and I wouldn't sell as much as I do."

Older crafters often underprice their art or craftwork for the above reason, but others who do place a high enough value on their time almost always

forget to include overhead expenses and the profit factor in the pricing formula I presented earlier. Many people believe that the best way to set prices on
crafts is simply to double, triple or even take ten times the cost of materials,
but there is a big flaw in that theory and it has to do with the time it takes you
to produce an item.

If something costs you $2 in materials, and you can make 6 of them in an
hour and get $4 each, that would yield a gross profit of $12 for an hour of your
time. But if each item takes an hour to make and costs you $2 in materials, a
doubling of the price of materials would yield a pitiful profit of just $2 for
your labor. As you can see, time is everything.

Let's really dig into this problem. Let's say you're producing a product that
takes three hours to make. You've been selling it at $25, subtracting the cost of
your materials (let's estimate they are $5) then dividing $20 by three hours
and feeling pretty good about making $6.66 per hour on your craftwork. But
that is not the right way to figure it.

Let's look at what happens when you get businesslike and take into account
your overhead expenses (let's estimate them at $5), and factor in some profit
(ten percent of the selling price). And while we're at it, let's look at what a
difference it would make in your year-end profits if you raised the selling price
another $10:

$ 25.00	Selling Price	$ 35.00
– 5.00	Cost of Materials	– 5.00
– 5.00	Overhead	– 5.00
– 2.50	Profit	– 3.50
$ 12.50	(divided by 3 hrs.)	$ 21.50
$ 4.17 *per hour*		$ 7.17 *per hour*

When you sell something for $25, you end up with a net figure of $12.50 or
50 percent of the retail selling price. But when you increase the price by $10,
you end up with a net figure of $21.50, or 61 percent of the retail selling price.
That's because your materials and overhead costs remained the same. It's rather
like the difference you pay when you buy only a small amount of printing.
The printer has to get all his overhead costs and expenses out of that first run,
so if you order only 500 copies of something, you end up paying all those
costs. If you order 1,000 copies, however, the second 500 copies might cost
only half what you paid for the first 500 copies.

Isn't it interesting how a $10 increase in the retail price of a product almost
doubles the hourly wage? You might want to try this pricing exercise with each
individual item in your line to find out which ones are the most profitable.

Certificates of Authenticity

Do you create one-of-a-kind pieces that sell on the high side? Artist Leslie Miller, who does a lot of custom-design work, says it's often difficult to justify her prices to new clients. "Until they begin to work with me, they do not understand the amount of time, talent and vision that goes into creating their one-of-a-kind treasures, so I spend a lot of time educating my customers and ensuring their trust in me."

One way Leslie does this is by issuing a "Certificate of Authenticity" for each piece she creates. It describes the piece itself and the materials used to create it. Using her computer, she prints on preprinted sheets of certificate stock available from paper supply houses. The certificate is enclosed in its own presentation folder along with a snapshot of the artwork and her dated signature.

"Commission work can be very time consuming and mentally exhausting," says Leslie, "but when I find someone I want to continue working with on a custom-order basis, I include a gift or discount certificate with delivery of their paid-in-full order. My 'thank-yous' have included notecard sets, brass-etched keyrings and coffee mugs bearing images I have created. My customers find these items a pleasant surprise, and I often get new orders from them as well as new customers by their word-of-mouth advertising."

Leslie's "incentive items" quickly became a business of their own. She now sells her mugs individually and in sets and is expanding her designs and adding an order/catalog sheet to her deliveries.

If your financial goal is merely to earn extra income, an hourly wage of $7 per hour would amount to a tidy sum at the end of the year, as you can see from the figures below. However, if your goal is to build a full-time homebased business that might eventually support your family, you should aim for an hourly wage of $25 to $30 per hour, minimum. About the only ways to make this kind of money are to produce high-priced products, get into wholesaling or sell a product or service that does not entail so much labor. (See Chapter Fourteen for other ways to profit from art or craft skills besides making finished products for sale.)

To estimate how much money you might be able to make in a year, first figure out how many hours you might be able to spend producing crafts. Then multiply that number by your hourly rate. In the above example, if you could produce crafts 20 hours a week 50 weeks a year, that would be 1,000 hours of production time. If it took you an average of three hours to make each product in your line, you could produce only about 333 units a year. If, however, you could design a product that would sell for the same price and could be made in an hour or less, the number of units you could make would jump to nearly a thousand per year. Here is a visual illustration of what I've just said:

A product that takes 3 hours to make:

- On the $25 product, a profit of $2.50 per item × 333 items made in a year = $832.50 plus 1,000 hrs. × $4.33 per hour for labor = $4,330, for a total of $5,162.50 per year.
- On the $35 product, a profit of $3.50 per item × 333 items made in a year = $1,165.50 plus 1,000 hrs. × $7.17 per hour for labor = $7,170, for a total of $8,335.50 per year (or $3,173 more).

Now look what happens if you triple your production by making a product in only one hour instead of three:

- On the $25 product, a profit of $2.50 per item × 999 items made in a year = $2,497.50 plus 1,000 hrs. × $13.00 per hour for labor = $13,000, for a total of $15,497.50 per year.
- On the $35 product, a profit of $3.50 per item × 999 items made in a year = $3,496.50 plus 1,000 hrs. × $21.50 per hour for labor = $21,500, for a total of $24,996.50 per year (or $9,499 more).

If you're making lots of crafts but aren't making lots of money, maybe it's time to analyze every product in your line, pull out the unprofitable items, create some new products, and bring your prices up to the point where you are truly making a profit from all the hours you are putting into your endeavor.

As you can see, pricing a product at $35 instead of $25 makes a huge difference in year-end profits even when it takes three hours to make a product. By tripling the number of items produced in a year, however, the figures shoot up to an impressive level. (See "Production Strategies" elsewhere in this chapter for ideas on how to increase the number of items you make each year.)

Paring Costs to the Bone

The easiest way to increase profits is to lower costs. For years, a common complaint of craft sellers was that they couldn't obtain supplies at wholesale because the policy of manufacturers and distributors in this industry was to sell only to storefront businesses. Now, however, the Hobby Industry Associa-

tion (HIA) acknowledges that craft designers and "converters of craft materials for the gift market" comprise a legitimate market. Although professional crafters are now invited to attend HIA trade shows, the companies who exhibit here may or may not sell to them. Those who do are likely to have high minimum orders of $200 or more.

Professional crafters may find wholesale minimums lower at the new "Professional Crafters Trade Shows" now being presented in various cities each year. These shows are produced by *Craft Supply Magazine* in cooperation with the Association of Crafts & Creative Industries (ACCI). To gain access to one of these shows, crafters need only prove they are in business.

When trying to buy supplies by mail, a professional approach will make it easier for suppliers to sell to you. The quickest way to ensure that your letter to a manufacturer or wholesaler ends up in the wastebasket is to write it by hand on paper torn from a yellow tablet, steno pad or notepaper with butterflies all over it. To get wholesale prices, you have to look like you're really in business. Even when you request a wholesale catalog on business stationery, some companies won't send a catalog until you complete their Dealer Information form. The policy of most manufacturers and wholesalers is to sell only to companies with a valid sales tax number, exemption certificate or vendor's license.

Tip

If you can't meet the minimum quantity requirements of some manufacturers, ask for the names of distributors and dealers near you. Local dealers may give you a 20 percent discount on supplies ordered in quantity if you present yourself as a legitimate business owner. (Regular orders from you might help a small retailer order in greater quantities for lower prices and increased profits.) Don't approach a shop owner as an ordinary customer, however. Phone first for an appointment, one business person to another.

In addition to shopping for bulk supplies and new wholesale sources, many crafters report they are adding craft products to their line that incorporate natural or found items, such as wild roses, grasses and weeds, old jewelry, wood scraps and recycled materials.

Keeping Track of Costs

Marina Pittman, who has been selling at fairs and country markets for three years, has a good system for recording the costs of each project as she makes it. "When I buy craft supplies, I make sure each item has a price on it before I put it away. When I am working on a project, I take out a project sheet (see illustration) and as I work, I record the supplies I've used and the cost of each. When the project is done, I know exactly how much it cost to make and that helps me price my crafts. On the project sheet, I also include fabric samples and pictures and any notes concerning how popular the item was, customer comments or any changes I should make if I make more of the same item. I then file each project sheet in a binder for later reference."

PROJECT
Pattern Source _____
Pattern _____ Completed _____
Begun _____ Price Sold _____
For _____
Fabrics & Supplies

Notes

Swatch Samples

Michelle Blunt browses resale shops in search of salvaged lace, buttons, fur trims and woolens for the jointed teddy bears and tree ornaments she makes. She suggests adding character to items by attaching a hang tag that conveys a story or history of the item. "Many recycle crafts were developed during World War II due to shortages and the war effort. A research of these could be profitable when the story behind it is attached to your product. The same is true with many pioneer crafts and heirlooms."

Sell It at Double the Price

If you can't sell something at a certain price, try reverse psychology. Don't lower the price, raise it! Yes, you may lose some customers, but your higher price will automatically attract a totally new audience of buyers.

Once there was a woman who started a teddy bear repair service. When she eventually decided to do something else, she thought she had an excellent strategy for killing her bear business: she would simply double her prices to discourage customers. To her amazement, business increased. As one customer explained, "I was reluctant to bring my antique teddy to you before because your prices seemed suspiciously low. Now I'm confident you can be trusted to do the job."

After reading this story in one of the author's magazine articles, artist Grady Harper reported on his experience:

"One of my full-sheet paintings just never would sell even though it seemed to be the main attraction in my exhibit at all of the shows. After reading your pricing article, I decided to follow your suggestion about doubling prices instead of lowering them. I increased the price of my painting from $325 to $750 and it was purchased after being on display only a few hours."

—an excerpt from *Homemade Money* by Barbara Brabec (Betterway)

When to Raise Prices

Most sellers automatically lower prices when things won't sell, but they rarely stop to think that the problem may be that prices are too low to begin with. Buyers have preconceived notions about what things should sell for. Something priced too low, when compared to items of similar quality offered by others, may make them suspicious. If you are thinking about dropping a product you like to make because it just isn't profitable, try offering it to a new audience at double the original price and see what happens.

I learned from experience that you can double your prices and still get orders. In one of my magazine columns, I offered one of my self-published books at $11.45 ppd. Due to a typographical error, the price appeared as $22.45. Nevertheless, I received almost as many orders for the book as I had received when it had been offered earlier at the correct price. I had to make a lot of refunds, but the lesson was invaluable. Clearly a certain percentage of my readers felt this particular book was worth twice what I was charging for it.

Many crafters selling in the 90s have reported that products priced at $10 continue to sell best. There seems to be something magical about the figure of $10 that has appealed to buyers through the years. Even when times are hard, it remains a price that seems affordable to most of us. I am concerned, however, that so many crafters seem to think that, because times are hard, products must be priced at $10 or less, even as low as $2 or $3. If you can make a profit on a three-dollar item, that's fine, but lowering prices on something that should sell for $10 or more is rarely the solution to sluggish sales. As stated earlier in this book, the real secret in selling more of what you make is *to make more of what people want to buy.* There will always be people with money to spend. The serious crafts seller will make every effort to find such buyers, employing new selling strategies while also improving the quality of his or her product line.

While today's buyers are more price conscious than ever, they still want top quality and they're willing to pay for it when a product gives them something they want or need. It's time to raise your prices when your production, selling or overhead costs increase, when you notice that others are selling similar products at a higher cost, and particularly when you can't keep up with the demand for a particular product.

Cletus Bushnell was unemployed with no income at the time she began to sell her throw rugs of recycled double-knit polyester clothes and fabrics. Soon after she started to sell, she told me that her hobby had suddenly turned into a fun and profitable home business. "I'm still new at selling," she says. "When I gave my family rugs as gifts, they showed them off, and that's all it took. The orders began pouring in. I could not keep up so I raised my prices to $25 and still got backlogged with orders. I actually need help at this point. The possibilities are mind-boggling. My expenses are minimal and the profits are great!"

Barbara Melkert makes 30" scarecrows of raffia and old jeans that she sells for just $9. At shows, customers fall over themselves trying to buy this item. "At one show, people were behind my table taking scarecrows out of the boxes," she says. "The lady in a booth next door said it reminded her of when people fought over nylon stockings in World War II."

Barbara said she arrived at her price by taking a three-times markup of her materials cost of $2.75, but it seems obvious to me that she is not getting a fair return for all the time she must be investing in this item. If people love it this much, they will pay more to own it and Barbara should raise her prices accordingly.

Is Wholesaling in Your Future?

If you produce high-quality work, sooner or later a shop owner is going to stop by your booth and ask for your wholesale price list, so you might as well prepare for this eventuality. And now you come to the hardest part of my pricing lesson: If you don't set your prices high enough to begin with, you'll never be able to offer a shop a 50 percent discount, which is standard and absolutely necessary if a shop owner is going to realize a sufficient profit to stay in business.

In checking the retail price lists of craft sellers in small towns, I've often advised them to leave their price list alone, except to change its heading from "retail" to "wholesale." Yes, it's true, many crafters could double their present retail prices if they simply changed their marketing outlets and began to sell to established shops in larger cities.

It's not hard to test the wholesale waters. Deborah Ann Kirkaldy used to sell at fairs only. Now she advises others, "Pick up some shops that will buy wholesale. Promote your product, even if it means giving a store a small sample of your product to see how it would spark interest. It works. I've done it."

If you do decide to wholesale, you'll have to stop messing around with your prices. Develop a line and price each product high enough to yield a profit *when offered at wholesale prices*. If you want to sell that product at the retail level, you must offer it at the same price that retailers are selling it for. Nothing upsets a shop owner more than discovering that a craftsperson is wholesaling an item at the same price they're selling it to consumers at a fair. Craft sellers are self-defeating if they decide to become wholesalers and then go to a fair and sell at less than retail prices. They are then underselling their dealers. Only by maintaining your retail prices at all times can you hope to realize the profit that is rightfully yours, and only by operating in a professional manner can you hope to maintain good business relations with your shop customers.

The temptation to lower this price is great, especially when you think the shop has set a too-high price on an item to begin with and you would be happy with less. But as soon as you lower a price, shop owners may begin to get comments like these from customers: "I saw this same item at a local fair for only $15. Why should I buy it here for $25?" If this happens, the shop will stop buying from you.

One solution to this problem is to have two different lines: one that you sell exclusively to shops at wholesale, and another that you sell only at craft fairs, boutiques, craft malls and so on. If two separate lines aren't possible, consider changing your materials. For example, use pine for the line of lower-priced wooden items you can sell with success at craft fairs, and produce the same designs in walnut or other fine woods for items sold through shops. Or use one kind of fabric or fur for soft sculpture items sold at a fair, and a more luxurious fabric or fur for items sold to shops. If you make a product in two sizes, consider offering the smaller, lower-priced items at fairs, and sell larger items of the same design exclusively to shops.

Selling in Hard Economic Times

In early 1993, readers of Barbara's "Selling What You Make" column were surveyed to learn how the 1992 recession had affected their sales. In general, readers reported that craft fair buyers did a lot more looking than buying in 1992, and when they did buy, they didn't spend as much as the year before. Buyers seemed most interested in practical items that could be given as gifts. In trying to meet consumer needs, 83 percent of survey respondents said they had priced most of their wares under $25, and items under $10 usually sold best.

In stark contrast, the rest of those surveyed said they successfully sold items priced from $25-$200. Many commented that the recession didn't affect their sales to any degree. In fact, several reported an increase in sales in one of the toughest economic years many crafters have ever known. This proves once again that it is not necessary to lower one's prices in hard economic times because there will always be some buyers with extra money to spend. The real secret to sales success is, and always will be, having products consumers want or need. Price is not the most important reason for lack of sales. More often than not, the fault lies with the product itself and the fact that people just don't need or want it.

Production Strategies

Of course, wholesaling requires a different mindset, more aggressive marketing strategies and different production techniques. You don't have to become a factory, making hundreds of the same item, but you do need to think in terms of producing dozens of the same item. To satisfy strong creative urges, some professionals produce one-of-a-kind pieces for sale at fairs and shows while wholesaling a commercial line to shops. Perhaps this idea would work for you, too.

If you alone plan to produce everything you sell, you'll have to get your workshop or studio organized for maximum efficiency. Set up an assembly-line operation that will enable you to work on twelve or more items at a time. You may not derive as much personal satisfaction from working in this way, but I guarantee you'll produce a lot more

in the same amount of time. Further streamline your production methods by eliminating some of the time-consuming detail work that may please you but has little effect on the salability of an item. Also look for technological solutions to special production problems you may have. For example, could a design be silk-screened instead of hand-painted? Could cutting be done by laser instead of saw? Could you cut hours of labor by buying a component part instead of making it yourself? Order a collection of craft supply catalogs to see how many precut and presewn parts are available.

Tip

Many craft sellers have solved their production problems by hiring homeworkers to do some of the routine production work— cutting, painting, sewing, gluing, packaging, affixing labels, tags, etc. To avoid problems related to the hiring of independent contractors, some crafters farm out piecework to sheltered workshops (such as Veterans Industries) that hire disabled workers.

Time Management

Before you automatically say no to the idea of moving from retailing to wholesaling, tally all the hours you normally spend on show correspondence, packing for a show, traveling to a show, unloading, manning your booth, repacking after the show, loading the car, traveling home and unpacking again. Whew! That's a lot of time and work, isn't it? Now imagine how nice it would be if you never had to leave home to sell and could spend all these hours just producing crafts for sale. With all this extra time, you could probably quadruple your production, and if you could turn your retail price list into a wholesale list as I explained above, you could also quadruple your annual income. Think about it.

Pricing Tips

■ Offer an assortment of items priced in a broad range. "Your merchandise should be on a scale from rock bottom up to Mount Everest," says a seasoned show seller. "That way, you get some change from everyone's pocket."

"I always make sure I have several items under $5," says Jami Burns. "This seems to draw people to the booth and gives them the opportunity to look at (and hopefully buy) the higher-priced items. For the holidays, I try to have at least one item at $2 that can be used for party

Pricing by the Inch

One of the most difficult things to sell at a profit is needlework. One professional needlepoint artist told me she charges by the square inch. "This is one case where that famous rule of thumb (three times the material price) cannot be applied," she says. "I scale my prices to stitches per inch, the finer the stitch, the higher the price. I give the stitch count with it (e.g., 1 square inch of 12-mesh canvas is 144 stitches = price). I began with a figure of 60 cents per inch and gradually increased it as time went on."

favors or thank-you gifts. I price them at $2 each or six for $10 to encourage larger purchases."

■ Offer a quantity price to customers who buy several items of a kind. Decorative painter Susan Young sells a papier mâché heart box for $7.50, but when customers buy six or more as gifts, she discounts the price to $6.50 each.

■ Give a small freebie item with the purchase of a higher priced new item. "This helps to promote the new item and gives you a chance to get rid of old, lower-priced items that have been around too long," says Jeanne Swartz. "Customers love to feel that they are getting more than they are paying for."

■ Don't apologize for your pricing. "While explaining my prices," a woodworker reports, "a new customer who brought in a nice-sized order said, 'I didn't come because of the price. I came because I heard you were the best.'" A craftswoman agrees: "When you explain your pricing, it sounds like an apology and opens the door to dickering. Often as not, your prices are as low as you can afford to go, so don't create a problem."

■ Raise the price on any "hot sellers." When you can't keep up with the demand for a particular product you're selling at a crafts fair, try adding $2 to the item's price the next time you do a show. If it still sells like hotcakes, increase the price another $2 and keep increasing the price as long as the item sells at a rate that is satisfactory to you. You may be astonished to learn just how much you can get for some of your better items.

Shirley Miller learned an important pricing secret one Christmas when her best-selling item was a cinnamon stick Santa that could be used as an ornament or a pin. Originally, Shirley priced this item at three times the material cost, but it sold so fast at the first show that she raised the price. "I was hoping it wouldn't sell out so fast because

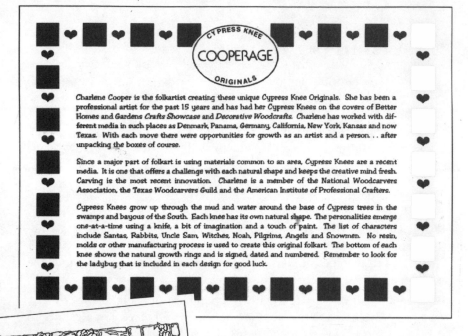

COOPERAGE
CYPRESS KNEE ORIGINALS

Charlene Cooper is the folkartist creating these unique Cypress Knee Originals. She has been a professional artist for the past 15 years and has had her Cypress Knees on the covers of Better Homes and Gardens *Crafts Showcase* and *Decorative Woodcrafts*. Charlene has worked with different media in such places as Denmark, Panama, Germany, California, New York, Kansas and now Texas. With each move there were opportunities for growth as an artist and a person... after unpacking the boxes of course.

Since a major part of folkart is using materials common to an area, Cypress Knees are a recent media. It is one that offers a challenge with each natural shape and keeps the creative mind fresh. Carving is the most recent innovation. Charlene is a member of the National Woodcarvers Association, the Texas Woodcarvers Guild and the American Institute of Professional Crafters.

Cypress Knees grow up through the mud and water around the base of Cypress trees in the swamps and bayous of the South. Each knee has its own natural shape. The personalities emerge one-at-a-time using a knife, a bit of imagination and a touch of paint. The list of characters include Santas, Rabbits, Uncle Sam, Witches, Noah, Pilgrims, Angels and Snowmen. No resin, molds or other manufacturing process is used to create this original folkart. The bottom of each knee shows the natural growth rings and is signed, dated and numbered. Remember to look for the ladybug that is included in each design for good luck.

Above: One way to get higher prices is to have high-quality printed materials. Folkartist Charlene Cooper has created this impressive card to acquaint her customers with her Cypress Knee Originals. Shown here in reduced size, the original card is 5 x 7 inches and printed in red ink on white stock. This is an excellent example of how to share the story behind your art or craft while also making your product seem more valuable to customers.

About the Artist:

When you work with Vickie Canham, you'll discover she is ready to bring your ideas into reality. With more than ten years experience creating quality porcelain pieces and custom ceramic tiles, she has worked with artists from the United States and from around the world.

Vickie is a member of the World Organization of China Painters and the Columbia Area Home-Based Business Network. Her work has appeared in *The China Decorator* and *The British Porcelain Artist*.

The Artistic Process:

Hand-painted porcelain began more than 2,000 years ago in China. An artist applies translucent layers of mineral-based paints to the porcelain surface using an oil-based medium. The paints are then kiln-fired into the glaze creating a lasting, personal work of art. Ceramic tiles do not fade or wear off, and they are easy to clean and maintain. Bring an air of elegance into your home with custom ceramic tile.

Vickie Canham offers a complete service which includes tile selection, custom painting, and installation.

4445 Roemer Road
Columbia, Missouri 65202

314 442-8033

Left: Vickie Canham also has an impressive "artist card" that gives her credentials and explains how she creates her unique porcelain tiles. Her card measures 4 x 8 inches and is printed on a pumice-colored stock that has flecks of green and lavender in it. The border artwork is printed in a pale green and the center text is printed in lavender.

I didn't have time to make more," she says. "To my surprise, they still sold out just as quickly."

Don't overprice your items. "Customers are intelligent," says Joan Monostory. "The fact that a wreath similar to yours sells for $40 at Bloomingdale's doesn't mean you can get the same price on yours when it's sold at a crafts fair. (The same logic holds true for beginning artists who paint beautifully but have not yet acquired a reputation as an artist.)

Explore new markets for some products. If you can't get the price you need on a particular product, don't stop making it. Just look for a new market for it. The same item offered at different fairs or shops across the country might sell at a much higher price, depending on the economy of the area, the sophistication of buyers and the way the product is presented to them.

Start a pricing reference file or scrapbook. Check magazines on the newsstand that showcase American handcrafts, clipping ads for products similar to yours. Clip descriptive listings from mail order gift catalogs. Record what others are charging for your type of crafts at fairs, craft malls and gift shops. Your pricing task will be easier once you know what "the going prices" are for items similar to yours.

Never feel guilty about taking a larger profit on something you have produced easily and quickly because this may allow you to make another item for sale that gives you great pleasure, yet yields little or no profit.

Recommended Reading

Crafter's Guide to Pricing Your Work by Dan Ramsey (Betterway Publications, January 1997).

The Crafts Supply Sourcebook, 4th edition, by Margaret Boyd (Betterway Publications). Includes over 2,000 product listings neatly arranged in two sections: general arts, crafts and hobbies; and needlecrafts, sewing and fiber arts. Each listing includes a description of products available at retail or wholesale prices, along with the supplier's name, address, catalog and ordering information.

The Doll Sourcebook for Collectors and Artists edited by Argie Manolis (Betterway Publications). Incudes listing of suppliers of raw materials and manufacturers who buy artists' designs.

Homemade Money by Barbara Brabec (Betterway). Includes a lengthy chapter on pricing that includes several pricing formulas and tips on how to get higher prices for everything you sell.

● *Selling Your Dolls and Teddy Bears* by Carol-Lynn Rossell-Waugh and Barbara Giguere (Betterway Publications).

● *The Woodworker's Guide to Pricing Your Work* by Dan Ramsey (Betterway Publications). How to calculate the value of your time, materials and craftsmanship. Helpful to all crafters, but of special interest to those who do woodcrafts, carvings, folk art, turnings, clocks, furniture and cabinetry.

CHAPTER SIX

Fun and Profit at Fairs and Shows

Thousands of new sellers enter the crafts fair arena each year, and many quickly reach the point where they are earning a substantial amount of money doing what they do best and love most.

No one knows for sure how many art and craft fairs are presented annually, but many states now present hundreds of shows every year. In talking with Bill Ronay, a publisher of arts-and-crafts-show guides for several southern states, I learned there are more than 600 quality events a year in Georgia alone. By estimating the number of exhibitors at each show (from 100 to 700) and the dollars being generated at each show, Bill figures crafters are pouring more than $30 million dollars a year into Georgia's economy. Multiply that times fifty states, and you begin to get an idea of the importance of art and craft fairs to the American economy.

Selling through consumer fairs and shows is one of the fastest growing merchandising trends in small business commerce, says Susan Ratliff, author of *How to Be a Weekend Entrepreneur.* She estimates there are 10,000 quality shows that generate $50 billion dollars annually. Bill Ronay thinks the number of craft fairs could be as high as 20,000 a year if one were to include all the tiny local shows, home sales and church bazaars.

In years past, crafters had difficulty finding good craft fairs. Now many publishers offer advance show listing information in both print form (subscription newsletters and magazines) and electronic form (craft sites on the Internet's World Wide Web). This information is national in scope and generally includes

Craft Businesses Often Bloom Quickly

When Teresa Niell entered her first craft show at a local church, displaying the topiaries and wreaths she had been making for a year, she had no idea this would lead her into a profitable business. She was both surprised and flattered when a woman in charge of decorating a hotel in the area asked if she could produce sixty topiaries in two weeks.

"I had to tell her no," Teresa told me. "I just did not have the resources at the time. But that got me going. I did all my homework and my hobby quickly blossomed into a business named the Topiary Garden."

Teresa converted a spare bedroom into a workroom and went on to lease space at a craft mall and wholesale to a gift shop in Dallas. "I have been having a wonderful time with all of this," she says. "I absolutely love what I do. Having people tell me how creative I am and that I do great work is a wonderful bonus in doing all this. I think I have finally found the one thing I wish to do with my life. I may not make a million but I'm having a great time!"

the name and date of each upcoming event and who to contact for entry information. Some publishers include expected attendance or sales figures from previous shows. If you have a computer and use a service such as America OnLine, CompuServe or Prodigy, you can access the Internet and World Wide Web to find publishers who have established sites especially for professional artists and craftspeople. (See Chapter Eleven for more about this topic.)

The Advantages of Craft Fair Selling

A good craft fair offers many opportunities to see, to touch, to learn, and to be entertained. Crafters who sell at shows go not just to sell but also to meet other creative people. They enjoy exchanging information and ideas and observing new techniques. Sometimes a craft fair becomes a pleasant vacation away from one's studio or workshop.

Even when sales at a fair are poor, there are benefits from this kind of selling that can't be obtained in any other way. Nowhere else can you get the kind of customer feedback to your work that you get at a craft fair. After exhibiting in a show, you will be completely exhausted, but you will also be exhilarated, and you will probably find yourself making plans for the next event on the way home. Yes, if you do one show, you will want to do another! That's because craft fairs are infectious by nature, and the kind of fever they carry is the kind you'll be happy to catch. Pleasures aside, there are several real advantages to craft fair selling. Here you can

Test your prices

Get consumer reaction to various products

Learn which designs, colors or products are most appealing to buyers

Do market research by visiting the booths of other sellers

Expose your work to retailers who might want to buy from you at wholesale

Take custom orders for higher-priced items you wouldn't want to make in quantity

Meet new craftspeople and exchange information, ideas and techniques

Lose some of your shyness

Gain confidence and experience in selling.

What to Know Before You Go

Here are several questions you should answer before entering a show. In parentheses after each group of questions, you will find a reference to where these questions are discussed in this or other chapters:

❑ Am I meeting all the tax and legal requirements involved in crafts fair selling? Do I need any kind of license? Are the rules different for me if I'm just a hobbyist and not really in business? (See Chapter Four.)

❑ What kind of show is it? Indoors, outdoors, juried, non-juried, country, contemporary, themed? How does my work compare to other work likely to be in the show? (See "Different Types of Shows" in this chapter.)

❑ If the show is juried, what will I have to do to be accepted in the show? (See "Show Promoters and Juried Shows" in this chapter.)

❑ How important is my craft booth to making sales, and what should I know before I create my display? (See "Designing Your Display" in this chapter.)

❑ Can I increase sales by demonstrating my art or craft during the show? And how can I get past my fear of facing the public to sell? (See Chapter Seven.)

❑ What kind of sales and attendance figures are available from previous shows, and how can I use these figures to estimate the amount of merchandise I should take to a show? (See Chapter Seven.)

The Difference Between an "Art Sale" and a "Crafts Show"

"Having participated in several arts and crafts shows and sales in different parts of the country, I can find only one major difference between an art sale and a craft show," says Stephanie Frewert. "The first serves champagne while you're setting up the evening before, and the second offers you coffee and doughnuts the morning you arrive with the chickens at six A.M. to lay out your wares. Either one could be the best sale of your career if it has been accurately tuned in to its clientele. Match the buyer with the seller and the labels don't matter."

Different Types of Shows

There are so many different kinds and types of art and craft shows, fairs and festivals that it's almost impossible to describe them. There are little shows and big shows, indoor shows and outdoor shows, juried shows and non-juried shows. Some shows feature contemporary art or crafts, some have only traditional or country items while others may sell only one kind of art or craft, such as miniatures, dolls or woodcarvings.

Some shows are costumed events with a special theme, such as Early American, Victorian, Ethnic, Renaissance, Pioneer or Native American. Others are themed around holidays such as Easter, Thanksgiving or Christmas, or are tied to a local community event such as a flower show, music festival or food fair.

Outdoor shows and fairs may be held in a park or parking lot, on the sidewalk in front of a shopping center, in a town square, at the county fair grounds or other open country area. Indoor shows are usually held in a school, church or civic center, in an individual's home, or in a shopping mall or exposition center.

Some shows are open to the public while others are juried (see below). Any widely publicized craft fair will attract an interesting variety of exhibitors, including hobbycrafters who are trying to break into the field or get additional selling experience, part-time sellers who have other jobs and count on craft fairs for extra income, and craft professionals who rely on such shows for a living.

Some shows are organized by crafters themselves while others are sponsored by a local art or craft organization, chamber of commerce or other civic group. Most of the professional juried arts and crafts shows, however, are produced by some 250 to 300 show promoters who do this for a living. "Like craft fair sellers, show promoters come and go," says Dave Cook, editor of *Sunshine Artists* magazine. "I figure there is an annual turnover here of at least

25 percent." Following is a brief discussion of the different types of shows you might consider entering:

Street Fairs and Church Bazaars

Such events generally attract beginning sellers and consumers who are looking for low-priced merchandise. Entry fees may be as low as $20. While such events can be great fun and are good for getting your feet wet as a seller, they are often unprofitable.

Serious sellers eventually find they need to stop doing small fairs and concentrate only on larger ones, preferably those that are juried events (see below). "It takes just as much time to set up, build inventory, and sell at a tiny show as it does a big one," says a crafter who has been selling at fairs for two years. "And the big ones mean so much more in terms of exposure and volume-dollar sales."

"My last show was a large one with 125 craft exhibits," says Paula Hamby, who explains why she stopped doing church bazaars. "Over 8,000 people went through this show in two days, and my sales shot up eight times over what I was doing at the small shows. Now I know that I was simply exhibiting in the wrong kind of shows!"

Tip

"To sell more, avoid wasting your time at church and school boutiques that are poorly advertised, inadequately run and strictly for the profit of the organization holding the event. Look instead for juried shows in their third year, with an admission of at least $1 to get in."

—Kathleen Haer

Juried Art & Craft Shows

In a juried event, hopeful exhibitors must submit slides or photos of their work to prove it is of a type and quality desired for a particular event. In addition to a show's entry fee, there is often an extra, nonrefundable jurying charge. Nationwide, it seems that entry fees for small shows run between $50 and $125. More prestigious shows that attract thousands of people, however, may charge $300 to $500 per day or more.

Shows that are juried tend to have a loyal following of buyers because such shows have gained a reputation for high-quality art and crafts. This is particularly true of the annual craft festivals sponsored by art and craft organizations and associations throughout the country in which only members are allowed to exhibit and sell. Other juried shows, including those presented in shopping malls, convention centers and county fairgrounds, are open to sellers nation-wide. Because of their high quality and buyer following they often have more applicants than exhibit booths or spaces. Many of these shows have between 200 and 700 exhibitors and attract 30,000 to 50,000 people.

Tip

"Be selective about the shows in which you will participate," says a professional basketmaker. "Look for a juried show with strict quality guidelines, and inquire as to how many of your type of craft will be participating. I prefer to be the only one who is doing baskets unless the look is entirely different."

Mall Shows

Professional artists and craftspeople have mixed feelings about mall shows (juried events held in shopping malls nationwide). Being indoors is a great advantage over an outdoors show, but mall shows are not without problems. For example, if you try to do one of these shows alone, there is the problem of leaving your site unguarded as you bring in your merchandise. Although security is always promised, theft is not uncommon after the exhibit is closed for the day. Make sure your products are appropriate for this retail environment. Otherwise, after you get set up to sell, a nearby retailer may complain that your wares are causing them to lose sales. (Those who sell clothing and jewelry may not be accepted in mall shows for this reason.)

Before entering a mall show, ask how the show will be advertised. Some show promoters do this job while others leave it to the shopping mall. If advertising is poor, most of the people who come to the mall during the show will be there for some other purpose. They may see the craft exhibits as an interesting attraction to their shopping day, but any purchases they make are likely to be made on impulse, and only if they can be charged.

Tip

If a mall is loaded with people, it may be difficult for some to see your exhibit. One seller suggests stringing a banner across the top of your display that clearly tells people what you are selling. Another suggests displaying some objects on a tall stand or book-shelf so they can be seen above people's heads.

Present Your Own Crafts Show

In Canada, Jarmila Vik has increased her market by renting a community hall for her own craft fairs, which she presents in April, May, October, November and December. "The hall holds seventeen tables," she explains. "I keep six for my own products and rent the rest to other sellers whose products complement my own. No admission is charged so the rental fees must be sufficient to cover the rental of the hall, printing costs of promotional flyers and classified ads in community newspapers. Often I send an article to the local paper about the exhibiting craftspeople or new crafts that will be available. This usually results in publicity, and our fairs are always well attended." (If you decide to organize this kind of sales event, make sure each exhibitor collects and pays his or her own sales tax.)

Renaissance Fairs

These outdoor events offer consumers a mixed package of food, entertainment and crafts exhibits or demonstrations. To sell here, you will need to design a special and very sturdy booth in the medieval theme. This could cost up to $2,000, says James Dillehay, author of *The Basic Guide to Selling Arts & Crafts*. "Since you rent the space for most of the weeks of the show, you become a lessee or tenant," he says. "Management also takes a percentage of your sales. Sales can be slower than other kinds of craft shows because the renaissance fair is often an entertainment event first, and a place to buy crafts second."

Consumer Attractions

Be wary of shows that use artists and craftspeople as a drawing card for other events such as antique shows, concerts, outdoor picnics, horse races or carnival-type attractions. As one veteran craft fair seller told me, "We soon learned that the big celebration with the beer tent and carnival rides was not conducive to good sales."

A note about county fairs: While this is not a place to sell handmade items, putting work in a county fair exhibit is how many hobbycrafters get started selling. Thousands of people may see their work and the crafter and his or her family will take special pride in any ribbons that may be awarded. Often, this experience gives the timid seller enough courage to enter that first crafts fair.

Flea Markets

In recent years, flea markets—sometimes called swap meets—have enjoyed a great revival in America. Every product imaginable is now being sold through such markets. Presented in both indoor and outdoor settings, the quality of such markets can range from terrible to terrific. Entry fees may range from $20 per day to several hundreds dollars a month. Flea markets are popular because they offer bargain prices and a chance to barter, a fact that makes them one of the least profitable markets for the average crafts seller. But there are exceptions, says Susan Ratliff, who told me about one event in her area that draws over 45,000 tourists each weekend. "Of the 4,000 vendors who sell at this market, about one-fifth are crafters," she says. "I consistently see people who are selling items such as wooden coyotes, cactus mug holders, handpainted T-shirts and other tourist-type novelty items."

Show Promoters and Juried Shows

Let's say you want to enter a juried show. You send away for the application and, as you begin to complete it, you wonder if you're going to be accepted or rejected. Remember this: As a seller, the most important thing is not just that your work be up to the standards required for a particular show, but that the show itself meets *your* requirements. Being juried out of a show doesn't neces- sarily mean your work is not good, *only that it is not appropriate for sale at this particular show.* Try another one.

Your Photographic Presentation

If a show promoter rejects you for reasons you don't understand, the problem may not be with your craft, but with the way you are presenting it to the show promoter, explains Marsha Reed, publisher of *Craftmaster News,* a California show calendar. "Many promoters are getting very picky, but the thing they look at most is what your display may look like. When you send in photos of your work to be previewed for the shows, you should be as professional as possible. If you are not good at taking pictures of your product you may wish to hire a photographer to do the job for you. It will pay off in the long run."

Where to find an affordable photographer? Marsha suggests calling the pho- tography department of local colleges. "By going to the colleges you get stu- dents who charge a fraction of what they will charge after graduation. Many will work for free, just for the experience or to make a great portfolio for themselves. The colleges will send their best student because the school's repu- tation is riding on that student."

Different Shows, Different Results

"Don't judge the value of attending shows by just one event," says Teresa Farber. "My sales vary greatly depending on the area of the show. It's important to attend shows in different areas because what someone purchases in a metropolitan area is not necessarily what will sell in a rural area. I don't have any one item that sells exceptionally well at every show. For example, at a recent metropolitan fair, I was selling Victorian door pulls as fast as I could take them out of the box, while at the next show in a rural area, my best seller was hobby horses."

What Show Promoters Want

Craft show promoter Heidi G. Hutson says show promoters want "a special person who wears an optimistic smile despite torrential rains, sweltering heat, or buyers aimlessly roaming aisles searching for 'nothing in particular.'" In an article for *ShowGuide,* Heidi offered these tips on how to find favor with show promoters:

- Complete the show application neatly and professionally. Follow directions, sending exactly what the promoter asks for—nothing more, nothing less.
- Offer unique, quality crafts. Don't try to sneak in imported or commercial items.
- Be cooperative with show management and other exhibitors and attentive to your customers.
- Don't leave a show early. This is a mark of unprofessionalism that will irritate the show promoter (who will never hire you again) and hurt your fellow crafters.

I would add another: Don't bring small children to a show with you, then let them run around creating problems for other exhibitors. Like shop owners, craftsellers are *retailers,* and shop owners don't bring their children to work with them.

Fairs That Charge Admission

Some crafters feel it is a mistake for fairs to charge admission. "This hurts the crafters," one complains. "The only ones making any money are the ones running the craft fair. A family of four that has to pay $12 or more to get in may not have money to buy crafts."

Other crafters think that some show promoters charge too high a price for their spaces. "Some of the finest crafters have given up the show circuit as a result," says a craftswoman in Vermont. "Crafters complain the show promoters don't advertise enough. Customers complain about the admission price because a show is really a place to sell, not a show."

The logic behind charging admission at a show is quite sound. In fact, it is the same as that used by mail order sellers who qualify their prospects by asking them to send a dollar for a brochure or catalog instead of giving it to them free. Mail order sellers have learned that only those with a serious interest will send the dollar, while show promoters have learned that only serious shoppers will pay to get into an art or craft show. This qualification process automatically eliminates many curiosity seekers who never buy anything.

There will always be some promoters who are greedy, some who think they can "clean up" by sponsoring one high admission show in their area. Only the best show promoters survive, however, so in deciding whether to be in a show that charges admission, find out how many years the event has been held and how many exhibitors and shoppers have attended in past years. In many areas of the country, well-established shows that charge admission are the ones that attract the same serious shoppers year after year.

Designing Your Display

In designing a crafts display booth, you should strive to

1. Capture the attention of prospective buyers
2. Encourage them to stop, browse and get out without feeling trapped
3. Make it easy for you to sell to them

As you design your display, keep in mind how you're going to get everything packed into your vehicle, unloaded at the show, and back home again. Also consider who will help you with this work as well as cover base for you during the show when you need to take a break or have lunch. When the crowd gets heavy, you may need someone to help make sales, wrap purchases, watch for shoplifters or keep children's hands off fragile merchandise.

An eye-catching display will help you make sales, and it need not be expensive to be effective. For your first show, keep your display simple and portable. With each new selling experience, you'll automatically gain insight on refinements and improvements that can be made to grab buyers' attention and increase sales. "One's first display will never be the ultimate display because with growth many things change," confirms a seasoned show seller.

Packing Tips

Moving all the individual items you plan to sell—without damaging them—can be a challenge in itself. One crafter uses baker's bread trays to move merchandise from show to show. These heavy cardboard trays (available through box outlets or paper supply houses) have handles and stack inside each other. Another seller uses banana boxes she gets from her grocer because they have hand slots for carrying and can be carried two or three at a time when lightly packed with smaller boxes of merchandise. Other wooden boxes or crates might do double duty for packing crafts and for display. Consider covering boxes with indoor or outdoor carpet. This will give a suitable background for display, and the carpet serves as a shock absorber for crafts in transit.

Barbara's "SPECIAL" Formula

Here's my "**SPECIAL**" formula for a good display. It should be:

S afe

P ortable

E ffective

C olorful

I maginative

A ppealing

L ively

Safe

Carefully critique your booth for customer safety. Will it stand up to the press of a crowd or a hard wind? What displays might fall over or break? Could your whole display topple, taking your neighbor's exhibit with it? You can save money by constructing your own display, but if you're not certain about its stability or balance, seek professional advice.

If something should fall and injure a customer or another's property, the financial responsibility will be yours.

While on the topic of financial responsibility, I'll remind you to always ask
show promoters what protection you will have against theft or damage to
your crafts booth if it must be left overnight in a shopping mall or park. I
recall one couple who told me they entered a large shopping mall show and
lost everything when the mall caught fire one evening. They never thought it
would happen to them, so they had no insurance for such a thing.

Damage to craft work sometimes comes in strange forms. A woman who
exhibited corn dollies in a week-long outdoors festival lost hundreds of dollars' worth of work one evening to squirrels who must have nibbled all night
on items displayed on one table. Inclement weather can also cause loss. Any
outdoor show is a calculated risk, so always be prepared for both wind and
rain. Never leave your work unprotected in a tent, because even new tents
have been known to leak, and water can also seep in under the tent flap,
ruining anything on the ground.

Portable

The ideal display will take little space in a vehicle, be easy to pack, transport,
set up and dismantle. Teddy bear designer Jan Bonner, who has traveled the
craft show circuit for many years, says a good crafts display fixture "must be
portable, modular, easy to set up, neutral in color, and durable." She uses
break-apart bookshelves that look like a ladder. Three, seven foot-long pieces
fit along the inside wall of her van. The board shelves stack down the center.
All other necessary supplies can be stacked on top and around these fixtures.
Her first purchase was collapsible bookshelves, which proved to be expensive,
bulky and too heavy for her to transport alone. They also took up too much
space in her van.

The average exhibit area is about ten feet square, but your display should
be flexible in case you have to fit it into a smaller area. It should also be
adaptable to changing conditions. (Example: How would you handle the challenge of tree roots, uphill slants, or pillars with electrical outlets?) "Prepare
for surprises," advises an experienced seller.

Before trying to build your own booth, read craft magazines to spot ads
from manufacturers who offer a variety of portable, modular, lightweight display booths and canopies, folding tables, collapsible carts and other quick-
assembly display units. Tents and canopies generally feature snap-joint frames
and they can be personalized with your business name and/or logo. An added
advantage is the protection they offer from sun and rain. Before buying a canopy
(expect to pay between $400 and $900), visit some craft fairs and talk to the
exhibitors who use them to see how satisfied they are with the particular

brand or model they're using. (Companies who make canopies, tents and other display items for craft fair sellers advertise in such periodicals as *Sunshine Artists* and *The Crafts Report*.)

Tip

"Be prepared to maintain and repair your exhibit," reminds Jan Bonner. "Carry a tool kit filled with extra hardware, tools and leveling blocks as well as rope and anchoring stakes for outdoor shows. Constant setting up and tearing down can cause a great deal of wear and tear on any fixture."

Effective

Design your booth to keep customers exactly where you want them, whether it's in front of you, down the center of your booth or all around you.

An effective display will include merchandise that is displayed at several different eye levels (flat on a table, in containers, on one- or two-foot-high table props, portable riser displays, wall shelves or free-standing panels).

If you plan to hang artwork or other items on two sides of a wall unit, remember that you can see only one side at a time. Objects out of sight can easily be spirited away by mischievous children or light-fingered adults.

Remember that not everyone in a crowd will be honest. Display small, expensive pieces such as jewelry in a closed case. Or, instead of just laying jewelry on a piece of velvet or some other suitable background, make a fabric-covered A-frame display board that allows for tying items down, to be removed only when sold.

If you sell things that need to be touched or viewed close at hand, and customers do not have access to your work, you may be losing sales. In this case, you might consider an open display that allows customer entry, instead of trying to sell to them over a table or counter. Try to give this kind of display the illusion of a small shop, but never let the display itself overpower your work.

Tip

"More is not always better," says Phyllis Johnson, who makes and sells scarecrows year round. "Don't cram your entire stock into your booth. We see in a triangle. Even a table, with shelves to create a triangle (wide end at bottom) is better than shelves straight across and loaded with product."

Colorful

To display vividly colored art or craft objects, place them against pale or neutral background colors. Give plainer pieces a background that emphasizes their shape or texture. When displaying individual pieces, also think *contrast*. For example, try glass against brick, straw with calico, fiber on wood, metal on acrylic, silver on velvet.

Carefully plan the use of color for table coverings, your costume and accent areas of your booth. Be careful that the overall impression of your display does not compete with your products for prominence. Sheila Young, who designs and sells hand-loomed, personalized hats and mittens, planned her display around the colors used in her brochure, which are beige and red. She uses a beige table covering, a red backdrop for her hats, and a red, natural wicker basket on the table to hold her brochures. Her costume consists of one of her hats and a beige apron with three pockets that has her name and logo monogrammed on it. "As I walk around looking at other displays, I am always advertising without saying anything," she says. "The consistency of the same display and uniform makes it easy for customers to remember me and describe me to friends. It also makes it easier to strike up a barter with other crafters."

The way you use color in your display will help people remember you. "The public buys color—they are moved by it," says James Dillehay, author of *The Basic Guide to Selling Arts & Crafts*. "Sure, you will always find a market for natural-colored work, but without the diversity of a wide and luxurious selection of color combinations, you can't compete with the vast array of products vying for your customers' dollars."

Imaginative

Emulate, but do not duplicate the successful-looking craft displays you see at other shows. Add your own special touch to make your display different from everyone else's.

Look at your products with an objective eye to find a theme you can build on. Do you use ethnic designs? Practice a historic craft? Does your work fall into a particular period (Victorian, Early American, etc.) or is its style contemporary or country in nature? Can you build a theme around color? Shapes? Can you create an attractive vignette? (Ideas: dolls at a tea party, rocking horses inside a fence, soft sculpture animals in a woodland setting.)

Teddy bear designer Jan Bonner uses a tabletop gazebo for an attention grabber. In the spring she may highlight her bears in a tea party while a summer display may feature a wedding. The gazebo can also be broken into smaller modular pieces to make two bay windows for turn-of-the-century colonial-style shows.

How The Craft Scene Has Changed in Recent Years

"There are a lot more shows now than there were ten years ago, and many more exhibitors at each show. Many craftspeople complain that the over-abundance of shows is making this type of selling less profitable than it used to be because the number of prospective craft fair buyers has not increased in proportion to the number of shows. Craftspeople are making fewer sales now than in the past and their annual profits may also be lower because their sales have not kept pace with the ever-increasing costs involved in craft fair selling (entry fees, jury fees, display costs, travel expenses, raw materials costs, etc).

"There are lots of fabulous artisans out there—people of talent, just as many as ever—but there are also more low-end sellers than ever before. Something that really bothers us and all the show promoters are people who buy imports and try to pass them off as their own creations."

— Dave Cook, editor of *Sunshine Artists*

"An inviting presentation table/display will attract lookers and buyers," says Nanci Luna. "Lookers turn out to be buyers when they see something they like and the price is right. When an item looks good in its setting, it can bring a higher sales price. I make and sell Victorian crafts and I use a crushed velvet table cover with Victorian accents to bring attention to my items. I also use a Battenburg lace umbrella and beads for accents."

Appealing

The foundation of your crafts display is just part of the challenge in making a good exhibit. Within the booth or display area, you will need a variety of appealing display props, organizers and attention-getters. Flea markets and antique shops will often yield delightful finds in the form of old hat racks, small trunks, shelf units, baskets, etc. Small items often need to be displayed in a bunch. Check your home for appropriate containers, from decorative bowls and coffee mugs to baskets, flower pots and small crates and boxes. Nature items, from driftwood to hay bales, may greatly enhance displays of country products. Browse fairs and shops for more ideas. Note the texture and type of backgrounds behind certain products, the color combinations or the interesting accessory items used to hold or hang things. In stores, look at the kind of display cases and shelf arrangements used.

Decorative painter and designer Susan Young always asks show management if she can bring a small table lamp or two. She uses a surge protector/extension cord and one or two low-watt tasteful lamps that complement her table covers and some of the items she's selling. "The extra light really shows off detail work and draws customers, who wonder what's on 'the bright table over there,'" she says. When permissible, Susan also uses a string of novelty or seasonal lights in her display. For example, she has a set of white bunny lights for showing a table of Easter designs. (Susan's Easter exhibit is a real attraction, due partly to the three-foot tall animated bunny in the center of her table.)

Tip

"At craft fairs, bag your customers' purchases in clear plastic shopping bags," says Susan. "As they carry away their goodies, other people see your work!"

Do your products all look alike? If so, don't put everything out on display at once since many handcraft buyers like to think that what they are buying is unique, not mass produced. On the other hand, if you produce in quantity, yet make each item a little different in color or design, customers may appreciate seeing your whole selection so they can choose the one item that is just right for them. Experience is the best guide here.

Lively

Attract and appeal to buyers by teasing their senses with things in your exhibit area that move, sparkle, shine, make subtle sounds or release delightful scents. Make turntables revolve, let music boxes play, use mirrors to reflect, move wind chimes or mobiles with the aid of a battery-operated fan, throw a spotlight on featured products, use lighted display cases for small items, and so on. "We always use four or five swing arm lamps to light our display because the lighting in most places is terrible," says Deborah Ann Kirkaldy, who makes sewn, stuffed animals and other items from her own handmade felt.

Sachet packets might be intermingled with stitchery or sewn items, while spicy potpourri balls could be hung alongside Christmas ornaments. The idea is to prompt people to say or think, "Look!" "Listen!" or "What's that scent?"

Tip

Want to add a little activity to your booth? Barbara Schaffer recommends that you always have a raffle box for a special prize or discount on a craft item. "This also gives you a mailing list for future contact," she says.

Display Props and Attention Grabbers

Most crafters build their own interesting shelf arrangements, display cases, background walls and display accessory items to accentuate their particular art or craft. Commercial display units are often discarded after a while, so if you see one you like, ask the shop owner if you could have it when they're through with it. Here are examples of other things you might try, some of which are pictured in a nearby illustration:

- A-frame stands can be made by framing and hinging two sheets of quarter-inch plywood. Add stability with a chain at the bottom.
- Small modular units for special displays can be constructed from standard plumbing pipe and three-way elbow fixtures (see illustration A).

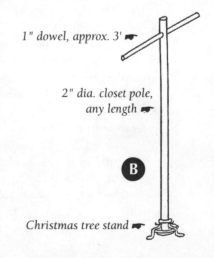

A

- Panels are adaptable to most any craft and are easily made in any size or shape from pegboard, lattice or other light-weight materials. They are generally painted or covered with a textured fabric such as burlap. Craft items can be hung on decorative hooks, placed on shelves or tucked into hanging baskets.
- Cardboard or plastic boxes can be used first as containers to carry merchandise to a show, then as display props.
- A variety of decorative easel stands and holders are available from companies who supply gift shops. They are great for displaying decorative plates, pictures and many other items that need to viewed in an upright position.
- Poles are good for making floor or table stands to hang things on. Drill a one-inch hole near one end of a two-inch-diameter closet pole to any height desired, and stick a one-inch-by-three-foot dowel rod through the hole. Mount in a Christmas tree stand (see illustration B).
- Stepladders can be a good display prop for crafts that sit or hang, and they can be brightly painted or especially decorated to coordinate with a particular craft. For example, a rosemaler decorated two

1" dowel, approx. 3' 🖝

2" dia. closet pole, any length 🖝

B

Christmas tree stand 🖝

ladders, then placed shelves on the steps to provide an excellent display for the back of her large walk-in booth.

■ Look for folding or specialty tables that allow for different configurations. Cover them imaginatively and completely to allow storage of merchandise underneath.

Tips on Protecting Displayed Items

Many shoppers carelessly handle items that can't take much handling before they break or become shopworn. In addition, people at fairs are often eating, drinking or smoking around a booth, further complicating exhibitors' problems. People who sell quilts and other fabric crafts are especially concerned about this problem. Here are some suggestions on how to handle it:

■ A quilter has a sign in her booth that says, "Smoking is hazardous to my quilts!" She provides a sand base ash tray in her booth and assertively tells people not to smoke or eat in it.

■ A crocheter puts each of her items in a plastic bag, keeping just one sample of each item for touching and examining. Later, these samples are offered at reduced prices or discarded.

■ To discourage people from picking up her stuffed fabric items, Shelley Adam makes fold-over cards to place beside her products. Each card (6" wide by 7" deep, folded in half) is decorated with a fabric shape that matches her products so shoppers can quickly see the price of items without handling them. (See illustration.)

■ Denise Lipps uses a sign that says "Food, drinks and cigarettes make me nervous because it takes approximately 100 hours to produce a quilt." (A similar sign might also dissuade people from handling soft sculpture, dolls and other fragile items.)

■ Another quilter displays one brightly colored open quilt in the back of her booth. On the center of her table is a portfolio of her designs, plus a couple of quilts in clear plastic bags. A note attached to each bag says, "Do not remove from package. Please see a salesperson for assistance." When showing a quilt, she takes it out in a way that many people can see it, but only one or two people at a time can touch it.

Recommended Reading

The general craft business start-up guides listed in chapter 1 all contain chapters on selling at fairs and show. These books will also be helpful:

● *How to Be a Weekend Entrepreneur, Making Money at Craft Fairs, Trade Shows and Swap Meets,* 2nd edition, by Susan Ratliff, Marketing Methods Press).

● *How to Put on a Great Craft Show, First Time & Every Time!* by Dianne & Lee Spiegel (FairCraft Publishing).

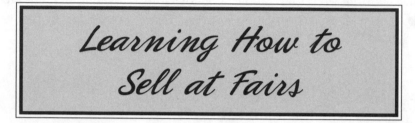

CHAPTER SEVEN

Learning How to Sell at Fairs

A Formula for Success: Quality Crafts + Affordable Prices + Attractive Booth + Friendly Attitude + Nice Personal Appearance + Effective Sales Strategies = Good Sales at a Fair

While selling does not come easy to most creative people, it should not be viewed as something scary. If you have a difficult time hawking your wares because you're shy, the good news is that you will become less and less shy the more people you meet face to face.

After her first experience at selling, a woman told me that while she was scared, she soon found that she enjoyed selling as much as crafting. "I also found that after selling many items, one negative response to my merchandise could very well have sent me home never to show my face or craft again. It was at this point that I had to learn not to take rejection as personal affront."

If you plan to enter a few shows this year to earn a little extra money, remember that you will be competing with many others who are trying to earn a part- or full-time living from the sale of crafts. Although the competition from such professionals may be stiff, beginning sellers with nicely-designed and beautifully crafted work can achieve good sales if they put a little time and money into the creation of a good display and learn some principles of selling.

Barbara's "SELL IT" Formula

This little SELL-IT formula will help you remember what to do when you're trying to learn how to sell:

S mile

E ntertain

L ook

L isten

I nterest

T alk

Smile

People are always drawn to friendly-looking people, so when you notice someone who's looking your way, make eye contact with that person and *smile!*

"I've observed adult crafters slumped in a chair reading with a booth full of customers," says Phyllis Johnson, Just Scarecrows. "I have also observed my teenage grandson attending my stand (he has nine years' experience) while I'm looking around. He always stands, always smiles as he greets people. He's courteous while making a sale or not making the sale. My customers have commented on his behavior during shows. It's not hard to smile and it sure boosts sales."

Tip

Do not sit in a chair and then get up as customers approach your booth, advises one seller. "This gesture is threatening to some. I have best results when I stand behind my display," she says. "If I must sit (as everyone needs to during a long day), I face the chair at an angle to the approach of my customers." Another option would be to sit on a high stool so that your eye level is close to that of your customers. Standing from this position will not seem threatening to customers.

Entertain

Many sales are lost by craft sellers who sit like lumps in their booths, arms folded across their chests in boredom. No sales? No wonder! It takes *action* to get sales! Successful salespeople in all fields *move;* they don't sit around waiting for money to fall into their laps.

Some fairs may not allow craft demonstrations, but for those that do, this can be a very good idea because many people go to craft fairs to be entertained. When you demonstrate your craft, you are automatically entertaining your audience, and if you can give people something no one else is giving them, they will give you not only their attention, but sales.

Tip

"Curiosity is a wonderful thing," says needleworker Judith McKinney. "I discovered I could increase my sales (115 percent at one show) by demonstrating. When people see a few other people gathered around a table, they want to stop and see what's going on. Even if they don't buy right then, they see my work and learn of the custom services I offer."

One of the most entertaining, demonstrating craftsmen I ever met was a Pennsylvania blacksmith named Harry Houpt. At folk festivals, he always drew large crowds with his rhythmic "musical anvil," which he played with a hammer before fanning the forge and demonstrating his blacksmithing skills. Then he would make a miniature horseshoe, all the while talking about life and the lessons it holds for all of us. Everyone would listen, especially the children, one of whom would be the lucky recipient of the newly-created horseshoe. When he finished his demonstration, people flocked to his exhibit to buy.

☞ **TRY THIS:** Think of some little "something" you could make from scraps to occasionally give to children as an attention-getting device. When you see bright-eyed children who seem entranced by something in your display, give them something to keep or just hold for a few minutes. Strike up a conversation with them, telling how you made the object or something about the material it's made of, or some interesting thing about your craft's history.

Now you are being entertaining, and this will automatically attract the attention of nearby adults, bringing them into the conversation and nearer your displays as well. Once your prospective customers discover that you are as interesting as your work, you will automatically increase the odds of making a sale. (Yes, you *are* an interesting person or you wouldn't be involved in crafts to begin with!)

Look

Watch people as they approach your exhibit. Try to discover what interests them most. If they merely pause before passing by, pay attention to what they were looking at when they paused. Is something lacking in this area to draw them in? When people pause, and then stop, observe which objects they pick up to examine. During the show, take time to observe the exhibits of other sellers, paying particular attention to those that have the largest crowds. What seems to be attracting so many people, and how can you employ the same idea in your own booth?

☞ **TRY THIS:** Study the reactions of people as they look at your work. Do these reactions make you feel that your crafts are priced too low, too high, or just about right? Although your feelings here are an excellent guideline in pricing, you should exhibit in two or three shows before making drastic changes in your prices.

Tip

Children have a lot of influence when it comes to buying something. When shoppers failed to take interest in her exhibit of dolls at a fair, Sara Weber began to strike up conversations with children who were looking at them. "Eventually I got the attention of enough mothers to sell out," she said. "But before I did, a cameraman from a nearby TV station was there, and he took a picture of me and my dolls and I was on the news the next night."

Listen

Pay attention to the questions and comments people make while in or near your exhibit. Such remarks will provide clues on what you need to do to increase sales or correct a problem that may be deterring sales. Brace yourself for negative feedback from critical people who do not appreciate fine craft work. It's hard to take criticism, but you need to listen to your critics to get new ideas on how to improve your work or make it more salable. Just don't take it to heart.

"Customers behave differently from year to year," says Mary Jane Jenrich. "I have a small group of customers who follow me to shows because they know I'll always have something new. It's important to listen to people and watch them to note the like or dislike on their faces. The hard part is not taking their dislike to heart, but learning through their teaching."

If you get really annoyed at someone, you might quote Zeuxis (400 B.C.). Once, when he was criticized for something he had done, he said (smugly, I'm sure), "Criticism comes easier than craftsmanship." Remember that the next time you overhear a discouraging word, and smile to yourself. Your most appreciative buyer may be right on your critic's heels.

Interest

Give your customers reasons to buy. People don't go to a crafts fair with a list of items they plan to buy, they go to browse and have fun. To sell to them, you need to plant some "Buy Me!" suggestions in their subconscious. Mary-Jane Guest has the right idea. She sells decorated brooms, wreaths and ornaments, along with her best-selling item, a special slip-through scarf with many uses. Her sales increased when she began to place gift idea cards by various items on her table.

"I use 4-inch square cards folded in half like a place-card," she says. "I print different things on them such as 'Secret Pal?', 'Gift for Teacher,' 'For someone who has everything,' 'That special someone,' etc. You'd be surprised how many people see these signs and say things like, 'Why, Grandma would love that,' or 'I forgot we need a teacher's gift,' or 'I never thought of something like that for my niece.' Sometimes people just need a suggestion or a little nudge."

Here are other examples:

- "A small sign near a product will give people ideas on how to use a product," says Chris Daley, who uses signs such as "Great for stocking stuffers!" or "Use as a pot holder or a teapot cover."
- Try a "Great Gift Item!" sign to remind people of an impending gift obligation, or a "Limited Edition" sign to suggest the collectibility of a particular item.

■ Since few people can resist a bargain, offer one. Artists might place a "Save by framing it yourself!" sign over a bin of unframed prints to encourage sales. Or, on a wall display of various items, you might advertise, "Your choice, $10 each." (Having to make a choice means people will linger longer in your area, giving you additional time for a sales pitch.)

The way items are displayed can send messages to buyers that either encourage or discourage sales. For example, small stacks of fabric say "Thumb through—we're interesting," while the same items stacked too high may make buyers fear the stack will collapse if touched. Representative samples of related items on a table suggests "There is more where these came from," while a table cluttered with too many unrelated items is the mark of an amateur seller. If your crafts can be handled without damage, encourage prospective buyers to pick them up. Sometimes the very feel of an object in the hand will prompt a purchase.

Tip

The desire to buy can be snuffed out in an instant by things totally unrelated to your work. For example, nonsmokers may avoid the displays of exhibitors who smoke, while clothes-conscious individuals may be turned off by a seller's inappropriate dress or untidy appearance. Timid buyers may fear aggressive sellers, while gregarious people may resent exhibitors who appear aloof. You can't win them all, but you can strive for a happy medium that will appeal to most of your buying audience.

TALK IT UP: Sales often begin with simple conversation, and you don't have to *sell*, just *talk*. (This will be easier to do if you remember that some buyers are probably as shy as you are.) When someone appears interested in a particular object, volunteer some interesting information about the product's unusual materials, origin, name or usefulness. This will encourage bystanders to ask questions and give you the chance to share your enthusiasm and sell without really trying. Be prepared to handle all questions that may arise, from "Do you sell on consignment?" to "Can you make it in blue, instead of red?" and "How soon can you deliver twelve dozen?"

"I hear a lot of complaints about low sales from other crafters," says Marla King, "but I watch how these people talk and interact with their customers and I am not surprised by their complaints. I am very talkative and friendly with all prospective customers. Sometimes I don't sell anything, but they always get a business card and they know I do special orders."

If you decide to take a custom-design order, remember that some people will order something, then decide later they don't want it after you have spent several hours and many dollars in materials. That's why you need to either (1) ask for a down payment sufficient to cover your actual costs (to be kept if the customer later cancels) or (2) make sure your custom-designed item is something that can be sold to someone else.

Selling Tips

Part of the secret in learning how to sell is understanding what makes the average person buy. For example, most people want comfort, ease, luxury and convenience. They may also like to buy things, even when they can't afford them. Appeal to these instincts, and let people know how your products can satisfy their needs and desires.

As a seller, it is your job is to make your customers feel important. Although you may feel like the star at a crafts fair (having created all those beautiful things), it's the customer who counts. If your sales are good, figure that you're doing something right, and keep doing it. If they're not so good, look at your work more objectively, not as its creator but as a prospective buyer. Try to figure out what's wrong with it. Ask yourself if you would buy it at the prices marked. If not, why not? Then ask yourself if you are making what you want to make because it gives you pleasure to do so or if you are producing crafts with buyers in mind. It is *their* needs, not yours, that must be satisfied if you are to succeed as a seller of handcrafts.

"I've been going to craft shows for the past six months with no luck at all," writes a frustrated reader. "People look at an item, pick it up, say it's cute, and walk on. I know my prices are okay because other people sell similar items for even more. I have noticed that the items that do sell are usually priced under $5, and anything else just sits there."

This reader crochets baby blankets, makes cross stitch pictures, grapevine/ straw wreaths, keychains and straw hats. She has a passion for crafting and doesn't want to give it up, but wonders what she ought to do differently to sell more of what she makes. Without seeing her products, her display, or the way she presents herself in her exhibit, it's impossible to know why her items aren't selling. She may be trying to sell products that are too readily available from other crafters. Or maybe her products are okay and the problem is that she is trying to sell them in the wrong places.

What Sellers Hear Most Often from Browsers

"These are cute. . . how do you make them?"

"This is nicely done . . . but I won't pay that for it."

"Pretty . . . you do good work . . . could I have the pattern?"

"Beautiful . . . but I don't have the money."

"Lovely . . . but I really don't need it."
Crafter's lament: "If I only had a dime for every compliment I got!"

If your sales at fairs are less than satisfactory, don't give up. Many other crafters have been in the same boat and gone on to enjoy success. "Do as many shows as possible and don't worry about profits when you're just beginning," advises Anne Pape. "You need to experience what it's like, sample the different types of shows, talk to other craftspeople, watch the competition, watch what people are buying. These things are just as important as those first sales."

"Don't get discouraged at shows," adds Roseanne Strazinsky. "At one show, it was a couple of hours before I finally had my first sale, and it was for a $1.50 item. But my second sale, half an hour later, was for $100—four sweatshirts. That woman's purchase made my day."

"Keep practicing your craft," urges Joan Monostory. "I remember a tole painter whose items were very amateurish three years ago, with poor sales. Now that she has perfected her craft, she is a top seller in our area."

"Hang in there!" says Karen Willard, who makes corsages. "People have money to spend. You just have to find an item they can't do without." I know more of you would like to hear what Karen says she hears a lot: "Where will you be next, so I can bring more money to shop with?" Karen courts her customers by regularly sending them a list of shows where she will be selling, and in this mailing she always offers a special new item or something on sale that can be pre-ordered and picked up at a show (or shipped later, if preferred).

☞ **TRY THIS:** To increase sales, Jeanne Swartz suggests giving a small freebie item with the purchase of a higher priced new item. "This helps to promote the new item and gives you a chance to get rid of old, lower-priced items that have been around too long," she says. "Customers love to feel they are getting more than they are paying for."

Gail Norman of Rag Bag Originals doesn't say much when other crafters complain about poor shows and sales because her sales were good even in her first year of selling. She buys preprinted towels for golf, tennis, fishing and bowling, then monograms them freehand at craft shows. People love to watch her do this, and a purchase is contagious. The towels sell for $15 and are her "bread and butter" item—the guaranteed seller that enables her to spend time on the more creative but less profitable items that fill the rest of her booth.

"I have items for sale that are not like things found in other booths," she says. "My patterns are original, I use beautiful, hard-to-find fabrics, and I'm always demonstrating what I do. Those who want to copy can purchase my patterns and raw materials. Those who want to learn can attend my classes, and those who can't do crafts buy my finished product. So I cover all the bases and make more money."

Linda Jackson has learned the importance of conversation with customers. "When a customer tells me she loves my product, I reply, 'Thank you, I've sold so many and my customers just love them—these are all I have left.' Every time, I sell another. I call it the 'power of positive selling.'"

Financial Tips

How will you accept and store money received from sales at a fair? Be sure to hide your cash box from view. Example: A seller who uses rustic apple crates to display her work turns one of the crates toward the back of the table with the open end toward her. This serves as a sales counter, with her cash box, pen, paper, cards and other items hidden from customers' view.

Another crafter told me how she designed a special "money apron" with a secret zippered pocket to hold checks and large bills. This pocket was covered by a larger cobbler pocket. Smaller pockets were added to hold dollar bills and change. Here are some special tips on accepting payments from customers:

Accepting Cash. When customers pay with cash, never put a large bill into your cash box until change has been given. Don't give people an opportunity to say, "But I gave you a twenty, not a ten." Prove the fact by showing them the original bill, still lying outside your money box. (Remember, there are con artists everywhere.)

Accepting Checks. If you take a check for merchandise, be sure to ask for identification and note the individual's driver's license number on the check. Also get a telephone number and address if it's not printed on the check.

Some retailers ask customers for a credit card number as a credit reference. But many consumers now refuse to do this because giving their credit card number to another individual leaves them open to fraud. And having this number does a crafts seller no good since a bounced check can't be covered by charging the same amount to a customer's credit card. Therefore, what you might want to do is simply ask to *see* a credit card for reference. Check the name, but don't copy the number.

Finally, don't cash checks for anyone, and don't let them write a check for an amount larger than the purchase, requiring you to give change. To protect the checks you do have, endorse them on the spot, "For deposit only."

Accepting Credit Cards. Although you might like to offer your customers the privilege of charging their purchases to a credit card, you may find it difficult to obtain merchant status from your bank. The situation is improving, but because many banks still consider homebased businesses to be risky, merchant status is often difficult to get. Curiously, the smaller your community, the easier it may be to get this service. If you're known in your community, have a good credit history or a track record as a business owner, you may have no problems at all.

If you don't expect to make many charge card sales, but don't want to lose sales because people have come to a fair without cash or a checkbook, you might opt for a manual system where you write out charge slips by hand and imprint them with a little machine the bank will rent to you for a couple dollars a month. This is the system I use. I resisted getting merchant status for many years, thinking it was just another business aggravation I didn't need, but I have to admit that in my first year of using this service I made many sales I wouldn't have made otherwise. Buyers do appreciate this convenience.

Today there are electronic systems that enable serious craft fair sellers to take charge card sales at a fair and check the customer's credit on the spot. Some craft sellers have reported this is "the cat's pajamas," so keep this in mind as your business grows. Several organizations catering to the home-business community now offer merchant card services, which is another reason why it may be advantageous for you to join a small business organization.

Coping with Copycats

"A big problem the craft world faces is that there is so much duplication of designs," a basketmaker told me. "Any new idea is quickly copied by crafters and then offered for sale at lower prices. Before long you can see the same item at every other booth in every craft show around."

What's interesting about this statement is that I first heard it twenty-five years ago. Nothing has changed in this department, except that people have become more bold in their copying.

Taking Custom Orders

"The crafters who bring home the most money are the ones with a diverse inventory," says Eleanor Holt, who does tole painting on wood cutouts and makes "sure money" by accepting special orders. "That's money in my pocket and customers are getting something made especially for them," she says. "Many crafters think this is a bother and almost get insulted because a customer wants something a little bit different from what is already made, but shoppers are so individual. We need to listen to what they are saying."

After selling at fairs for a while, Jeanne Swartz, who owns Gifts From the Heart, noticed that many fair shoppers were repeat customers, while others were referrals. "Others had taken my card and later ordered something they had seen at one of my shows," she says. "I've found that young, newly married working women are my best customers because they are excited about decorating their new apartments or homes. They like everything to match, so I get a lot of custom orders from them."

Every craft seller hates them: the people who saunter up to a booth, pull out paper and pencil, and begin to copy the designs found on exhibited products, or worse, snap pictures.

One crafter told me that at the last show she did, there were signs around the building stating "PLEASE: NO PHOTOS OR SKETCHES," but people ignored them, and she had two people in her booth sketching her work.

Another crafter reported in a magazine article that she has had some very rude and inconsiderate people stand in her booth and draw right in front of her. "I made them mad when I asked them to leave my booth," she said, "but at least they left."

☞ **TRY THIS:** If you see someone with a camera taking pictures of you or your booth, ask for identification. Unless that person is with a newspaper or magazine, tell him or her to stop taking pictures at once. If your craft designs are copyrighted, emphasize that you have the legal right to sue anyone who copies your designs.

The minute you put a good idea out there, the public will copy it. So the secret is to come up with new ideas every year because then you'll be ahead of the copycats. By the time they get around to copying you, you have new merchandise. Phyllis Johnson sums it up nicely: "As soon as you have a new design or product, get it out there, saturate your market area all the while dreaming up something new or a new twist on the old."

What to Do When Things Aren't Selling

What should you do when you've created something you think is wonderful, but no one wants to buy it? You have three choices: Stop trying to sell it, change it or make something else. Here are four ways you can change a product to make it more appealing to buyers:

1. Change your prices
2. Change the materials being used
3. Change your colors or designs
4. Change the name or function of your product

As explained in Chapter Five, the price you place on a product has a great deal to do with whether it will sell or not. Before you even think of lowering the price of a hard-to-sell product, try first to change it in some way to make buyers feel it is worth more to them.

The type and quality of the materials you use in your work automatically determine your market and the prices you can charge for it. Some materials are ordinary or plain, while others are unusual or luxurious. When you elect to work with common materials, buyers may expect your prices to be common as well. When you use luxurious or exotic materials, however, you automatically attract more affluent buyers.

For example, you can either make teddy bears for children, using inexpensive washable furs from your local sewing store, or make designer bears for collectors, using expensive imported fur such as mohair. Whereas a teddy bear for kids might sell for $15 to $25, collectors will pay ten times this price for a one-of-a-kind bear. If you make furniture or wooden accessories, you can either use a common wood like pine and price it for the general public, or use uncommon or exotic woods that will appeal to buyers with bigger pocketbooks.

Even when you are using the right materials for a product, it may not sell if your colors or designs are wrong for the times. Stay aware of what's hot and what's not where colors are concerned, and strive always for more originality in your designs.

What you call your products has a great deal to do with whether they will sell or not, so try calling them something other than what most people might call them. For example, let's assume that you make wheat weavings. They might sell at higher prices if you presented them as "Wheat Art Sculptures" or "WheatArt Collectibles." That's because some people automatically expect to pay more for a product if they feel they are buying "art" instead of "craft." To further illustrate, a wheat weaving affixed to a plaque might be perceived as "craft" while a wheat weaving in a shadow box behind glass might be considered "art." (And the extra benefit is that this product won't be soiled after it has hung on the wall for a couple of years.)

To change the function of a wheat weaving presently being sold as a plaque, consider placing it in a box with a recessed top so the arrangement is permanently preserved under glass. Such a box could be lined in leather or turned into a velvet-lined jewelry box. Now you've not only changed the function, but the name as well. And by adding a high-quality music mechanism that might add less than $10 to your materials cost, you could easily ask four times the price for this product because now the product has become a *handcrafted music box.*

Wheat weavings also make charming Christmas ornaments. The same people who aren't interested in another picture to hang on the wall may find it hard to resist buying another ornament for their tree. Or, think jewelry, always of interest to most women. Think pendants and earrings and designer pins, and remember that the quality of your metal findings will determine the price you can ask for jewelry. People will always pay more for gold-plated or sterling silver jewelry.

As you can see, price, material, color, design and a product's name and function all work together where sales are concerned. Apply the above logic to your craftwork and see what happens.

Make Something Else

Sometimes this is the only logical solution to sluggish sales. Consider the following letter I once received from a woman who crochets:

> I am not progressing in my moneymaking endeavors. I crochet and I have been trying for ten years to make it pay for itself, but at no time have I ever made a profit. I make the selling price three times the cost of materials, and I do not charge for my time, yet somebody is always sure to say an item is too expensive. A baby sacque and cap sells for about $20. Imagine what the true price would be if I tacked on the cost of the eight hours or more it took me to crochet it? To say I am beginning to get discouraged is putting it mildly. However, my natural optimism tells me there is a pot of gold at the end of the rainbow, so I keep plugging away.

I understand this crocheter's reluctance to give up her favorite craft, but if she wants to make money (and I don't mean just sell things, but make a *profit* from the hours put into them), she must begin to think in new directions. Profit rarely comes from making crocheted baby booties and other ordinary items because thousands of women know how to make them, and too many are selling them at giveaway prices at local fairs and bazaars. The serious crocheter interested in making money cannot compete in this kind of market, so the obvious thing to do is explore a different one by offering a different type of product.

For example, instead of using fine thread to crochet common baby items, consider crocheting small (three- to five-inch) pictures of dogs, cats, Victorian ladies or flowers as stand-alone designs that could be framed under glass. Now you're talking "contemporary art" that could sell for $25 or more. Consider jewelry, too. How about a miniature work of art that could be "framed" inside a pendant? Or, move into the women's clothing area by making vests of luxuriant thick yarns that could sell for $125 or more in an exclusive women's clothing shop.

A reader in West Virginia who makes pine cone wreaths also wonders why people aren't buying. "Many people tell me my work is the most beautiful, original and professional looking of its kind," she says. "Although it is priced below other work of inferior quality, people still won't buy. Why?"

Maybe it's because pine cone wreaths are too common in West Virginia, or maybe wreaths are considered a seasonal (Christmas) item by most buyers, or maybe buyers think they can do this craft themselves. It's hard to tell, but what is obvious is that this crafter is going to have to go outside her own area to sell with any success because she is meeting buyer resistance.

If it were me, I'd first raise my prices to allow for wholesaling, then I'd make the effort to drive to the nearest large city to seek out high-quality shops that might place orders. I'd also begin to study available resources to find Appalachian or country shops in other areas of the country that cater to tourists. I'd also think about making up kits of materials and instructions for people who want to make wreaths themselves. Finally, I'd start thinking about other products I could make from pine cones, concentrating on products others aren't selling.

Tip

Instead of waiting for a pot of gold that may never appear, make some changes. As someone once said, you cannot expect different results if you keep doing the same thing. Creative ideas will come if you will make the effort to stretch your imagination. To do this, pay attention to what others are doing. Read. Network. Experiment. Turn left instead of right. Ask "what if?" and "why not?" Dare to be different!

Whatever your craft, if you're not selling at a profit after a certain length of time, it may be that you're simply in a rut on the wrong road to sales success. Let this be your signal to stop and think about new roads you might explore. As any successful seller will tell you, changing directions in midstream is all part of the fun of selling what you make.

Reselling Earlier Buyers

A successful strategy used by many craft fair sellers is to send a postcard announcement of their next craft fair appearance or a new brochure to everyone who has ever purchased something at a fair. If you do the same shows each year, many of your customers might come back to see you if you send them a personal invitation. Sales at a fair will always increase in proportion to the number of years you have participated in that event. The better your customers know you, the more apt they are to buy from you. A mailing list will also be handy should you later decide to hold a home boutique, start classes or start selling crafts through your own mail order catalog.

Beginning with just 250 names, Kay Nelson began to send follow-up announcements to her craft fair buyers. At first she addressed the cards by hand. Three years later, with the help of a computer, she was sending announcements to nearly 5,000 customers and racking up extra sales at every show as a direct result. A study of her sales revealed that up to 85 percent of her show sales were from customers who had received her mailings. She now announces her spring and fall shows and new catalogs to her entire mailing list twice a year.

Once you have a list of customers who are familiar with your work, instead of asking them to order something by mail, send them a letter sug-

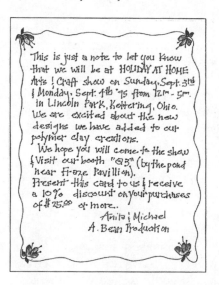

To promote upcoming fairs and shows, Anita and Michael Behnen print announcement cards like the one above. They use lightweight ivory stock printed in black ink. The card measures 4¼ x 5½ inches (which means it can be printed economically, four to a page, then cut). The flowers in each corner are hand-colored with red, gold and green felt-tip pens during in the evening while watching television. This little bit of color makes the card very appealing.

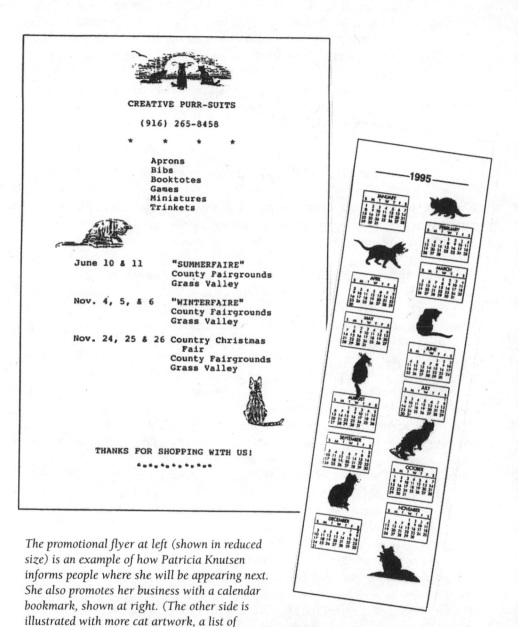

CREATIVE PURR-SUITS

(916) 265-8458

*   *   *   *

Aprons
Bibs
Booktotes
Games
Miniatures
Trinkets

June 10 & 11   "SUMMERFAIRE"
                  County Fairgrounds
                  Grass Valley

Nov. 4, 5, & 6   "WINTERFAIRE"
                  County Fairgrounds
                  Grass Valley

Nov. 24, 25 & 26 Country Christmas
                  Fair
                  County Fairgrounds
                  Grass Valley

THANKS FOR SHOPPING WITH US!

1995

The promotional flyer at left (shown in reduced size) is an example of how Patricia Knutsen informs people where she will be appearing next. She also promotes her business with a calendar bookmark, shown at right. (The other side is illustrated with more cat artwork, a list of products she makes, and her business name and address.)

"Using copyright-free graphics, I have designed all my printed materials," she says. "I make up the master copy and have one of the local quick print shops print them. I save money by cutting them myself."

gesting they place an order now for pickup at your next fair appearance. This idea has worked well for Suzanne Malafeoste. "I bring an inexpensive guest book to all craft shows, asking customers for their names and addresses," she says. "Twice a year, I send everyone a list of all my upcoming shows—one for fall and winter, one for spring and summer. I give these customers a 10 percent discount when they come to my next show, and I've had 30 percent repeat sales so far. Once a year I also run a 20 to 30 percent-off sale on leftover fall and Christmas items after my last show on December 8."

Keeping Craft Show Records

It's important to make a written record of all sales. Try using a simple carbon-interleaved sales slip book. For each item sold, write its name or code number, any information such as size or color that you wish to monitor, price and applicable sales tax. (Consider the use of removable price tags that bear the code numbers of items in your line—helpful for tallying sales by category at days end.) Keep one copy of the sales slip and give the other to your customer. By keeping detailed records of each product sale you make, you can learn which of your products sell best and which sizes, styles or colors are most popular. This information will enable you to plan for future shows.

How can you estimate the number of sales you will make at a show? It helps to know how many people are expected to attend. At one time, teddy-bear designer Jan Bonner figured she made one sale for every 75 shoppers at a show, but as her prices have increased, her percentage of sales has decreased. "The more specialized your product, the more potential customers needed," she says. As competition from other bear sellers has increased, Jan has continued to raise her prices and eliminate smaller shows that are not targeted exclusively to teddy bear collectors. "If I'm going to enter a non-targeted craft show, I figure I need an expected audience of at least 25,000 for the show to be profitable. Even then, I would not expect to sell more than a hundred bears at such a weekend show."

That translates to a mere .004 percent, so when a crafter complained to me that she was making only one sale for every ten people who showed interest in her exhibit, she had no idea how well she was doing. Making one sale out of ten translates to a 10 percent sales response, which is unusual to say the least. Another beginner complained that she had "five lookers for every buyer," but that's a 20 percent buy response, which is *phenomenal*.

As a mail order book seller, if I could consistently sell a book to one out of every five people who asked for my brochure, I would be delighted, not to mention rich. More often than not, I'm lucky to get an order response of only 5 percent. Beginning crafters would be lucky to get a similar sales response at shows.

YEAR _____

MOE'S TOLES & MORE

SALES INVENTORY RECORD

EVENT DATE: _____

LOCATION: _____

ITEM	QUANTITY SOLD	(COST)	SELLING PRICE	PROFIT

TOTAL SALES $_____   TOTAL PROFIT: $_____

NOTES: _____
_____
_____
_____
_____

Maureen Gragnani, Moe's Toles & More, designed the above form (shown in reduced size) to keep track of items that have been sold, and the amount of profit each one has yielded.

Beef Up Your Inventory

To avoid running out of merchandise the second day of a two-day show, beef up your inventory on small, inexpensive items. Also create a special display of sample items that can be ordered at the show for later delivery. "But never commit to a certain delivery time that is unrealistic," advises Suzi Fox. "It is so easy to stick your foot in your mouth and over commit." Suzi, whose best-selling items are $10 mini mop dolls, has learned the importance of planning and stockpiling merchandise during her off-season. "Last Christmas, I was not prepared for the shows I had agreed to do and I had to work every available minute just to come up with an adequate amount," she says. "It was very frustrating to know that I could have made four times the money by being organized."

Let's look again at Jan Bonner's percentage-of-sales figures. Now this isn't a formula written in stone, but if Jan knows that 75,000 people are expected to attend the next show she is doing, she can at least estimate that she might make 300 sales at this event (75,000 x .004). Much will depend on the price range of her products, of course. The lower her prices, the more items she can expect to sell.

Perhaps you could use the above percentage figures as a starting point in estimating sales you might make at a show. To learn how well (or poorly) you are doing at craft fairs, start recording the following information on each show you do:

■ Name and date of show and where presented.

■ Number of sales you make at the show. (Individual items, not dollars).

■ Total dollars generated at the show.

■ Number of people who attend the event. (The figures you get from a show promoter are apt to be on the high side, but any estimate will be better than none.)

■ Number of exhibitors.

■ Other pertinent facts. (Professional craft sellers keep very detailed records about every show they enter because this information helps them decide whether it will be profitable to enter the same show again in the future. Note such things as the weather, current economy, amount of advertising or publicity the show got and any other factor that you think affected your sales.)

How to Estimate Sales at a Show

Once you have some figures to work with, start a worksheet to record the figures you will get from the following four-step arithmetic process. I believe that your ability to keep and analyze craft fair sales records will have much to do with your success as a crafts fair seller. Few if any crafters keep the kind of records I am suggesting here, but this is the same kind of arithmetic that I and other mail order sellers use to calculate the profitability of a direct mailing. I may be wrong, but I believe you can do the same thing with fairs and shows.

Whenever I plan a mailing of any kind, I can closely estimate the number of orders I will receive because I have kept detailed response records of every mailing made in the past. By knowing the percentage of people who normally order, and the dollar amount of my average sale, I can estimate the number of orders I will get from a new mailing. By multiplying this figure times the size of my average order, I can estimate the total dollars any mailing is likely to generate. By comparing this to what it will cost me to do the mailing, I can then decide whether a particular mailing is likely to be profitable or not.

If you would like to try this idea, here are the figures you should record on your "Sales Analysis Worksheet." (see sample worksheet nearby).

1. After each show, tally your sales and divide the total dollars by the number of sales you've made. (Not the number of individual items sold but the number of customers who have made purchases.) This will give you the dollar amount of your average sale. Let's say you sell a variety of items priced from $5 to $50. The following examples illustrate how your average sales figure might change from show to show:

Craft event #1: $ 182 divided by 24 sales = average sale of $ 7.58
Craft event #2: $ 436 divided by 30 sales = average sale of $14.53
Craft event #3: $ 1,468 divided by 40 sales = average sale of $36.70

To find the size of your average sale for all three shows, total the three average sale figures ($58.81) and divide by three ($19.60). Thus, with a range of products priced between $5 and $50, it would be reasonable to expect that your average sale at any future show would be approximately $20.

Sales Analysis Worksheet

Name of Show	Event #1	Event #2	Event #3	Average
Date of Show	Dec.14, '97	Jan. 23, '98	Apr. 10, '98	
Total Sales	$182.00	$436.00	$1,468.00	
Divided by **Number of Sales**	24	30	40	
Equals Average Sale	$7.58	$14.53	$36.70	**$58.81 ÷ 3**
Average of Several Shows				**=$19.60**
Number of Sales	24	30	40	
Divided by Number of People Attending Event	2,500	10,000	25,000	
Equals Sales Response *Percentage*	.01%	.003%	.002%	**.015 ÷ 3**
Average of Several Shows				**=.005%**

Calculations:

1. To get SIZE OF AVERAGE SALE, divide total sales by number of sales.

2. To get SALES RESPONSE PERCENTAGE, divide the number of sales by the number of people attending the event.

3. To estimate NUMBER OF SALES AT NEXT SHOW, multiply expected number of shoppers by your latest sales response figure.

4. To estimate NUMBER OF DOLLARS AT NEXT SHOW, multiply estimated number of sales times dollar amount of your average sale.

2. After each show, divide the number of sales by the number of people in attendance to get a percentage figure of your average sales response. Examples:

Craft event #1: 24 sales divided by   2,500 shoppers = .010 % sales response
Craft event #2: 30 sales divided by 10,000 shoppers = .003 % sales response
Craft event #3: 40 sales divided by 25,000 shoppers = .002 % sales response

To find the average, add all percentage figures (.015) and divide by three to get .005, which is less than half a percent. Adjust this *average sales response figure* as you continue to do shows. The more shows you record, the more reliable your figures and estimates will become. (As you can see, I've used very conservative sales figures. I'd be delighted to hear that your sales response figures are higher than this.)

3. To estimate the number of sales you might make at your next crafts show, multiply the expected number of shoppers by your latest average sales response figure.

Using the above average sales response figure of .005 percent and an estimated 7,500 shoppers expected, you would multiply 7,500 × .005 to get 38 sales (rounded off).

4. To estimate the number of dollars you might generate at your next crafts show, multiply the estimated number of sales times your average sales figure. Using the above figures, you would multiply your estimated 30 sales times your average sales figure of $19.60 to get a total of $745 in expected sales.

There is yet another figure (factor) that will affect the number of sales, and that is the number of exhibitors at a particular show. For example, if 5,000 people attend a show populated by 200 exhibitors, it's only logical to assume that each exhibitor will make more sales than they would if the show were to have 400 exhibitors. That's why you should also keep a record of the number of exhibitors at each show in which you appear. Even though all these figures will be mostly rough estimates (since you'll never know for sure how many people attend any given show), they are nonetheless valuable. After a while, a study of these figures will give you a reliable picture of what you can expect to sell at any given show, and this will help you figure out how much merchandise to take to each event.

Evaluating the Profitability of Shows

Once you've done a round of art or craft fairs, you will probably plan to enter some of the same shows again the following year. To decide which shows were the most profitable, you will need to keep additional records. For each show, keep track of your booth fees and travel expenses so you can calculate an "expense percentage figure" for each.

For example, if your expenses for a nearby show were $150 for the entry fee and $120 for gas, motel and meals, total expenses would be $270. Divide this figure by total sales for the show—let's say they were $2,872—to get an expense percentage figure of 9 percent. On another larger show several hundred miles away, your booth fee might be $395 and travel expenses $600, for a total of $995. If your sales here were $3500, your selling expenses would be running 28 percent of sales, which common sense tells you is too high for profitability. In comparing the two shows, you can see that the smaller, nearby show was more profitable, even though overall sales were lower. When you do this show again you might increase sales by improving your display and selling methods and taking a larger inventory of products, some priced a bit higher than before.

I like the simple formula used by many professional artists and crafters. They look at what it costs to enter a show and figure they need to sell ten times this amount to cover all their expenses and yield a profit. For example, if the entry fee for a show is $250, professional crafters figure their gross sales should be $2500. Whatever method you use, it's important to keep track of expenses. If you don't, you will never be certain whether you are making a true profit or not.

NOTE: My research shows that the rule-of-ten is common in retailing. A tried-and-true profitability formula for retailers is to keep their rent at 10 percent of sales. Craft mall sellers aim for sales of 8 or 10 times their booth rental, and pushcart sellers know that this kind of selling won't be profitable unless they keep their lease rental fees to no more than 10 to 15 percent of gross sales.

CHAPTER EIGHT

Selling Handcrafts from Home

If you must stay close to home or don't want all the work involved in doing craft fairs, selling from your home or that of a friend may be the perfect solution for you.

Do you dream of owning a little craft shop of your own up on Main Street? If so, you're not alone. Most crafters think a gift or craft shop would be lots of fun, but few have any real understanding of how much time and money it takes to start and operate a retail store. Instead, they tend to see the romantic side of retailing, imagining themselves at work at their craft behind the counter, talking to customers from time to time as they browse in the store. They look forward to decorating the shop for holidays and figure they will rack up extra profits from the sale of their own work.

Unfortunately, it doesn't work that way. Running a shop is a full-time job. Constant interruptions from customers make craft production difficult if not impossible. "The extra walk-in traffic I originally anticipated was more of a headache than it was worth," says one crafter who opened her own shop after years of selling monogrammed products from home. "Being a sole proprietor, I found it difficult to work with the interruptions during the day, and working outside my home was definitely a hardship for my family. That's why I moved my business back home."

While I would never encourage anyone working alone to open a shop uptown (or downtown, as the case may be), a cooperative craft shop is another matter entirely and a topic I will discuss in Chapter Eleven. For now, however, let's explore ways to have the fun of retailing without the financial responsi-

bilities and worries of a regular retail shop. This chapter explains how others
are selling directly from home and how you can sell from home, too, through

* Your homebased shop or studio
* Open house sales
* Home parties (Party Plan Style)
* Holiday boutiques

Shops and Studios in Town

Before opening any kind of shop in your home, check with local zoning officials to see what's allowed or disallowed in your community. (Refer to my
earlier discussion of zoning in Chapter Four.) Even in residential areas that
prohibit business signs and homebased business activity, many artists and
craftspeople sell from private studios or workshops, present one-day open
houses, give home parties and run weekend boutiques. When held only a
couple of times a year, such sales are rarely a problem because zoning officials
view them in the same light as garage sales.

Tip

Since most zoning problems occur when officials receive complaints from neighbors, a big key to success in selling from home
is never to annoy neighbors with too much traffic or noise.

As homebased businesses continue to sprout up in communities all over the country, zoning officials are beginning to wake up. Usually, outdated laws are changed only
at the insistence of home-business owners in the area who
band together to make a presentation to city officials.
Many individuals simply ask for and get a zoning vari-
ance or "special use" permit. After operating a pottery
studio in Horseheads, New York, for eight years, Carolyn
and Archie Richards expanded their business by opening a Bed and Breakfast in their home. Because this business was desirable to their community, the village board
changed the zoning ordinance to accommodate them.

When zoning isn't a problem, and your homebased
shop or studio is open to the public at all times, you may
have a different problem. "How do you get the public to

Shop Ownership: Weighing Pros and Cons

A couple in New York who had a shop in their home for a while sold at craft fairs and kept their shop open only at night and on weekends. There was a lot of business during the summer months when tourists were in town, but in time the couple found their shop sales to be less profitable than craft fairs. After moving to a new location, they decided to stop wasting their time and space with a home shop and began to sell through a local consignment shop instead.

This is just a reminder that while home shops may be fun, they do take up space in your home that your family might like to be using. And, you may quickly tire of giving up your evenings and weekends and always being at your customers' beck and call. Before opening a shop, carefully weigh the advantages and disadvantages of your own shop versus renting space in a craft mall or other retail shop.

accept an in-home shop?" asks Peggy in Louisiana. "In my experience, people do not like to come to a private home to shop. I have a small sign out front and you walk directly into my shop, not my home. My living room is wall-to-wall shelves and is definitely set up as a shop, yet I have watched people drive in and then leave when they see the shop is in my home."

Peggy ventures a guess as to why people react this way. "They may feel they are going to go in and a little old lady is going to pull out several items in a box from under the bed and try to sell them," she says. "Or they may think they will be pressured to buy, or that they are intruding into your privacy."

This problem will resolve itself in time if you work to bring visibility to your shop. In the end, the success of most home shops will turn not on how much paid advertising is done, but on how much word-of-mouth advertising you get.

Tip

To build local visibility for a home shop, get involved in community affairs, which often leads to publicity in the local paper. Donate items for raffles, asking that your home shop be mentioned as the contributor. Send special invitations to local clubs and organizations, offering them a "private showing" and a special discount on purchases. Make it easy for satisfied customers to give you word-of-mouth advertising by asking if they would like a few business cards, flyers or brochures they can pass on to friends.

A Back Yard Studio

Susan Young lives in the small community of Madison, Alabama, north of the city limits. After leaving her job with a Fortune 500 company to pursue her decorative painting, designing and folk art full-time, she soon tired of selling crafts at fairs. Like many others, she didn't like the hassle of packing merchandise, loading the van, driving long distances to fairs, fighting the weather and working such long hours. The idea of a home show was exciting to her, however. "This kind of selling is a wonderful way to test the waters," she says. "I held my shows in the dining room and the success of my first sales made me feel I had a good market for my work and real potential as a crafts designer."

The Peach Kitty Studio
Decorative Painting
and Folk Art

Before long, Susan decided she just had to have a little shop of her own. After doing research, she designed a 12 x 16-foot wood structure to be built in her back yard. "Being outside the city limits, I did not have zoning problems, and I learned I wouldn't even need a building permit if I didn't build a permanent structure on a concrete slab," she says. "I was only reminded to be sure the building ended up on our property and not the neighbor's."

Although Susan's Peach Kitty Studio is impermanent (meaning it could be picked up and moved if necessary), it has all the comforts of home, including a tile floor, baseboard heaters and air conditioning. "Some people might call it a glorified garden shed just perfect for the riding lawnmower," she jokes, "but it's exactly what I wanted." The studio is open seven days a week from 10 to 5 P.M., but Susan discourages drop-in visitors by asking them to call first before coming round. She does much of her designing in the studio, but most of the actual production of craftwork is done in the house where there is more room and better climate control.

Selling to Clubs from Your Studio

In Annandale, Virginia, Susan Fox Hirschmann, a potter, writer and speaker, offers her studio as a meeting place for charity, hobby or religious organizations, then provides the evening's entertainment by showing a video of herself working at her crafts. (Lacking a video presentation, you could simply show people around your studio, giving a brief demonstration of how you do your craft.)

In an article for *The Crafts Report,* Susan emphasized that many different groups—book clubs, garden clubs, civic home associations and library clubs—are likely to be interested in craftspeople as speakers. The more unusual your

This sign graces the entrance of the driveway to the Charles and Liz Davis home in Dundee, Kentucky, where Dolls by Liz are handmade.

This is a juried craft
of the
Kentucky Craft
Marketing Program
and was skillfully crafted by
Ky Folk Artist
Liz Davis
10978 State Route 69 North
DUNDEE, KY 42338
Phone (502) 276-5018

Above: A "Kentucky Crafted" hang tag used by Liz.

Right: A small "artist information card" Liz includes with all purchases and also uses as a general promotional tool. Shown full-size, it is printed in black ink on tan card stock.

Liz Davis has been designing and producing hand-made dolls for over 25 years. An Ohio Countian, her work is being collected across the U.S. and internationally. Liz's dolls are said to "reflect a healthy respect for the past, and a contemporary sense of humor." Fiddleing Fifi is a limited edition–signed, numbered and dated by Liz. The doll is dressed in a cotton-blend print dress, holds a mahogany-toned wood fiddle and bow, and has a button music-box attached at her back. Fiddleing Fifi was created to honor bluegrass music's West Kentucky heritage.

Entertaining Tour Groups in Your Shop

As the owners of a Rosemaling studio in Wisconsin, Audrey and Ray Punzel got tremendous word-of-mouth advertising in their area by inviting tour groups into their home shop when they weren't out selling at craft fairs. Situated on a rustic road by a lake, their home shop was inviting and they entertained many a busload of visitors before they finally stopped doing this sort of thing. The strategy they used is still timely, however, and may be an idea you can use.

"Factories have sales meetings and other local groups are always looking for something interesting to see and do," Audrey told me. "We simply let it be known that we had an interesting attraction for visitors. As each bus arrived, I would give a little introductory talk before asking the group to split in half. Ray would take half the group into our home and show them our collection of articles from Norway while I entertained the rest of the group in my shop and display room. After explaining the art of Rosemaling, I would encourage people to browse and make purchases. We usually ended up with hundreds of dollars in sales and customers from many states and Canada who later gave us word-of-mouth advertising.

work, the better. "The idea is to bring people into your studio to educate them," she says. "I purposely leave my credit-card terminal and receipt book in plain view with a UPS shipping chart. I explain what services I provide, be it custom, phone order or special packing for one-of-a-kind pieces. They get the message. Often the attenders will not buy right away, but ask me to put a piece aside for them. Spending a few hours discussing your work can net you lots of new customers," she concludes.

Day Care Center and Gift Shop

Several years ago, Ginger, the owner of a day care center in California, told me of her plans to open a year-round gift shop in a small room directly off her living room. Finding her idea interesting, I filed her letter and came across it as I was writing this book.

Ginger said she had found a good market for her rag dolls, stick horses, Christmas stockings and other handcrafted gifts and was working on her crafts in the evening, on weekends and two hours each afternoon while the kiddies napped. "I plan to cater to the two dozen parents I see regularly," she told me "Where else can a busy working mother leave off her child, pick out a gift, and at the end of the day pick up both the child and a gift-wrapped purchase? I think this idea may be unique enough to work, and I think word-of-mouth will be my best advertising. If things go well, I'll follow up with a weekend boutique next Christmas."

I lost touch with Ginger so I don't know how successful her ideas proved to be. Beginning with only two dozen prospects, her income from craft sales would have been limited initially. Yet, if every mother brought a friend with her, and every friend told someone else, it wouldn't have taken long to build a good customer base. Ideas like this are always worth exploring because there is so little to lose, and the financial risk is virtually nil. I'll bet Ginger's first holiday boutique was a smash success, and I wouldn't be surprised to learn that the gift shop and boutique indirectly convinced more parents to use Ginger's day care services.

Shops and Studios in the Country

It's easier to open a shop in a rural area or farming community because there are usually no zoning laws to worry about. You may have to get creative, however, to entice people to drive miles out of town to visit your shop. Following are ideas that have worked for others.

The Only Shop for Miles Around

"You have to do a little advertising and give great service to get good word-of-mouth advertising from customers," says Linda Tvedt, who had a shop in her home for five years. She lives three and a half miles out of Wilbaux, Montana, a community of 660 and the only town in the county. "There is no place to buy a gift unless you drive seventy miles to the next town, so local business was always good," she told me. "I was open only by appointment and people usually called before coming out. I did a lot of custom orders and it was not unusual to get a call at 7:15 from someone who needed a gift for a party at eight o'clock."

In time, Linda's business took over every room in the house and there was more work than she could handle. She had to make the difficult decision of pulling back to an easier lifestyle or moving her shop out of the home. When she was offered an interesting job as activity director in a nursing home, she decided to close the shop and go back to doing crafts part-time.

Expanding Studio Profits with Classes

Many craft producers who sell finished crafts from a homebased studio or workshop increase their profits by offering classes and selling a line of related supplies and materials. (Bringing people into your studio for classes automatically builds word-of-mouth advertising for your handcrafts.)

Bobbie Irwin, a weaver who has lived in many parts of the country, learned something interesting when she offered her weaving classes in a small community of only a thousand people. "I thought I would quickly saturate the local market after teaching one or two classes," she said. "Instead, I found that one class perpetuated another. Friends see what folks are learning and then want to learn themselves. That's one advantage to living in such a small community. The locals are desperate for new things to do, and my classes are always well received."

Hosting Local Clubs

You don't have to live in the city (like potter Susan Hirschmann) to work with clubs and organizations in your area. A story from my *Creative Cash* book offers a good example of how to attract shoppers when you have an unusual home and shop off the beaten track. For years, Ginnie Wise and her husband, Ernie, sold their crafts at fairs and shows and had a gift shop in their home. Their 240-acre property in Ohio included 65 acres of river bottom that flooded yearly, yielding many pieces of driftwood each spring. Ginnie would invite local clubs in the area to hold meetings at their home and shop. Afterward, Ginne would give a little talk about the farm and explain how she gathered driftwood, dried mosses, wayside grasses, pods and rocks to make a variety of natural gift items for her shop. Sales were always made when club members browsed the shop before leaving.

Christmas Shop on a Farm

The best way to ensure the success of a shop in the country is to live on a busy highway. Glenda and Jim Cox own a farm in Canada about fifty miles from Vancouver. Nearly 4,000 cars a day whiz by. After years of attracting crowds with their annual Christmas display, Jim suggested it might be a good idea for Glenda to open a Christmas shop in the tack house.

Thus, in 1990, with absolutely no retailing experience, Glenda opened her Christmas Cottage seven weeks before Christmas. Regular shoppers off the road and publicity on opening day brought so many customers that Glenda had to rush out and buy more goods. Sales response that first year was so great that a second showroom was added to the shop the following year, and Glenda purchased an even greater quantity of merchandise from suppliers she found at wholesale gift and craft shows. Sales quadrupled within four years, and all of Glenda's family and friends are now involved in the business.

The only advertising Glenda does is put a sign at the end of the lane and place a small newspaper ad during her selling season. She believes the success of her shop can be attributed to the fact that she sells a mix of commercial gift items and selected handcrafts. "There are just too many shows in this area to sell handcrafts only," she says. "What my customers seem to like most is the fact that I have something for everyone. We sell everything associated with Christmas plus non Christmas gift items and gourmet food and drinks. I am certain that a shop specializing strictly in handcrafts would not have been as successful."

More Sales through Open Houses

If the idea of a homebased shop is impractical or simply not appealing, how about an occasional open house to supplement your other craft sales? Many creative people have found this a profitable way to sell their products. You may hold an open house in your home or that of a friend. You simply send information to a select list of customers or prospects, inviting them to the open house to see your product display. Just before the event, you might telephone several of your best customers to remind them to come with a friend. Open houses a couple times a year are a great way to resell regular customers while acquainting new people with your art or craft and any custom design services you may offer. Whether you sell products during an open house or simply take orders for later delivery is a matter of choice unless such sales are strictly prohibited in your community.

Tip

Always check with local authorities before publicizing an open house event. In some areas, zoning laws prohibit any kind of business that involves inventory. In others, a seller may take orders in the home, but it would be a violation of the law if the customers walked out the door with merchandise they bought during the open house. (Later deliveries are a simple solution to this problem.)

Home Parties vs. Open Houses

Cheri Lynn Gregory used to sell her gift baskets through home parties held during a specific one-hour period. She increased sales simply by switching over to marketing through open houses. After scheduling several basket parties for specific one-hour periods during the Christmas holidays, only 10 percent of the invitees showed up. "So I tried a different tactic for Valentine's Day," she said. "I switched to three-to-five-hour open-house parties and nearly half of all invitees showed up. I think people may prefer the low-pressure atmosphere of a stop-by-any-time-and-browse open house as opposed to the be-here-and-buy party. Since all my presentations are at the homes of friends or family members with whom I can sit and talk all day, the open house style is perfect for me."

Open House Boutique

Ruby Tobey of Wichita, Kansas, does watercolors, paintings and one-of-a-kind-collector plates. She also publishes poetry books, bookmarks and calendars illustrated with her sketches. For nearly thirty years, she has sold her work through fairs, consignment shops and open-house boutiques held in the spring and fall. They run from Friday through Sunday from 10:00 A.M. to 5:30 P.M. (Staying open any longer than this is a waste of time, she has found.) Most of Ruby's gift items are priced between $5 and $20, and sales for a weekend are generally around a thousand dollars.

Until recently, Ruby's sales were held in the basement. (She used to joke that the best thing about her open house was that the basement got cleaned really well once a year.) Now that the kids are grown and gone, Ruby has turned the living room into a display room, and her studio is now in a bedroom off to the side.

Ruby is a perfect example of how to make a steady income from your art or craft over a long period. Getting rich was never the goal, she says, but her work has kept her mentally healthy and the extra income from her art has given Ruby a delicious feeling of independence. "Get your nerve up and try a home sale," she advises beginners. "It will give you the chance to get to know people you wouldn't meet otherwise, and it's better than selling at fairs because you have the undivided attention of your customers without all that work."

Open House in Your Homebased Shop

Susan Young, mentioned earlier, presents open house sales in her back yard Peach Kitty Studio two or three weeks before all the major holidays. She sells originally designed gifts and decorative accessories she calls "painted pleasures and tiny treasures." Because Susan has always made it a point to capture the names of customers and interested prospects, she has a growing mailing list that now receives her open house announcements.

Tip

Susan advertises by posting brightly colored posters on all the community bulletin boards at the bank, grocery store and drug store. She also buys four days' worth of advertising in the local newspaper just before the open house. "Three days would be enough," she says, "but I was surprised to learn that the difference between running an ad for three or four days was only $1.50."

Open Houses in Other People's Homes

In Bremerton, Washington, Deena Nixon presents "Deena's Li'l Country Nook Home Parties," which are an interesting mix of home party and open house. "I work on a very simple arrangement with friends who offer the use of their home for a sale," Deena explains. "The hostess mails invitations that I provide—25 to start with, more if needed. Guests are invited to shop anytime between six and eight o'clock, and the hostess receives a sales commission that she can take either in cash or merchandise. Most take merchandise."

Unlike traditional party plans where all the guests show up at the same time, stay for an hour or two and place orders for later delivery, Deena sells directly, taking orders only for custom-designed items. She likes this kind of selling because she doesn't have to give a talk or sales spiel like party plan presenters. "Shoppers seem to prefer it, too," she says, "because they don't have to wait three weeks for their merchandise. They can drop in anytime during the open house period, buy what they want, and leave."

In the past two years, Deena has presented ten open houses during October and November. Initially, she offered her hostesses 10 percent of sales, but she found they worked harder to bring in guests when she gave them a greater profit incentive of 20 percent of sales. More guests, of course, means increased profits for Deena. She sells a country line of products that includes floral arrangements, seasonal items, resin figures and wooden toys and miniatures.

She has had sales of $300 with as few as nine shoppers. One of her most popular sellers is a set of six 1¼" blocks hand-painted with pictures of Noah, the Ark and its animals. She sells them for $6 (a price I feel is too low for such a clever product).

Formula for Calculating Open House Sales

A potter who announced a private exhibit of work in her home told me she sent postcard invitations to 100 customers on her mail list. Thirty people came to see her creations, and eighteen of them made purchases.

Take another look at those figures. This seller got a 30 percent response to her mailing, which is excellent, but she got a 60 percent sales response, which is extraordinary. Not everyone will do this well, so here is a simple, more conservative three-step formula to help you estimate how much you might make from an open house of your own:

1. Number of customer and prospects on your mailing list × percent who might attend (estimate 25%) = number of shoppers.
2. Number of shoppers × percent who might make a purchase (estimate 40%) = number of sales.
3. Number of sales × dollar amount of your average sale = what you might make in a couple hours' time at home.

Let's say you have the names and addresses of 75 people who have recently purchased your work at a crafts fair, and your average sale is $14.50. Using the above formula, you might expect to make $116 from your open house. (All figures have been rounded off.)

$$75 \times 25\% = 19 \text{ shoppers} \times 40\% = 8 \text{ people making purchases}$$
$$\times \$14.50 = \$116.$$

I grant that eight sales may not seem exciting, but I'm trying to show you that you don't need a large list of customers to get started in this type of selling. Of course, your sales may be larger than this if more people attend your event and make purchases. Or, if you happen to sell higher-priced items, such as paintings, ceramics, glasswork or jewelry, the profits from even eight sales could be significant. Finally, there is the probability that people who attend the open house but don't make a purchase will tell their friends about you and remember you later when they need a gift. Over time, you could develop a large following of customers without ever leaving home.

Party Plan/Home Party Profits

The party-plan method of marketing that Tupperware made famous has been popular in the crafts industry since the early 1980s. After manufacturers began to sell craft and needlecraft kits and supplies through home parties, craftspeople figured they could sell handcrafts this way too.

The party plan concept is simple. One crafter puts it this way: "I take my samples and catalog into people's homes, present them, and take orders for later delivery." A party can feature your own products or those of area craftspeople. Either way, the continued success of this type of selling will depend on your ability (1) to have enough merchandise for all the parties you can arrange and (2) to continually find new hostesses who can bring in new guests.

Ten Simple Start-Up Steps

1. Find a friend who will let you use her home for a party, usually for two hours on a weekday evening.
2. Send invitations to the hostess's friends and family. (The hostess provides the list, you print and mail the invitations). For a party to be profitable, you will need at least ten people.
3. Set up your display an hour or two before the party. (You don't sell these products but merely use them as samples to get orders you will deliver or ship later.) For maximum sales, offer products priced no more than $25 and include a variety of items in the $5 to $15 range.
4. As the party opens, you welcome the guests, thank them for coming, and present the hostess with a thank-you gift (one of your nicer craft items that everyone will ooh and ah over). Explain how the party plan works so others in the audience will want to hold a party in the future (and get a similar thank-you gift).
5. Give a little spiel about yourself and describe the products on display, suggesting how they might be used as gifts and passing them around whenever possible. (Label each product with its name, item number, price, and notations about other colors or sizes that may be available.)

Tip

Explain that there may be slight variations between the samples you are exhibiting and what people will receive, since no two handmade items will ever be the same.

Advantages of Home Party Selling

"The biggest advantage of selling your crafts through home parties is that you control how much you work by spacing out the party dates," says Chris Peters, a longtime home party presenter. "Of course you will have great parties and not-so-great parties, but this is no riskier than selling your work at craft shows. While you have to tote tons of items to a craft show and then bring them all home again if they don't sell, at a home party you only have to make an item *after* you get the order for it."

6. Halfway through your presentation, take a "fun break" to play little games and award some of your inexpensive craft items as prizes.

7. Wind down your presentation with information on how guests may order your products, the amount of deposit you require and who to make the check out to (you, not the hostess). If you have brochures, flyers or price lists, bring them to the attention of guests.

Tip

Some sellers ask guests to pay the full amount of purchase prior to receiving goods, but most people would be reluctant to do this. Having to pay only half up front will encourage more sales.

8. Close with information on how and when you will deliver their order, explaining that custom-design orders will take a little longer.

Tip

Some sellers promise delivery in two weeks while others take as long as three to six weeks to deliver custom-design orders. The closer you get to Christmas, however, the quicker most folks will want their merchandise.

9. While the hostess serves refreshments of cake and coffee, you take orders, chat with the guests, answer questions and encourage them to book a party. (Take your date book with you.)

10. Later, tally the evening's sales and calculate the amount the hostess has earned (between 10 to 20 percent of sales, payable in gift merchandise,

not cash). If you have booked some parties at this point, it is customary to give the hostess an extra $5 to $10 credit for each party.

NOTE: Some party plan presenters deliver merchandise to the hostess, who in
turn delivers it to customers. For this extra service, they increase the hostess
percentage from 10 to 20 percent (generally taken out in merchandise). Others give a certain percentage on sales up to a specific amount, and a larger
percentage for orders totaling more than this.

Parties in the Country

Party plan selling works as well in the country as it does in urban areas. Kim
Brandt, who lives in the country near Willshire, Ohio, got interested in home
parties after reading about them in one of my columns in *Crafts*. When she
began in 1987, she was the manufacturer, demonstrator and owner-operator
of Country Crafters. Recently Kim reported that she had four demonstrators
who now present parties, and she works with a growing number of crafters.
Kim no longer makes crafts for sale but spends 15 to 25 hours a week managing her growing homebased business. "This is still a part-time business," she
says, "because I want to be as much of a full-time mom as possible while
making an extra income. I sometimes do demonstrations, though, because I
enjoy getting out and showing off our products and meeting customers." Kim
recently expanded her business by offering fundraising parties to schools and
ball team organizations.

Many crafters increase their party plan profits by hiring friends to present
parties for them. In her first year of selling through home parties, a crafter in
Alaska told me she presented 33 shows between August and November, gen-
erating over $8,000 in sales. The following year, with three others helping her
present parties, she more than tripled her income. (This seller gave her helpers 25 percent of sales, and the hostess got 10 percent.)

"The one thing I wish I would have known before I began to give home
parties was how successful this idea would be," one crafter told me. "I gave 25
parties in my first month, and there was such a demand for them that I had to
turn down as many as I booked. Had I known this, I would have structured
the business to include an additional representative to present parties for me."

Home Parties Lead to How-To Book

Opal Leasure, a mother of five and a craftsperson for over twenty years, started
her Apron Strings crafts business in 1992 after her mother said, "You can do it,
I know you can!"

After considering her many marketing options, Opal decided she liked the idea of doing home parties best. Everything that could go wrong did go wrong at that first party, but Opal's sales were good enough to keep going. In time, she became so successful at giving parties that she wrote and published a how-to book on this topic titled *The Apron Strings Lady Did It . . . So Can You!* Her book includes Opal's success story, business start-up guidelines, party planning and sales success tips, and samples of printed materials needed in this kind of selling. (These include flyers, information sheets, thank-you letters, receipts, order forms, summary sheets and more.)

Opal's Apron Strings Country Home Parties are presented in the Madera, California, area where the average guest spends at least $20, and often a lot more. She sells both a country and southwestern line of products, with her best sellers being eucalyptus sprays, raffia swags and wreaths. Other products include birdhouses, dolls, hats, wooden and novelty items and a line of Apron Strings "Cow Babies." Opal estimates that she has gained over 600 customers in three years of doing parties. She counts a party a success whenever it leads to at least one new party.

Opal's roots are in the Ozarks, where she was taught the old-fashioned values that are now an important part of her business. She stresses the importance of not taking on so much work that your family suffers. "Managing is the key and controlling your work load is essential," she says. "If part-time employment is your goal, schedule only one or two parties per week. Just one party per week may generate two full days of filling orders."

How to Organize a Successful Holiday Boutique

Holiday or "seasonal" boutiques provide an interesting and profitable alternative to selling at fairs or through local shops, and they are generally successful no matter where they are held. It is not unusual for 25 to 30 sellers to gross $10,000 to $20,000 over a weekend, particularly if the boutique has become a regular annual event noted for high-quality merchandise. Usually presented in the spring or fall, boutiques are themed to holidays such as Valentine's Day, Easter, Halloween, Thanksgiving or Christmas.

"Boutiques can be very successful if they offer articles that are exclusive to the sale—not available anywhere else," says Barbara Griffin, who has produced several successful boutiques. "This technique adds an even more exclusive feeling to your show and can pique interest and sales," she says. "Boutique fever—that impulse to quickly grab a special item before anyone else can see it—will mean higher sales for all exhibitors. Offering an annual edition of a best-selling item (ornament, wreath, sweatshirt design, etc.) can also boost attendance and profits."

An individual may decide to present a holiday boutique alone or work with

Moving a Home Boutique to Larger Quarters

In thinking about moving a show out of your home, consider that you will have increased expenses from room rental and extra advertising to announce the change of location. One boutique organizer thought she would see significant increases in sales and customer turnout if she moved her boutique to the banquet facilities at a local restaurant/motel. Surprisingly, sales were no higher and many previous customers didn't realize the show at the restaurant was the same quality show they had been attending in this individual's home. Also, because products were spread out over a larger space, those who did attend felt the show was smaller.

In looking for a new site for your boutique, don't limit your thinking to schools, churches and restaurants. With so many vacant retail stores in shopping malls these days, it might be very easy to rent such a store in a prime location for a weekend or week-long boutique. Ten artists who had been doing in-home shows for eight years decided one year to rent the senior citizen library building for two days. Many boutiques have been presented in new homes for sale. (Realtors are delighted to have so many people see a home in such an attractive light.) One boutique presenter told me about her boutique, held in an old Victorian house on the National Historic Register that happened to be on sale at the time. Another said a historical mansion in her area was interested in hosting her show in the future because this would draw favorable publicity to the mansion.

a small group of friends. The sale can be something as simple as your own work displayed in a shoplike atmosphere in one room of your home, or a major exhibit of products spread throughout several rooms. Although these events usually start in someone's home, many become so successful in time that they must be moved to a school, church or other large building in the community. Sometimes successful boutique owners buy or build special buildings to house their growing enterprise.

Boutiques in a Barn

Milo and Ruth Tuma live a few miles outside of New Prague, Minnesota, population about 6,000. In 1979, Ruth decided to start selling her silk and dried flower arrangements by making fifty items for sale and displaying them in her home. She invited forty people to attend her little boutique and sold everything in two hours.

For the next few years, Ruth continued to present spring and fall Country

Boutiques in her home. As these events grew in size, however, the Tumas moved the boutique out of their farmhouse and into a new barn built especially to house these sales. Today, thanks to an aggressive advertising program, Ruth's boutiques attract up to 2,000 shoppers each weekend from all over Minnesota and five surrounding states.

Rubber stamp designs by Sue Brown, from her Wood Cellar Graphics catalog.

The spring boutique runs between eight and ten weeks, usually starting around the middle of March. "We're always working around Easter and Mother's Day," Ruth says, "but the spring boutique also features a large fishing section, men's gifts division and garden department with the latest spring flowers." The Christmas boutique opens in mid-September and runs four days a week through December 4. As many as 10,000 Christmas ornaments priced between $1 and $30 will sell during this period.

Ruth advertises in the *Minneapolis Star-Tribune* (which circulates through Minnesota and five surrounding states), plus local papers and the *Minneapolis–St. Paul Magazine*. Twice a year, she sends postcard reminders about the boutiques to her mailing list of customers, which has now grown to 10,000. She supplies her boutiques with products from 250 craftspeople taken on a 70/30 percent consignment basis. There are usually a couple hundred crafters on a list waiting to get in, but only twenty or so will be selected for each new boutique. "We jury all our merchandise," Ruth emphasizes, "accepting only those products that are superior in quality and design. It's hard to turn crafters away, but we know what our customers want."

Ruth believes that the success of her boutiques can be attributed to a combination of things. "We advertise heavily, everything we sell is handmade, and we have a wide range of products to fit everyone's budget. Our typical customer is a young married couple with two incomes. Some people spend as little as $15 to $25 while others may buy up to $400 worth of furniture or decorative accessories."

I asked Ruth if she thought the current craze for country products would die out in time. "No," she says, "it's here to stay. The young people are very interested in it and they're the buyers. They decorate their homes with country crafts because they are affordable. We plan to present our Country Boutiques for many years to come."

The Old Church Boutique

Since 1983, Anita Means has been helping artists and craftspeople in the Holmdel, New Jersey, area by presenting an annual Christmas boutique. It was held in a little cottage behind Anita's home until the zoning commissioner closed her down in response to neighbors' complaints about traffic and parking problems.

Anita then made an arrangement with the Monmouth County Historical Association for the use of its two-century-old "Allen House." Permission was easy to get, she said, after she explained how a quality crafts show like hers could bring needed publicity to the historical association and increase its revenue. She was given every room of the house to work with, and over a hundred artists and craftspeople helped her fill them with products.

In time, Anita and husband Tom decided to buy an old restored church to house her boutique. In addition to space for the boutique, there were sectioned-off areas that could be rented as office space to cover overhead costs. Before long they had turned the old church into a cultural event center that offered year-round classes, workshops and seminars focusing on traditional arts and crafts. A mini-boutique runs all year, and special spring and Christmas boutiques present the work of over 175 artists and craftspeople. Most are from the area, but some participants come from surrounding states.

This project received widespread support from the community and the old church is now on the National Register of Historic Places. Says Anita, "Our ancestors developed their creative potential as artists and craftspeople, and that is how they made a living. To be in a historic setting inspires us to reach inside to develop our potential."

Holiday Boutique Planning Checklist

Some crafters who work together to present a holiday boutique have firmly-established operating guidelines similar to those of craft cooperatives (discussed in Chapter Eleven). Most, however, have no formal legal structure and different people may be involved in a boutique from year to year. It takes a lot of planning and hard work to organize and present a successful boutique, and plans for a Christmas event should begin no later than March. Assuming you will be working with a few crafter friends, here is a checklist of things that must be done (not necessarily in this order):

❑ **Decide in whose home the event will be held, and in which rooms of the house**. If no one wants their house open to the public, consider using someone's two-car garage. One boutique presenter gave her garage an antique flavor through the use of old lamps, cabinets and tables covered with color-coordinated sheets. She decorated one wall with quilts, another with pegboard for hanging crafts, and another with the end rolls of newspaper acquired from the local paper.

❑ *Select an interesting name for your event.* Examples from my files include "Cottage Collection—Only by Hand," "Harvest Time Craft Sale," "Christmas by Candlelight," "Santa's Helpers Boutique," and "The Heatheridge Artisans Holiday Festival." Marketing consultant Silvana Clark suggests "The Mistletoe Marketplace," "Holiday Highlights" or "Trinkets and Treasures Boutique."

Ginny Hartger told me of three successful home craft sales she and her friends have been producing for over fifteen years in Grand Rapids, Michigan. After years of doing Christmas shows, one of which was named "Christmas by Candlelight," the group presented its first spring show, calling it "The Romance of Spring." It proved so popular they came back the next year with "Return to Romance." Their fall show was named "Down a Country Road."

❑ *Take care of tax, legal and insurance matters.* Check with local zoning officials to make sure your event won't violate local laws. Contact your state's Department of Revenue, Sales Tax Division, to learn how to collect and pay all required taxes. Check with insurance agents about liability insurance in case a customer is injured while on the homeowner's property. Make sure all crafters understand they must obtain their own insurance on merchandise consigned to the show.

Tip

Keep neighbors happy by giving them special early-entrance passes to the boutique and perhaps a 10 percent discount on purchases.

❑ *Decide who's going to do what.* The group organizing the boutique needs someone who will act as boss, taking the responsibility of overseeing and coordinating all the work being done by others. This will include the making and distributing of posters and flyers, writing and placing advertisements, planning, buying and serving refreshments, obtaining special decorations or display props, recording and marking incoming merchandise, arranging it for sale, setting up a cashier's table, arranging for Visa/MasterCard charge services, recording sales, and capturing customer's names and addresses in an address book. Someone will also have to take care of putting up directional signs on the day of the event.

Tip

Have at least two cashiers who do nothing but take money. Someone else should remove price tags and wrap parcels. To avoid having too much money sitting around, someone might need to make a couple of trips to the bank during the sale.

❑ *Decide how exhibitors will be selected.* Will you limit participation to your immediate circle of friends or invite other artists and crafters to exhibit and sell? Those who only sell and do not take part in organizing the event should be charged an exhibitor's fee or a percentage of sales similar to what they would have to pay in a local consignment or rent-a-space shop.

❑ *Decide what kind of crafts you will sell.* Will you jury outside sellers to avoid duplication of products or place limits on certain categories of items for sale? Remember that not all crafters are dependable suppliers, so it would be wise to get a commitment as to the type and volume of merchandise each seller plans to display. Otherwise there may be either too little or too much merchandise for available space. Once volume of merchandise is determined, you can more easily decide how much display space you will need and how long the boutique should run.

❑ *Estimate Expenses.* Expenses not covered by fees or sales commissions from sellers outside the core group will have to be divided accordingly. These would include postage, advertising and sign making; printing of flyers, posters and invitations; bags, tags and wrapping materials; sales books; guest book; decorations and refreshments. You may want to mark the house with balloons or banners or string lighting outdoors. A extra amount should be paid to the person who lends her home for the event to cover electricity and phone expense. To avoid damage to carpets (in case of wet weather), floor runners may be needed. (Allow for the possibility of accidental damage to furniture or other possessions in the home and perhaps the need to have carpeting cleaned afterward.)

❑ *Decide how you will promote and advertise your event.* Common advertising methods include distributing flyers, sending postcard announcements to a customer list, placing ads in local papers, (including "Pennysaver" publications), displaying posters with tear-off, take-along reminders attached, seeking announcements on cable television and sending press releases to area newspapers.

One boutique organizer said she rented a billboard at the fairgrounds for a week. Silvana Clark suggests publicizing your event by making colorful book-

Holiday Boutique

Date: ----------------------------

Time: ----------------------------

Place: ---------------------------

Happy Holidays!

If you don't want to design your own postcards, check out the colorful cards in the Cranberry Junction Designs Catalog from Eleena K. Danielson of E. & S. Creations. (See Chapter Thirteen for examples of hang tags offered by this company, whose address is included in that illustration.)

marks that the library and local bookstores could place on their counters.

❑ *Set up an inventory system that accurately records all items consigned to the show*. For example, you might assign a letter code to each seller and a number code to each craft item. Note these letters and numbers on price tags and later transfer them to the sales slip at the time of purchase. You could then tally any sales commissions due you at the end of the show. (Several boutique organizers have told me that, in a one or two-day show, it is common to sell at least half of everything on display.)

❑ *Plan how crafts will be displayed for sale*. Excluding furniture and lighting, remove from the sales area everything that isn't for sale. Display ideas that work at craft fairs also work in a home boutique. For example, avoid placing items flat on table tops. Intermix items according to color, texture and size or arrange products in a mix that gives buyers an idea on how they would look if displayed in their own homes. Use interesting pieces of furniture for contrast, baskets for small items, bookcases for collections of small items. Put only large items on the floor.

Tip

During the show, increase sales by moving things around to make sure all items are seen, especially if crowds are heavy. Buyers aren't receptive when it looks like everything has been picked over, so make sure that holes on tables or shelves are quickly filled in with additional craft items or rearranged to look full.

❑ *Plan future events*. Holiday boutiques are rarely one-year events. Instead, they generally run for years, becoming more profitable with time. In New Jersey, a one-day boutique that began in a woman's home soon grew to two-day sales in a local store. The last I heard, the boutique was running for a full two weeks, and gross sales were at the $80,000 level. Over 200 craftspeople were selling through this boutique and paying the organizer 20 percent of their sales.

CHAPTER NINE

Craft Malls and Rent-a-Space Shops

If you can produce in volume but don't want to wholesale your crafts, selling through craft malls and rent-a-space shops may be the perfect answer for you.

Rental space has been available to artisans, flea market dealers and antique sellers for years, but everything changed in 1988 when Rufus Coomer opened the first Coomers Craft Mall in Azle, Texas. He was the first to refine the unique craft marketing concept that would sweep America in the 1990s and forever change the way craftspeople sold at the retail level. By the end of 1995, Coomers was the nation's largest retailer of American handmade crafts, gifts and decorations for homes and offices, with 30 malls in nine states and annual sales of over $25 million. More Coomers malls are planned for the future, with six to be opened in the next two years.

As retailing entrepreneurs across the country began to copy Coomer's profitable idea, the popularity of craft malls spawned similar, yet different, types of retail handcraft shops that are discussed later in this chapter. Artisans were quick to see the advantages of selling in malls and other rent-a-space retail outlets. Now, instead of selling only at craft fairs or consigning merchandise to craft shops, they could:

146

Some 8,000 crafters currently sell through Coomers malls. "Most are hobby sellers operating from their kitchen table," says Linda Coomer, "but we also have many craft professionals, some of whom are selling more than $100,000 per year through our malls alone."

The Coomers Internet Web Site, introduced in March 1996, includes photographs of store locations available for exhibiting crafts. To learn how to sell your crafts through any of the malls in the Coomers chain, mention this book when you ask for their "National Crafters Network" package. Write to Coomers, Inc., 6012 Reef Point Lane, Ft. Worth, TX 76135. (Illustration by Nancy Hester.)

- Rent an affordable amount of shelf or booth space and get the benefit of a shop atmosphere without the problems of consignment selling
- Have control over how their wares were displayed
- Enjoy year-round sales and regular monthly payments without the hassles involved in setting up fair exhibits
- Sell in many different stores across the country and deal with mall owners and operators entirely by mail through special remote stocking programs.

Many see craft malls and rent-a-space shops as the greatest thing ever to come down the crafts pike, but this kind of selling is not for everyone. To succeed here, you must produce a large quantity of merchandise that is competitively-priced and in tune with market needs. You also need to understand the industry to avoid its pitfalls.

Industry Overview

Most craft malls are individually owned and operated. Only a few have expanded with outlets in other locations, and there are no other chains similar to Coomers. Although there may be a thousand or more malls in existence, there is no central organization to monitor this industry's growth or police the way individual malls are being operated. Where there is no control, there are bound to be problems. Because there is no guidebook on how to start and operate a crafts mall, everyone who has ventured into this field has been flying by the seat of their pants, making up rules as they go along. It is not surprising, then, that there are no standards in the industry as to rental fees, booth sizes or service charges. Because each mall or group of malls has established its own fees, services and method of operation, craft sellers ought to investigate several malls before signing a lease. Coomers Malls have set a high standard for the industry but not every mall operates so professionally or efficiently.

Like some consignment shop owners in years past, some people who have jumped on the "craft mall bandwagon" are inexperienced retailers or business managers. A few have opened craft malls as much to sell their own work as to sell the work of others. One reader told of a mom-and-pop mall that lasted only eighteen months. "The owners tried to help but they were more interested in selling their own crafts than ours," she said. "All their advertising featured their clothing more than our crafts. When they closed, I searched for a month until I found a mall run by an owner who was devoted to making money for exhibitors. She did extensive advertising, promotions and appearances by guest celebrities daily. She also had booths in craft fairs and displayed our crafts to lure people into the store."

A few craft mall entrepreneurs have been less than ethical. One crafts newsletter reported on a fellow in Oklahoma who opened several malls, skipped town leaving his investors and crafters holding the bills, and then went to another state where he opened new malls. No one is keeping track, but a number of malls have come and gone in the past couple of years and more are sure to come and go in the future as the industry matures and settles down.

American Craft Malls

Two of the first Coomers Malls in Azle and Burleson, Texas, are now known as American Craft Malls and are owned and managed by Phillip Coomer. (See illustration.) Phillip believes the future of craft malls will probably follow a course similar to the development of craft shows. "We're going to have a few very professional chain-type craft malls and hundreds of smaller, independently owned stores. I believe they can all be equally successful."

Phillip was the first mall owner to promote his crafters with a site on the World Wide Web. Anyone who sells in either of his malls gets an extra bonus in the form of free advertising on "The Professional Crafter" web site. (See also "Marketing on the Internet" in Chapter Eleven.) Whereas the number of remote sellers in most malls is about 5 to 10 percent of the total, in Phillip's malls that percentage has jumped to 25 to 30 percent. "So many new suppliers have found us through our web site," says Phillip, "and these out-of-town people have really got the pack-and-ship stuff down pat. They are true profession-als who produce in quantity and deliver the kind of products we want to sell. We're de-lighted to have them because their sales tend to be higher than those of local craftspeople, many of whom sell only for extra in-come."

Look for "The Pro-fessional Crafter" on the Internet. For infor-mation on how to work with American Craft Malls through their National Crafter Program, mention this book when you contact Phillip Coomer at American Craft Malls, Box 799, Azle, TX 76098.

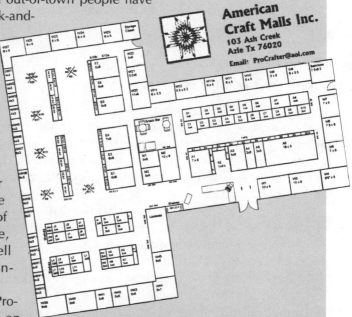

American
Craft Malls Inc.
103 Ash Creek
Azle Tx 76020
Email: ProCrafter@aol.com

Tip

Beware of "Crafters Wanted" ads for malls not yet open, and don't give anyone up-front money to reserve a space. There have been reports of crafters who have lost their deposit money to unscrupulous individuals who didn't follow through on their promise of opening a craft mall.

How to Select a Good Craft Mall

Craft malls come in all sizes, from small shops of 3,000 square feet to super malls of 20,000 square feet. All malls operate alike in that they rent space by the square foot, but that's where the similarity ends. Monthly rental fees, service fees and sales commissions vary considerably, along with size of exhibit space and benefits offered to sellers. In comparing craft malls, consider the following things:

Location and Size of Mall

If you are checking out a local mall, visit it to see how many people are shopping there at different hours on different days of the week. Is the store in a heavily-trafficked area? Does it regularly attract tourists? Is it a new community? (Coomers has found that it's good for business to locate a mall in neighborhoods where new homes are going up because people like to decorate them with arts and crafts.)

Consider the size of the mall not only in relation to its location but in terms of number of booths. In reading craft mall descriptions, I found a mall of 17,000 square feet with 250 spaces, one with 11,000 square feet and 500 spaces and another with 3,000 square feet and 200 spaces. What this tells me is that the display spaces in some malls are much smaller than in others. Always ask yourself whether the size of the mall and number of exhibitors seem right, whether the display space is large enough for your kind of crafts and whether shoppers have enough room to move about.

Booth Size and Monthly Rent

Some basic booth sizes are 3 x 3, 4 x 4 and 8 x 8 feet. To increase profits, however, some malls may try to squeeze extra booths into a space just to get the additional rent from crafters. You might think a 3 x 3 foot space at $85 is a better deal than a 4 x 4 foot space at $115, but is it? By comparing the square footage of a booth to the monthly rent, you will find that the 3 x 3 space costs $9.44 per square foot while the 4 x 4 space is $7.19 per square foot (3 $\times$ 3 = 9 square feet; $85 $\div$ 9 = $9.44 per square foot). It's interesting to compare figures like this, but you also need to consider a mall's location. Ultimately, what crafters are charged for rent is directly tied to what a mall owner must pay to operate the building itself. The higher these costs, the higher the monthly rental fee will be. In some cases, a smaller-size booth in an expensive, higher-traffic area could be two or three times as profitable as a larger booth in a mall with lower rent fees.

Number and Type of Sellers

If a mall can accommodate 200 artisans, find out how many are presently represented by the mall. If it has been open for some time and is only filled to 75 percent capacity, there may be a problem. One sure sign of a successful mall is its being filled to capacity with a long waiting list.

Some malls will rent space to any seller, including antique dealers and others who sell commercial goods, making them less desirable outlets for high-quality handcrafts. A mall that sells only handcrafts is likely to jury all its sellers by asking to see samples or photographs of products that will be offered. (Most high-quality craft fairs are juried, so you should expect this in a high-quality mall.)

Lease

Read the lease carefully before you sign it to make sure you understand your responsibilities and legal obligations. You'll have to pay the rent whether your crafts sell or not. Initially, most malls require a three- to six-month lease and ask for a deposit to cover the last month's rent. Some malls require renewal for the same length of time while others allow it on a month-to-month basis after the initial lease period. If you have never sold in a crafts mall before, you might lessen your financial risk by leasing your first booth before the holiday or peak tourist season.

Sales Commission

This seems to vary from 4 to 8 percent. A low percentage here may be offset, however, by extra fees discussed below. One mall owner I spoke with takes 7 percent, but only after crafters have made two times their rent.

Service Fees

Some malls charge for every little thing. There might be a 3.5 to 4 percent charge on credit card purchases plus an additional fee for advertising or other special services. (In comparison, Coomers charges a single monthly fee that includes credit card payments, layaways, special orders, computerized check-out and accurate reporting of inventory records.) If you think any of the service fees are unfair, check out some new malls. One seller reported that she and several fellow artisans pulled out of a shop in Vermont when the owner suddenly decided to impose a flat fee for processing credit card sales whether a crafter's purchases were charged or not. The shop owner figured this was fair since 70 percent of her sales were on credit cards. The crafters didn't agree. In the end, the shop suffered.

Payments/Sales Reports

All sales are made by the mall; crafters do no selling. Some malls make monthly payments; others pay every two weeks. Some malls have computerized their business and offer detailed sales reports of what has sold while others are doing sales reports manually.

Merchandising Assistance

Most craft malls leave it up to crafters to decorate their booth, but if you're not good at this, look for a mall with a merchandising specialist who can advise and assist you. All malls have some kind remote stocking program set up to enable them to work with sellers outside their area, but there are some problems here. (See lengthy discussion on this topic elsewhere in this chapter.) Some malls will restock a booth at no extra charge, but most seem to be charging a flat $10 restocking fee.

Insurance

Unless a craft mall is located in a shopping center, you are not likely to have any fire insurance coverage on the handcrafts you are displaying there. (Shopping malls mandate all stores to buy liability and fire insurance on their contents whether they own the merchandise or not.) While the chance of fire may be slim, this is a risk you will have to take unless you can secure coverage on your own. If not, it would be prudent to limit the amount of merchandise you put into a single mall. (Refer back to Chapter Four for the names of two organizations that offer policies that protect against loss to both unfinished and finished works at home or away.)

Security System

Is the mall well lit? Does it have a camera-security system or at least a strategic floor plan that discourages shoplifting? Are children allowed to roam freely and play havoc with displays? Bless the mall owner who has set up a special area for children to play while Mom shops! (See discussion, "Two Problems You Must Deal With.")

Restrictions

I was astonished to learn that some malls do not allow crafters to use hang tags bearing their name and address because they are afraid other shop owners will come in and steal away their renters. Instead, they make crafters use the shop's tags. If you are renting space, you should be able to display your products as you wish. Hang tags add a professional touch that increases sales, so if a mall makes this kind of demand, it is actually harming your ability to make sales. If a mall tells you that you can't put hang tags on your products or put your business cards on display in your exhibit, find another mall.

Tip

Once you get started selling in different states, mall owners are likely to start coming to you. "Other mall owners pose as shoppers when they check out the competition," says a successful seller. "When they see products they like, they look for hang tags and business cards so they can contact craftspeople directly and invite them to sell in their mall."

Ask a mall if you are restricted to selling only your own merchandise. If the space being offered is too expensive or too large for you to keep filled, you may be able to sell with a friend whose work is compatible with yours. Some sellers have increased their profits by becoming a vendor for several crafters who don't want the responsibility of maintaining their own rental space in a mall.

Crafter Benefits

Are you getting any special benefits from the mall owner? "Some craft malls offer you space and wish you luck," says Coomers. "Look for a mall with expertise to help you develop your business." Crafters in the Coomers stores get a discount card for purchasing supplies, merchandising assistance, booth setup and seminars on specific crafting techniques. (See also "American Craft Malls" sidebar.)

Craft Mall Arithmetic

Some well-meaning but inexperienced mall owners have opened stores that are too large for their market area. They may figure their profits will be higher if they have more spaces to rent, but they don't stop to consider that there may not be enough customers for the number of crafters interested in selling. Before signing a lease with a new mall, check to see how much traffic it has, then do a little arithmetic.

Let's say a new mall opens in a small community, offering 200 spaces to local crafters at an average rental fee of $95 per month. At full capacity, the owners would figure to gross $19,000 a month or $228,000 a year. This may sound like a good way to get rich quick, but it doesn't work that way. If a mall can't attract enough buyers, its crafters won't stay. If everyone in a mall this size made even twice their rent in sales—and I'll bet a lot of sellers don't do this well—the mall would have to sell $38,000 worth of crafts every month. For sellers to make four times their rent (which is the minimum professionals say is needed for a good profit), the mall would have to sell $76,000 worth of product every month, or more than $2500 a day. If a mall's average sale is $25, to sell $38,000 worth of crafts every month, it would need to pull in an average of 50 buyers every day.

Here is another way to look at it. If a mall has 200 crafters and has monthly sales of $38,000 per month, it suggests that sellers are averaging only $6.34 a day or $190/month. ($38,000 ÷ 200 = $190/month.)

Patricia Krauss has sold through malls and done considerable research in this field for a how-to booklet she has published. From interviews with more than 70 craft mall owners, she learned that the people who run malls tend to be leery about giving direct answers to questions about sales volume. "Often, when I would ask how much the average vendor makes, a mall owner would reply in vague terms, such as 'It varies,' or 'It depends on what craft they are selling,' or 'It depends on the time of year.' No one provided me with any sales data," she said.

Patricia thinks the best way to get such information may be from crafters themselves. She suggests you walk a mall and collect crafters' business cards or phone numbers from their hang tags and call a few of them. "Ask if they have encountered any problems with the management and whether they are making at least two or three times their rent."

Some sellers are realizing sales of ten times their booth cost, but I believe most sellers will be lucky to get three or four times their rent in sales. In other words, if you are paying $40 per space in a small craft mall, you would be doing well to have sales of $120 to $160 per month. If you were paying $150 for space in a larger mall, you would need sales of $375 to $500 per month. To sell at this volume, however, you might need to display three or four thousand dollars' worth of merchandise.

Craftspeople who sell in malls have a lot of power because a mall can't stay in business without satisfied exhibitors. Its financial success depends not only on the quality of suppliers it can attract, but the number and quality of shoppers it can bring into the store. "We realize that without the quality crafter, our business would be nothing," confirms a mall owner in business for four years. "Therefore, our mission is to provide a quality environment for artisans and crafters to sell their quality creations. We know that if our crafters aren't successful, then we won't be either, so we make every effort to bring in qualified customers to buy our crafters' work."

If you are afraid to deal with malls outside your immediate area, your fears may be ungrounded. While it pays to be cautious in dealing with new outlets, you can't build your crafts business if you never try anything different. Generally speaking, it seems a good idea to limit the amount of merchandise you put into a new mall until you've established a good working relationship with it or have favorable recommendations from other sellers in that mall. Because more craft newsletters and magazines are now reporting on craft malls across the country, it's getting easier to find reputable outlets. In such periodicals, crafters often share their marketing experiences, recommend good outlets and warn against others.

What Sells Best in Craft Malls

Craft malls are providing an important additional outlet for people who have a good deal of product to sell. Although most malls have suppliers from other parts of the country, their primary goal is to bring their area's buyers and sellers together. If you have been selling with success at local fairs or holiday boutiques, it stands to reason that you will do well in a crafts mall in the same area. Try to offer items that are not being offered by other crafters in the mall, and also try to find the "magic selling price" that is low enough to be attractive to buyers and high enough to give you a true profit.

Tip

"Analyze the profitability of your mall outlets on a quarterly basis," advises Beverly Durant, who has sold in as many as 35 malls at a time. "I tally sales, add shipping costs, telephone costs, my booth rent and stocking fee. If I haven't made a profit at the end of the first lease period (generally six months), that mall is closed."

While many crafters are selling with success in craft malls, others have lost money. After signing a four-month lease with a Coomers mall, an artisan specializing in Victorian crafts reported on her unsatisfactory sales experience. "During the biggest shopping week of the year, I sold absolutely nothing," she said. "The only thing that seemed to be selling was cows and sunflowers, spray-painted coffee cans with cardboard tree cutouts and seashells glued into angel shapes."

The fact that Victorian crafts are popular in some areas of the country—and receive rave reviews from a craft mall jury—doesn't mean they will sell everywhere. Renting space in a prestigious store doesn't guarantee sales, either. When you specialize in a particular type of craft, you must pay careful attention to where and how you offer it for sale. Generally, the following items seem to be selling well in malls across the country:

- Seasonal items
- Traditional crafts and furnishings
- Country crafts, folk art and Americana products
- Small decorative accessories for home and office
- Dolls, toys and miniatures
- Crafty wearables, jewelry and accessories
- Novelty items and whimsical creations

For every crafter who complains of no sales, there will always be others in the same place who are selling everything they make. It always comes down to the same thing: To make sales you must make products that people *in that area* want to buy. "Too many crafters make what they want to make with little regard for what people want to buy, " confirms Linda Coomer. "They don't change with the times. They're still doing crafts that went out of fashion months or years ago, still using colors no longer in vogue or patterns and techniques that are old-hat."

Good pricing is essential to financial success at a crafts fair, but it's vital for success at a crafts mall because you've got to lay out the monthly rental fee whether you sell anything or not. Linda Coomer says the hottest sellers in Coomers malls are items priced around $6. The average Coomers shopper spends $34, however, which means that higher-priced items in the $40 to $60 range are also selling well. "You need to have a variety of prices on your products," says Linda. "Try to have items priced for everyone's budget: low, medium and high-priced. For example, a lot of school kids come in to find something for their teachers for $5."

Tip

As the owner of Mini Measures, Gina Casey has been selling in malls for several years. Her selling expenses average 10 percent of gross sales, which is excellent. This is the same ratio used by successful retailers everywhere.

Setting Up a Mall Display

How products are displayed in a mall has everything to do with whether they will sell or not. All the display tips and ideas you found for craft fairs in Chapter Six are applicable to a craft mall setup. In addition, it's important to regularly rotate your stock and freshen your exhibit. Some sellers report increased sales immediately after restocking or changing their display. That's because most malls have developed a loyal customer base that expects to see new merchandise every time they return. If your booth always looks the same, it will receive no attention from these repeat buyers. They not only want to see new products, but new products displayed in new and interesting ways. "Success starts with the way you present your booth," confirms Linda Coomer. "Keep it fully stocked—the more crafts you put in it, the better your sales."

"When selling locally, visit the mall every month and rearrange all the items in your display," advises Beverly Durant. "If an item hasn't sold at the end of 90 days, take it home and either redo it or drop it from your line." Here are some ideas on how to add pizzazz to your craft mall display:

1. Do special displays for each holiday, featuring products appropriate for that particular holiday.
2. Change your color scheme periodically to reflect changing seasons.
3. Change the way products are displayed by rearranging shelves or hangers.
4. Rotate any display containers in use (baskets, boxes, crates, etc.).
5. Experiment with paint, wallpaper, curtains, swags or mirrors.
6. To attract more buyers, display your best sellers or higher-priced items at eye level.
7. If sales are sluggish, move your display to a different area of the store (rent a different booth space.) Otherwise stay in the same place so regular buyers always know where to find your newest products.
8. Use signs to encourage sales (as discussed in Chapter Seven).

Sells Thousands of Miniatures Annually

While it is difficult to make a true profit on low-priced items, some crafters have figured out how to do it. Take Gina Casey, for example. Working at her Mini Measures business about four hours a day, six days a week, she produces thousands of miniature handsculpted items each year from a special

blend of Fimo and Sculpy mixtures. Her line includes fruits and vegetables, dolls, bears, cats and other items for dollhouses and people with shadow box collections. Her best-selling item in craft malls is a 1½-inch teddy bear.

"From $10 worth of materials, I can gross $300 in sales," she says. "It takes me only a couple of minutes to make one of my little teddy bears and I make hundreds at a time, pricing them at $2.50 each." Gina currently sells in five malls, which is all she can handle. "I've had lots of requests to be in others, but I also wholesale to a few shops in tourist areas and occasionally do craft fairs, too."

Gina got her wholesale buyers by placing an ad in *Folkart Treasures,* a consumer showcase magazine for handcrafts. (See "Selling Nationally through Catalog-Magazines" in Chapter Twelve.) Because her prices are so low, Gina gives only a 30 percent discount to wholesale buyers. She doesn't know what price shop owners are putting on her items, but I'll bet it's two or three times the price they are paying Gina. I have encouraged her to raise her $2.50 price to $3.50 because this small increase would not begin to deter buyers and would give her thousands of extra dollars of profit each year.

"I spend a great deal of time, energy and money on display and I think this helps convince people to buy," says Nancy Mosher, a crafts consultant and seminar leader in Ft. Worth, Texas. In addition to selling a line of products to help crafters succeed in business, Nancy sells her handpainted crocks, tin and enamelware in several craft malls. They sell well, she believes, because they aren't found in magazines, books or other craft outlets. "Spare no expense to provide the most attractive way to display merchandise in a mall," she advises. "Don't line it up like a grocery store shelf one by one, side by side, nor stuff your display so full that it looks a mess."

Barbara Massie of Cherokee Village, Arkansas, sells painted wood and stones in craft malls. Like Nancy, she also teaches and writes about crafts and has published several booklets for crafters, including one on craft malls. When selling in malls, she suggests grouping products and colors to attract buyers. "For example," she says in her book, "if you are selling pillows and wooden items, mixing up the items in just any way can create a look of confusion. But if you group some pillows together, then group the wooden items together, the visual effect is much more pleasing."

Tip

"The walls of a craft mall exhibit area are generally of white pegboard but may be painted or decorated in any way the crafter desires," says Beverly Durant. "Use colors that complement your crafts. Put small items in planter boxes and display others on glass shelves hung on the pegboard walls. Don't ever put anything on the floor—use wicker shelves or wooden crates instead. Drape fabric for accent. To display my angel dolls, I use ivory paint and wide ecru lace tied in a big bow that drapes down on one side."

Two Problems You Must Deal With

Two display problems you need to address are the possibility of damaged merchandise and theft.

Damaged Merchandise

If you make expensive items that can't be handled without damage, don't put them in a craft mall. "You cannot expect a manager of a gallery or craft mall to guard your work," says Joy Lapcewich, a professional artist who uses hand-spun wools, leather, beads and feathers in her wall hangings and baskets. When exhibiting at craft fairs, Joy has often seen people push her "Please, Resist Touching!" sign aside to pull on a bead or a feather. Some of her expensive beads and feathers have been cut off during the night, despite her display being covered. After checking out a particular craft mall, she passed on an invitation to sell there. "The store was beautiful and well lit," she says, "but there was only one employee up front to handle sales. A child in the store was playing on the floor with some beautiful handmade toys from one exhibit while another child was twisting a conch on a sweatshirt trying to get it off. The parents were right there, of course."

In every grocery store and shopping center, we see parents who let their children run wild, so you must take this into consideration when setting up a craft mall display. Goods within reach of young children are going to be handled. Other goods will naturally become shopworn as they are handled by adults. (You may want to reread the tips in Chapter Six for reminders on how craft fair sellers protect their work from excessive handling.)

Shoplifting

Be prepared to lose some merchandise to theft, especially in malls that are poorly lit, inadequately staffed or without camera security. Of course the only way to know if you have lost merchandise or not is to set up an inventory system, and I'll bet only a handful of craft mall sellers have done this. You should keep track of how many of each item you place on display, and as you receive payments from the mall with a list of items that have sold, mark your records accordingly. Periodically, take a physical inventory to see how many items are unaccounted for.

Tip

When a product turns up missing, check other booths. I can easily imagine a shopper picking up an item from booth 23, walking the aisle and then deciding when she's in front of booth 37 that she doesn't want that item after all. Is she going to walk back to booth 23 or even know it's important to replace the item there? I doubt it. Instead, she may lay it down in someone else's booth.

You would think that Gina Casey, the miniaturist I mentioned earlier, would have terrible shoplifting problems, but she doesn't. (See related sidebar.) She takes a quarterly inventory so she knows exactly how many items are missing from each store. "Curiously, fewer items are stolen during the heavy selling seasons," she says. "Most seem to disappear during the slow seasons when there are fewer shoppers in the store."

Last year, Gina lost about $400 worth of items against sales of $25,000, or .016 percent. Assuming that each of the shoplifted items were priced at $2.50, Gina is losing about 160 pieces a year, or about 32 pieces a year per mall. Because shoplifting comes with the territory, Gina figures this is a loss she can accept. It's also a formula that might help you estimate your own losses.

Most malls offer security tags or labels that can be attached to merchandise to deter shoplifters. There are different kinds, but each is imbedded with a magnetic strip that sets off an alarm when people try to leave the store with a stolen object. At five to ten cents apiece, this is cheap insurance. Unfortunately, it doesn't work for everyone. The problem Gina has is that her items are too small to be tagged. "The 1 x 2-inch labels have to be stuck on a piece of cardboard before being attached to my products," she says. "This takes a lot of extra time and is no guarantee of protection because they can be easily removed. For that reason, I rarely bother to tag the low-priced items."

Gina tried selling items in plastic bags, but she made fewer sales so she stopped doing it. "I think people want to be able to pick up and hold items before they buy, and putting them in plastic bags makes them seem more commercial," she reasons.

Tip

You could put small valuables on display in a locked case, but this may cost you a few sales, Patricia Krauss warns. "Some impulse buyers may be too impatient to wait for someone to unlock your case. If you do use a locked case, insist that only authorized store personnel unlock it. Crafters working in the store should not have access to it. You would be surprised at how many people think it's okay to unlock a case, hand the item to the customer, and let them carry it around while they shop. This defeats the whole purpose of having your valuables locked up. I now have a sign on my locked display case that says items removed from the case must be held at the check-out counter until the customer has finished shopping."

Remote Stocking Programs

Most craft malls offer a remote stocking program that enables crafters from other parts of the country to sell through their malls. This is a great service if you happen to live in an area that is devoid of craft malls, rent-a-space shops or good local craft fairs. It's also a good way to get your crafts into an area that may be hungry for your type of product. Some crafts have only regional appeal, however, so you always need to research a new market area to learn what's selling there.

Two disadvantages of running a remote booth are increased costs (shipping expense and phone calls) and problems in controlling your display. Within two years of beginning to sell in craft malls, Beverly Durant of Weatherford, Texas, was selling more than 70,000 angel dolls a year in 35 malls, most of them out-of-state. Initially she found remote stocking programs to be a godsend. Each time she opened a new mall, she would send a diagram and a photograph to the mall's remote representative, who would set up the display and send Beverly a picture to see if she liked it.

"I couldn't complain about the service I received," says Beverly, "because they did everything to accommodate me. They notified me when my stock was low and restocked my display each time I sent a new supply of merchandise. Problems developed over time, however. I would get a picture of my display every three months, and as time passed I became more dissatisfied with the way it looked. The people who were maintaining my display were trying, but they seemed to lack design sense and just couldn't comprehend how I wanted things set up."

In time, sales dropped in all of Beverly's out-of-state malls, convincing her of the importance of displays to sales. She gradually closed all of these outlets to concentrate on selling through fifteen malls (nine of which are Coomers) within a hundred miles from home. Although she appreciates the remote representatives who continually restock her displays as merchandise sells, Beverly has learned the importance of personally maintaining her displays with regular visits to each mall.

I might mention here that Beverly is something of a legend in craft mall circles where everyone knows her as The Angel Lady. Her first products were four angel dolls seven inches in size, made of embroidery floss or mop yarn and finished with ribbon, lace and other decorative items. Now she has more than a dozen items in her line, all priced between $5.95 to $14.95, with new products being introduced and sold by the thousands every year. She has become a whiz at figuring out how to turn out items assembly-line style, and her whole family and three outside employees are now involved in her business. "I can't say enough good things about craft malls," she says. "They have made me an independent person."

Beverly is enjoying her phenomenal sales success in craft malls, but she knows she can't keep producing this much merchandise every year without wearing herself to a frazzle. Her future plans are to limit the production of finished handcrafts and add a line of patterns and kits.

Variation on a Theme

In July 1993, after doing craft fairs for thirteen years, Debbie Nita opened The Craft About Store in Munster, Indiana. Originally, the store was planned to be a craft mall with rental space for local crafters. To encourage out-of-state sellers to try the shop, Debbie gave them the option of selling on a 60/40 percent consignment arrangement or renting space on a monthly basis ($25 to $70, depending on size of space).

Today the store has 90 crafters. Most of the local people rent space, but the out-of-town crafters prefer consignment. Several seniors, including a couple of women in their 80s, have found this to be a good outlet for their work. Only seven of the sellers are men, two of whom do fine woodworking. The store's average sale is $15 to $20 and the highest priced item in the store is $80.

"When I offered consignment as an option to renting space, my main goal was to increase sales," says Debbie. "But this proved profitable in more ways than one. In starting to take consignees from across the country, I gained a competitive edge I wouldn't have had as a craft mall owner featuring only the work of local sellers. These people sell the same merchandise at all the local fairs and malls while my out-of-town consignees send me merchandise that is unique to this area. Since I'm offering shoppers something they can't find elsewhere, I've developed a loyal base of customers who keep coming back to see what's new and different."

"If you can't maintain your craft mall display personally, you may get better service from a smaller mall," says Gina Casey. "It seems to me that the bigger and larger the mall, the less attention your exhibit receives." The five malls Gina currently sells through are all in Indiana, within 200 miles of her Remington, Indiana, home. During the fall and through the Christmas season, she checks all of them once a month. During slower periods, she goes every two months. "I have found that items shipped in between times to replace stock are often haphazardly placed on shelves or in the type-tray boxes I use instead of being grouped by kind, color or theme."

In summary, stocking programs are important because they enable crafters to ship in new merchandise when it can't be delivered in person. Greater sales may be realized, however, if you keep a close eye on the quality of your display through regular visits.

Beverly Durant attributes part of her sales success to the people who work in the malls. "When I go in, I make a point of speaking to every employee. I make friends with people who work there, send them Christmas cards, participate in store activities, donate items. When I leave, I always thank everyone for the help they have given me. In effect, these people are working for me, and I try to make them feel I really appreciate them being there. I think it has made a tremendous difference and my booth gets extra attention simply because everyone knows me."

When a Craft Mall Fails

Whether craft malls close because of poor management or market conditions, craftspeople are the ones who suffer most. As I was writing this chapter, one of my readers reported on her bad experience with a mall in Pennsylvania:

After leasing space with a mall for more than two years, the owner expanded by open-ing two other shops. When we signed our one-year lease agreement, we had to pay the first and last months' rental fee. Each month on the 15th, we were to get a printout of last month's sales and our check. Out of the check was taken a monthly lease fee, VISA charges, and an electronic deposit of check fee called EAT. We all questioned the EAT fee, but every month it was removed from our income. On our statement, we were told how many and what items we sold, but never told which items were paid by check, cash or credit card. The charge for VISA/EAT was just lumped together.

On January 15, the expected payment didn't arrive. I received my 1099 at month's end, and on the second of February I received a check for one-third of the amount owed to me. A letter explained that the craft mall owner was having financial difficulty. He asked us to bear with him. On our check stub it stated what our total sales for Decem-ber were, minus next month's lease fee and VISA/EAT charges. I pulled my items out of his shop on January 31, and on February 4, he closed all three shops. Those who left their merchandise in his shops were asked to bear with him as he dismantled his busi-ness, but other sellers got letters saying they were the reason he had to close, because they broke their contract by pulling goods out of stores.

What this man owes me is not a great amount—about $350—but in adding what he owes to all the crafters in all three stores, we estimate it comes to more than $300,000, not to mention all the sales tax he collected and didn't pay to the state. We all met to discuss the legal advice we had been given, but it looks like a lot of us are out a lot of money, and now we have no place to sell unless we go back to churches, organizations and four-day mall shows.

Two Tiny Shoppes All Her Own

In Bartlesville, Oklahoma, Claire Welch operates what she refers to as her "two tiny shoppes"—dealer booths she rents in two antique and craft malls in her area. They provide a monthly income as high as $2,500 per shop. She has increased the inventory in her booths by purchasing craft items from other sellers.

"Such outlets used to be solely antique and flea-market type stores," she says, "but crafters in our area have really taken to this idea. What I love about this type of selling is that I can stay home with my three children and have more time for producing the line of woodcrafts I wholesale to other outlets."

While shopping cart peddlers in large shopping malls may pay thousands a year in rent, Claire pays only about $65/month for an 8 x 7 foot space, plus a 10 percent commission on sales. She has had some shoplifting problems but doesn't fret about them. "Even with shoplifting losses, my expenses are still less than what it would cost me to travel to a craft show every weekend," she says, "and the time I save enables me to produce a greater volume of merchandise for sale."

Unfortunately, crafters don't have much clout in a case like this. Most will be lucky to get all their merchandise back. While many states have special laws to protect artisans when a consignment shops goes into bankruptcy (see next chapter), craft malls and rent-a-space shops fall into a gray area that is not currently covered by state consignment laws. About the only way to protect yourself against this problem is to keep a keen eye on the malls in which you sell and watch for warning signs of a mall in trouble. These might include

- Less than 75 percent occupancy
- No advertising being done
- Too little traffic
- Crafters pulling out
- Poor accounting of sales
- Inadequate explanation of charges being made
- Late payments

Rent-a-Space Shops

A few consignment craft shop owners were experimenting with the rent-a-space retailing concept as early as 1975, but crafters didn't catch on to the benefits of renting retail space until craft malls took the country by storm fifteen years later. Although craft malls and rent-a-space shops are similar in that they both rent space to individual sellers, there are some interesting differences.

First, rent-a-space craft shops are generally smaller than craft malls. Some are laid out like a mall (one display area after another), while others are set up like a regular gift or craft shop, with display controlled by the shop owner or manager. Shops that don't rent standard display areas may rent shelf space, wall space or a corner nook. They may also take handcrafts on consignment or sell a line of commercial goods. In some stores, crafters must agree to work in the shop or pay a higher commission on sales.

In Vermont, Sue Wilder of Wildbeary Crafts has found rental shops to be perfect for her. "It's a good deal," she says. "The shops are open seven days a week and they do a lot for us." She rents a 3 x 5 foot space in three different craft shops for from $27 to $35 a month. Two are set up like mini malls, the other is like a boutique shop. She sells a line of three-dimensional animal sculptures made from plastic canvas—cows that moo, horses that whinny, frogs that croak. Priced between $6 and $8, customers buy them for use as decorative accessories or refrigerator magnets (something many people are collecting these days).

Nancy Gray in New Hampshire likes the rental system too, because she only has to deliver merchandise, not arrange and sell it. "You can rent on a month-to-month basis and you can leave the shop at the end of any month if you've given two weeks' notice," she says. "Seasoned crafters get to show their work to a wider variety of people while new crafters can learn from the veteran crafters how to price their work."

The rent-a-space retailing concept has enabled many entrepreneurs to open shops that could not have opened as straight consignment shops. "I opened with only a thousand dollars," says a former shop owner in Savannah who later moved to another city. "I began with 30 crafters. Each paid $22 per shelf per month on a month-to-month basis and floor space was available for up to $100 a month. No sales commissions were taken. Word-of-mouth advertising was great and the crafters themselves promoted the shop."

Display is as important in the rental shops as in the craft malls. Diane Troutman of My Two Hands rents space in a Texas craft and gift shop. Something she has found to be successful is to feature a subject or type of craft each month or season. "For instance," she says, "one month might be angels, where

I would display handmade angels made from various materials. In the summer months I might feature watermelons or sunflowers. I keep a card displayed in my booth letting people know what the next month's theme is."

Tip

"Lower your stress by working several months ahead of the season," says Diane. "Ideally, during the Christmas months you should be working on Valentine and spring crafts while also producing additional Christmas merchandise that may be selling quickly."

Treasure Cache Gift Shops

Similar to craft malls, yet different, are the new franchise retail craft outlets now making their appearance in selected shopping malls and tourist areas across the country. Treasure Cache Inc. pioneered this new type of gift retailing with the opening of its first store in Holbrook, New York, in 1992. By the end of 1995, there were 26 stores in ten states, making Treasure Cache the largest chain of handmade arts and crafts retail showrooms. Additional stores will be opening in the future.

The Treasure Caché

"Treasure Cache stores are located in the finer regional malls and high-traffic resort areas," says President Richard A. Simeone. "Crafters might call them art and craft showcases or craft display showrooms, but customers see them as upscale specialty gift shops."

Although some craft malls are also located in high-traffic areas, the major difference between the malls and Treasure Cache stores is one of atmosphere. "The whole key here is not size of space, but location," Simeone emphasizes. "To succeed in this kind of marketing, artisans need to get away from the what's-the-size-of-my-booth mentality and understand that it is customer traffic and retail sales that drive this industry."

In craft malls, the whole concept is "this is your booth," with little or no consideration given to traffic flow or the public's buying habits. The sales impetus is on the person who rents the space rather than the one who runs the shop. In the Treasure Cache stores, however, sales become the responsibility of the shop owner, not the crafters who are renting display/sales space in that store. Because so many handcraft purchases are for gifts or home decor rather than items of necessity, they naturally sell better in an exclusive gift-shop atmosphere. "And crafters can get higher prices for their work in our shops than they can in a craft mall or at a fair," Simeone adds.

These showrooms display the works of artists and crafters who currently pay a monthly rental fee of $55 to $65 and a sales commission of 16 to 20 percent of the retail price. Although this is a higher percentage than that taken by craft malls, it may well be offset by the higher prices and greater volume of sales crafters can realize in this type of store. The typical price range in a Treasure Cache store is between $10 and $25, but some items are priced as high as $500 or more. Fire insurance coverage on all handcrafts in the store is an extra benefit of selling through Treasure Cache outlets.

"This business is inventory driven," says Simeone. "We look for a good mix of local people to give each store a local fair, but we are always interested in hearing from professional crafters in other parts of the country." To encourage suppliers interested in selling in five or more stores, the company has developed a National Distributor Program. "This is a membership type of arrangement, more of a team effort," says Simeone. "Instead of a monthly fee, we take 40 percent of sales. The membership fee paid by national distributors entitles them to display in every Treasure Cache store, subject to space availability. Most of the crafters in this program sell in fifteen or more stores."

Look for Treasure Cache on the Internet. For more information on selling through this chain of shops, mention this book when you write to Treasure Cache, 33 Walt Whitman Road, Suite 110, Huntington Station, NY 11746.

Crafter's Boutique Franchise

Crafter's Boutique is a new franchise program still in its infancy. The first shop opened in 1995 in Valley Stream, New York, where the corporation is headquartered. Watch for these stores to spring up across the country over the next few years. These shops are likely to be a cross between craft malls and the

Treasure Cache stores described above. Also targeted for high-traffic shopping areas, they will operate on the rent-a-space concept and will deal primarily with local crafters who will be responsible for stocking their own display areas. The content of these stores will be part handcrafts and part commercial items with some antiques taken on consignment.

CHAPTER TEN

Selling on Consignment

Selling on consignment is one of the oldest and most successful methods of marketing art and handcrafts. It is also the most controversial.

Many professional crafters would advise you against consignment selling, arguing that shop owners who won't (or can't afford to) buy your merchandise outright will not work very hard to sell it and will often ruin it in the process. Yet, for the beginner who can locate a good consignment shop, this is a great way to gain experience in the retail marketplace with less financial risk than with craft malls or rent-a-space shops. After reading this chapter and considering the pros and cons of selling on consignment, decide for yourself if this is the route you want to go.

First you need to understand the difference between selling your work outright and consigning it to a retail shop. When you sell outright (wholesale), you relinquish all control over your merchandise. Once you have been paid for it, the shop owns it and can sell it for any price it wishes. When you consign merchandise, however, you are merely transferring it to another who will act as your sales representative. You remain the legal owner of all consigned goods. If and when it sells, the retailer will withhold its standard sales commission and send you the balance. This can often take months, which is why some craftspeople prefer to wholesale their work. Although profits may be smaller, at least they get their money in hand quickly.

If you have previously sold only through craft fairs, you may think it is more profitable to sell directly to the consumer than through a shop that takes a sales commission of 35 to 40 percent. But is it? Much will depend on what you are selling, what it costs to make, and how quickly you can produce it. As I've emphasized earlier, if you were to take the time normally spent at fairs and use this time for production instead, you might find that your increased volume would more than offset the sales commission paid to shops and give you a larger profit at year's end.

Different Types of Shops and Galleries

Today there are hundreds of traditional handcraft shops and art galleries in the United States and Canada, many of which have probably been around since the 1970s, when America was enjoying its first great crafts movement. Some of these shops specialize in a particular type of product (country, contemporary, Appalachian, dolls and toys, etc.), while others feature handmade items of all kinds. Some shops operate exclusively on a consignment basis while others include a line of gifts or crafts purchased at wholesale.

Years ago, consignment shops were all the same: sellers left merchandise on consignment and when it sold, the shop owner took a percentage of the sale and gave the rest to the seller. In the 90s, a new breed of consignment shop has emerged, due in part to the popularity of (and competition from) craft malls and rent-a-space shops and partly because of ever-increasing overhead costs. Now, in addition to taking a higher percentage of sales, most consignment shops are also charging overhead or management fees and consignors may be asked to work in the shop or pay a higher percentage on their sales.

Bea Sheftel of R & B Country Crafts sells her sweatshirts in three Connecticut shops. "One charges me $10 a month plus 40 percent commission but doesn't give me any set space," she reports. "Another charges $5 a month and 40 percent commission and lets me display a limited amount of merchandise. Another charges $7 a square foot and gives me that space to decorate with crafts as I wish."

Once you get involved in consignment selling, you will find yourself dealing with shops that have different commission arrangements. One seller asks: "I work with two consignment shops. One works on a 60/40 percent arrangement, the other on 75/25 percent. If I offer my crafts to both shops at the same price, the second shop will sell my work for much less. Is that fair to the first shop? If I raise the price of my work to sell to the second shop, to keep both shops equal in their selling price, is that fair to the second shop?"

That's a good question. What's important here is that you establish a firm retail price on the items sold in both shops. To be professional, you must also sell at this price when you offer these items to consumers at a crafts fair. Consider the extra profit from your sales, and from the second shop, as "gravy." Don't be concerned about what is fair to the shops; be concerned instead about what is fair to buyers. The same item found in three different places should be offered at the same retail price. If you can make more profit from one shop than another, more power to you.

Tip

___

To find reliable consignment shops, you must subscribe to magazines and newsletters (in print or online) that serve professional crafters. Many shops and galleries advertise their special needs in publications such as *The Crafts Report* (Wilmington, Delaware), and subscribers often recommend good shops they have worked with. (To find such publications, check art and craft categories in one of the periodical directories mentioned in Chapter One.)

___

Most art and craft galleries now operate on a 50/50 consignment basis because their overhead costs are high and the products they carry tend to be unique, expensive, one-of-a-kind works of art that can't be wholesaled. Some galleries offer only fine art while others sell both fine art and crafts, including sculpture, weaving, woodworking, pottery, glass, metalwork and stitchery. Special exhibitions and sales are often held in galleries to promote the work of the artists and designers they represent. Commissions from architects and interior designers and custom orders from private collectors are just some of the special benefits connected with gallery exhibitions. Prestige is another.

Some consignment shops are also taking as much as 50 percent of the sale price. I sympathize with shop owners who are being faced with increasing overhead costs, but craft sellers have too many marketing options today to give 50 percent of the retail price to a consignment shop. This might make sense if you make mostly one-of-a-kind items and don't have any other outlet for them, but it makes no sense at all if you are producing multiples of a line of products that could be sold just as easily through fairs, boutiques, craft malls or rent-a-space shops. When wholesaling to gift shops, it is standard practice to offer them a 50 percent discount off the retail price, so why give the same amount to a consignment shop that may not sell your products for months?

The Benefits of Consignment Selling

The great advantage of consignment is that it enables individuals with limited capital to open shops that may provide important marketing outlets for local producers. None of today's most successful handcraft shops could have opened if, like regular gift shops, they had to buy all goods outright to begin with. The benefits to crafters are threefold. They can

1. Consign merchandise of their choice without the pressure of meeting a deadline date
2. Control the retail selling price of their work
3. Test the marketability of new or untried items

In fact, consignment selling is often the best or only way to market work of limited production or expensive, one-of-a-kind crafts and needlework. On the minus side, consignment selling means increased bookkeeping and paperwork for both shop and seller and, for the latter, merchandise is tied up but not sold, which presents cash-flow problems.

Consignment selling has its share of pitfalls, but Betty Schriever has learned that it can also be a wonderful way to sell crafts. She says the secret to success lies in selecting consignment shops with care. "One of the nicest and best shops in my area is owned by a woman who has turned a whole house into a shop," Betty reports. "She charges consignors only $4 a month and takes a sales commission of between 35 and 38 percent. After inspecting my work, she displays it where she thinks it fits best."

Betty lives in Sioux Falls, South Dakota where there are many one and two-day craft shows in the spring and fall, but she doesn't do fairs anymore. She prefers to sell on consignment because it's less work for her and her things are on display all year. "I especially like receiving a monthly check and a computer printout of items that have been sold," she adds.

Jeri Fry has been selling beeswax candles at Michigan fairs for five years, but when she put some on consignment in a combination antique/craft shop, she sold 371 pairs in just nine months. "This prompted me to look for new shop outlets and consider other marketing outlets, such as home parties, open house shows and a cooperative shop," she says.

It will be easier to work with consignment shops outside your area if you have professional printed materials that include illustrations or pictures of your work (see Chapter Thirteen). If not, be prepared to send a photograph that illustrates the quality of your work. Instead of sending a batch of unprofessional snapshots that have been developed at the local drug store, ask a friend with photographic skill to take a professional picture of a collection of your best items. Arrange them artistically against an appropriate background. Once you have a good negative, find a company that prints photographs in quantity.

Tip

Consider the cost of photographs part of your advertising and selling costs and don't whine if you don't get them back. You can enclose an SASE and ask a shop to return a photograph, but when you do this, you automatically mark yourself as a hobby seller that few shops will want to deal with.

What does "SASE" mean? It doesn't mean a "self-absorbed stuffed elephant," as I once heard someone say on radio. It means you are to include a Self-Addressed Stamped Envelope with your request for information or other reply.

Avoiding Consignment Pitfalls

Don't ignore new shops as a market for your work, especially if you are still trying to "get your feet wet," but do be cautious about dealing with them on a consignment basis until you're satisfied you have a good thing going. One hazard is that some new shop owners are as inexperienced as the sellers with whom they are dealing. Often, it's a case of the blind leading the blind.

You can greatly expand the number of shops you sell to by dealing with them by mail. On the other hand, you need to be careful in deciding who to trust with your handcrafts because you can't personally monitor what's happening to them in a far-distant shop. The longer a shop has been in business, the more comfortable you will feel about dealing with them, so always ask how long the shop has been in business before you ship your first order. Here are other tips to help you avoid common pitfalls:

1. Never consign merchandise without a consignment agreement. Reputable shops will use a standard consignment form. (See "Preparing a Consignment Agreement" below.)

Damaged Goods

Maureen Padgett has encountered some problems in selling beaded earrings and needlepoint tapestries through consignment stores. "I have had work that didn't sell in consignment stores returned to me in poor shape," she says. "In one case, my work was displayed in a window. That sounded great at first, until the unsold work was returned badly faded by the sun. In another case, work had been handled by many customers and was returned very dirty."

A crafter who avoids consignment shops adds: "If you can afford to get damaged merchandise back and have low sales, then consignment is for you. Some shoppers try to tear a product apart to see how it was made so they can try to make it themselves. The resulting damage is the responsibility of the crafter and not the store owner. That's why I now sell only to wholesale buyers."

2. Avoid consignment to shops that normally buy most of their merchandise at wholesale. Such shops who offer to take your work only on consignment may believe that your products are unsalable for one reason or another, and they will not work very hard to sell them for you.

3. Never consign more than a few items to a new or unknown shop until you have developed a satisfactory relationship with the owner or manager (based on prompt payment after the first merchandise has been sold) and see other indications that the shop is being well managed.

4. Your products will sell better in any shop when several pieces are displayed. If the choice is between several shops that only want a few pieces, or one or two that will take a good supply, pick the latter and offer a wide price range in the articles you consign. Obviously, the less expensive pieces will sell first, but your higher-priced pieces will encourage sales of the lower-priced items.

5. When you make a shipment to a shop, prepare two copies of a packing list that describes each item you're sending. Keep one copy and include the other in the shipping carton for the shopowner. This should prevent later disagreements about what was sent and received by the owner. If you ship more than one carton, reference on each the total number of cartons being shipped, and number each accordingly. Make sure your packing list shows which items have been included in each carton in case you need to make a claim for a carton that gets lost or damaged during delivery. (Insure each box accordingly.)

Get It in Writing!

"No matter how much you want to believe what you are being told and what you think you see, get it all in writing," cautions Nanci Luna. "Be sure every area of your consignment agreement is spelled out in clear English. Don't leave anything to chance or rely on verbal agreements. This includes doing business with friends. Don't ruin a friendship or take a chance with a stranger."

A seller in Pennsylvania warns against working with new consignment shops. "Get the consignment commission details in writing," she says. "I started in a shop that had no set fee and nothing in writing. After being there for a few years and becoming friends with the owner, I found it very hard to leave after she decided to double all prices. It took me two years to find the courage to tell her I was leaving, and why. We are still friends, but this spring when she opens her shop again I won't be there unless we agree on a much lower fee and I get it in writing."

Preparing a Consignment Agreement

A good consignment agreement will cover all situations that are likely to come up in your relationship with a shop. If any of the following points are not included in the contract you are offered, it may be that you are dealing with an inexperienced shop owner. In that case, you should get answers to all of the following questions and add appropriate clauses to the consignment agreement before you sign it:

Shopowner's Name

When you establish a relationship with a new shop, insist on getting the name of the owner, not just the manager. Shops have sometimes been known to close suddenly with owners and stock disappearing overnight and sellers left holding the bag. Other shops simply go bankrupt, with consigned goods being seized by creditors. If you don't know the owner's name, you won't have a chance of reclaiming your merchandise. (See "State Consignment Laws" sidebar.)

Shipment of Merchandise

Who pays the freight? Buyers are generally expected to pay shipping charges on goods they buy outright (at wholesale prices), but a consignment shop may expect you to absorb the expense for both shipping and insurance. (If you ship by UPS, your shipments are automatically insured to $100 without additional cost.)

Display of Merchandise

Will your crafts be properly displayed and not left in the storeroom after you bring them in (or ship them) on consignment? What guarantee do you have that they will not be carelessly placed in a display window for weeks at a time, to be faded by the sun? Discuss the matter of display in advance, noting in your agreement any special requirements you may have.

Insurance

What happens if your work is damaged, completely ruined, stolen, or destroyed by a fire or flood? Be sure to ask if the shop's insurance policy covers such loss. If not, you may wish to purchase your own insurance policy to protect against such loss or limit the amount of merchandise consigned to a particular shop.

Return of Unsold Merchandise

Ask how long your work will be on display and how unsold work will eventually be returned to you. Will it be returned at your expense? Must you claim unsold goods by a certain date or forfeit ownership entirely? (Some shops have a clause stating that if unsold merchandise is not claimed within 30 to 60 days after a notice has been sent, the shop can assume ownership of it and dispose of it any way it wishes.)

Pricing and Sales Commission

Consignors are usually expected to set the retail price on their merchandise, but sometimes a shop will ask consignors simply to tell them how much they want for an item and they will set the retail price accordingly. This arrangement, or the exact percentage the shop will retain as its sales commission, should be clearly stated in your agreement.

Payment Dates

How and when will you be paid? Monthly payments to craftspeople are customary for many shops, but there are many ways to keep consignment sales records, and the method of payment should therefore be spelled out in

State Consignment Laws

Theoretically, consigned goods remain the property of the seller until they are sold to the retail customer. In normal situations there are no problems. If an establishment goes bankrupt, however, consigned goods may be subject to the claims of creditors, and may be seized by such creditors unless certain protective steps have been taken by consignors. (This is according to the Uniform Commercial Code that has been adopted by most states.)

A standard consignment contract will not offer sufficient protection in a bankrupt case. In some states, artists and craftspeople have lost all their merchandise due to such seizures. (In one case I recall, an artist actually had to pay $10,000 to retrieve her own paintings from a bankrupt gallery.) Fortunately, several states now have consignment laws designed to protect artists and craftspeople. Those known to me are California, Colorado, Connecticut, Illinois, Iowa, Kentucky, Massachusetts, New Hampshire, New Mexico, New York, Oregon, Texas, Washington, and Wisconsin. There may be others I am not aware of.

If your state is not listed above, contact your state legislature to find out if it has a consignment law. If so, be sure to ask what kind of merchandise that law protects from seizure by creditors. Even when a consignment law exists, there may be a pitfall. Some states protect only "art," and handcrafts may not be included if they fall outside the area of painting, sculpture, drawing, graphic art, pottery, weaving, batik, macrame, quilting, or other commonly recognized art forms.

your agreement. In addition to a check each month, you should receive a report of the specific items sold so you can adjust your inventory records accordingly.

In Summary

Consignment selling is neither fish nor fowl in that it is neither retail nor wholesale selling. It is, however, an effective way to test the market for products you might consider wholesaling in the future. Interestingly, switching from consignment to wholesale selling may be more profitable than you realize. You may think you will make less money because you'll get only half the suggested retail price instead of the usual 60 to 75 percent you ordinarily get from consignment. However, you will gain in other ways, especially in the time department, and you will have fewer cash flow problems as well.

As one crafter explained it to me, "Instead of consigning $300 worth of merchandise to one shop and receiving $10 to $75 monthly checks trickling in over a year's time, I can now send three shipments, each worth $100 to three different shops and within a month have $300 in hand." She added that, within a couple of months after switching to wholesale, her monthly gross sales had doubled and her bookwork decreased by 80 percent.

CHAPTER ELEVEN

Innovative Marketing Methods

Opportunities to promote your business and sell at retail are everywhere. You need only stretch your imagination a bit to see them.

In previous chapters you have learned how to sell handmade products through eight of the most common arts and crafts retail outlets (numbers 1–8 on list below). This chapter discusses seven additional, unusual ways to market arts and crafts in your own community (numbers 9–16). Closing the chapter is a discussion on how to inexpensively promote your crafts business locally, along with a brief introduction to marketing on the Internet's World Wide Web. The following list will serve as a reminder of the retail markets discussed at length in this book:

1. Art and craft fairs and festivals
2. Home shops and studios
3. Open houses
4. Party plan selling
5. Holiday boutiques
6. Consignment shops
7. Craft malls
8. Rent-a-space shops
9. Local retailers
10. Service providers

11. Schools
12. Hospitals and clinics
13. Retirement centers and nursing homes
14. Military base
15. Pushcart merchandising
16. Craft cooperatives

Selling to the last eight markets on this list will require extra effort and creative thinking on your part, but I think you will find them worth exploring.
Success here will depend on your ability to take the initiative, make sales presentations, set up special displays or form cooperative marketing arrangements
with others. If you have discovered other innovative ways to market arts and
crafts at either the retail or wholesale level, I hope you will write and tell me
about them. I am always looking for interesting people to write about in my
magazine articles and books.

Selling through Local Retailers

You may be surprised to learn how many marketing opportunities await
you in your own back yard. Begin by taking a look at all the small retail businesses in your community—the hardware store, butcher shop, sports store,
beauty shop, drug store, clothing shop, convenience store, etc.—and note the
kind of sideline merchandise they offer. The owners of such businesses aren't
likely to come to you in search of products, but if you can show them how
they can make money by offering your products to their customers, you've
just opened the door to mutual profit. Ideally, you will offer products that
complement a particular merchant's line. Here are specific examples of how to
make this kind of marketing work for you.

■ *Gift Shops*. Gift shops are always interested in buying handcrafts at wholesale prices, but if you can't sell at wholesale or a shop isn't interested in buying
from you, they might consider renting you a bit of display space. When Judy
Reilly was selling her gift baskets by mail, she expanded her market by asking
a local gift shop if they would showcase a selection of her baskets and decorative woodenware in exchange for a 30 percent commission on sales. They
were happy to do this, and Judy sold quite a few baskets this way. Signs in the
exhibit area informed buyers that they could call Judy to special-order a basket or create their own baskets by filling them with items in the shop.

■ *Floral Shops*. Some floral shops now sell handcrafts as a sideline, and a
few have jumped on the "crafts mall bandwagon" by making space available to

crafters on a rent-a-shelf basis. Visit local floral shops to see if handcrafts are currently offered. If not, ask if the shop owner has any interest in renting you some space for your products. (In case you're thinking of offering your crafts to florists at wholesale prices, remember that floral shops traditionally buy only through distributors in this industry, or from exhibitors in floral trade shows. While you can probably sell to local florists through a personal sales call, a direct mailing to a national list of floral shops is unlikely to produce any orders.)

■ *Gas Stations and Convenience Food Stores*. At a time when local craft fairs were experiencing poor attendance and low sales, Elizabeth Parrott asked a local service station if they would be interested in displaying a small item she had made. Items were left on consignment and sales were good enough for Elizabeth to explore opportunities with other service stations, convenience food stores and local merchants. "This mode of merchandising requires time and expenditure of money for display preparation," Elizabeth notes, "but it is offset by the savings on bazaar booth space, travel and related expenses."

■ *Any Store with a Big Window*. An article in a crafts newsletter told of a crafter in a small rural community in Minnesota who has discovered a great way to market her crafts. She rents store windows for $25 a month and decorates them with her products, using themes appropriate for the season. She says beauty shops are best because they have windows just begging for decorations. (See also "Beauty Shops" in next section.)

Most retailers are hurting for business these days, so many would probably be happy to clear a window, or at least a portion of it, for a special crafts display. Such a display is going to attract attention from people who might otherwise walk on by, and once they get into the store to take a closer look at a crafter's products, they might buy something else from the retailer. This kind of win-win arrangement certainly seems worth exploring. If you try this idea, you will have to work out the details on how shoppers can actually buy your products. Will they call you to place an order you will deliver in person or ship by mail, or will the store owner sell items right out of the window, collecting the money and appropriate sales tax for you?

Working with Local Service Providers

Many businesses need employee or client gifts, so study your line and select one special item that you could make in quantity at reasonable cost to buyers. Then call some larger businesses in your area and make an appointment to discuss their needs.

■ *Ad agency*. One crafter was thrilled when an ad agency hired her to make a thousand dough Santas to be used as employee and client Christmas gifts. The fact that her Santa had an Old World look and specially designed enclosure card helped cinch the sale.

■ *Realtors*. Randall Barr, who used to sell his Birdhouse Clocks at craft fairs and now wholesales to shops, said his first large order was from a realtor who wanted to use his product as client gifts. Catherine Gilleland once marketed her gift baskets directly to consumers through local fairs and mail order. Later, she also found realtors to be a good market for her baskets, along with home party entrepreneurs who used them as hostess gifts.

■ *Conventions*. The convention market also proved lucrative for Catherine. Here, baskets are used as room amenities, speaker gifts and raffle items. After doing some market research, she found she could provide a variety of convention products and services, such as table centerpieces and imprinted items.

■ *Beauty Shops*. Have you ever though of taking a sample of your work to your favorite beauty shop? In rural communities and small towns where gift shops do not abound, this idea could be extremely profitable. To maximize sales in this market, concentrate on solving a gift need facing busy women, such as an upcoming graduation, birthday, anniversary, wedding or baby shower. In negotiating with the shop owner, first suggest a merchandise incentive (more economical than cash), but if this doesn't work, offer a 25 percent commission.

Suzanne Chiasson, who has found beauty shops to be a wonderful market for her handmade products, says there are four reasons why this kind of marketing works:

1. Women in a shop seem predisposed to buy things
2. Hairdressers, whose job requires them to be gregarious and sympathetic, are excellent saleswomen
3. Many of the same people come in each week, which allows them time to think about buying something and another opportunity to purchase
4. Repeat business is assured as friends ask about the products and order their own through the original customers

"Selling through beauty shops is also a good way to do market research," says Suzanne. "People will say just what they like and do not like when the maker isn't around. All you need is someone to report to you on what has been said. It helps to know a hairdresser personally, but if you don't, scout the local beauty shops to see which ones have space for product displays, then show them your stuff and make an offer."

Other Community Markets to Explore

Here are four innovative ideas on how to sell through schools, hospitals, clinics, retirement centers and nursing homes:

■ *Schools*. Melody Johnson once sold 40 straw-burlap scarecrows without even trying. Because she was a substitute teacher, she got the idea of taking a display scarecrow with her to different schools where she placed it in the teacher's lounge with a sign-up sheet for orders and colors preferred. "I was amazed to discover how many teachers, librarians, bus drivers and principals wanted not just one, but two or three," she said.

The easiest way to get a display of your products in a school is to know a teacher who can put in a good word for you with the principal. To get his approval, show how a display of your products will benefit the teachers (make holiday shopping easier) or the school (donate a percentage of sales to a special school fund).

■ *Hospitals*. Eileen Uribe told me of her interesting experience doing fundraising shows for a hospital that had no gift shop. Initially, she did this three times a year, but the idea proved so successful that she began to do it monthly. "I set up shop for one or two days and sell to employees and visitors," she explains. "My donation is 15 percent to the auxiliary department, and after only five shows, I've raised over $1300 for them. This is not a multi-vendor show, just me in the lobby." Before launching a wholesale and mail order business for her country line of antique lace and potpourri, Eileen owned a basket shop. When I last heard from her, she was planning to contact several hospitals with her temporary gift shop idea.

■ *Clinics*. From her own children, Andrea Warner learned that kids want things they have touched or played with. "The true test of a toy is if it can make a child happy when he or she is scared or sick—both big possibilities in any doctor's office," she says. "Parents will buy something that pleases a child under stress, particularly if the child shows great interest in it."

Following this logic, Andrea contacted a clinic in her area and asked if they would like donated toys for their waiting rooms. The only catch was that they had to post a list where their patients could see it, telling who made each toy and how it could be ordered from the craftsperson. The clinic did this and orders began to pour in. Later, when a new clinic opened, Andrea was asked to set up a similar arrangement for them. Craftspeople who donate toys handle their own sales and deliveries, and the items they donate stay donated, even if no orders result. "When you consider that you are getting unlimited publicity for the cost of one sample, it's a good idea," Andrea says. "Well-made items sell well because the parents can see that they are holding up to repeated playing." (See "Craft Cooperatives" below for another innovative marketing idea from Andrea.)

■ *Retirement centers*. Joyce Roark has found a terrific way to sell her custom-made jewelry. Her sales increased by 400 percent the year she raised her prices and began to sell her products at senior living retirement centers (not nursing homes).

"The people I sell to have difficulty going shopping," she explains. "They tire easily and they fear being knocked down by kids running in the stores and malls. The retirement centers furnish me with tables and advertising, and do not charge me a fee. I am only there for a couple of hours."

The products Joyce has developed for this market include decorated mini tote bags for room keys, bingo money and other items, tissue holders for the pocket, eyeglass cases and custom-made jewelry. She makes earrings and necklaces to match special outfits or will modify jewelry pieces owned by the residents. She adapts earrings, changes clasps on chains and necklaces that are hard for arthritic hands to manipulate, and cuts pendant chains to specific lengths wanted.

"My customers appreciate the fact that they don't have to spend hours shopping for the right piece of jewelry," says Joyce. "They bring their outfit to me and if I don't have something already made, I will customize a piece for it at no extra charge. People repay me by purchasing more of my products."

The first time at a facility, Joyce may realize about $50 in sales. Each time she returns, however, her sales increase, and she eventually makes at least $200 in that two-hour period. "Once people get to know me and my merchandise, they are repeat customers," she says.

This idea has proven so popular in Joyce's area (Baton Rouge), that she has been asked to return to these facilities from October to December so residents can do some of their Christmas shopping. Because those with arthritic hands have a hard time wrapping gifts, Joyce began to offer a selection of paper and ribbon and a gift-wrapping service. This led to invitations to offer the same service in nursing homes.

Selling Crafts on a Military Base

If you happen to live on a military base, here is an idea that might work for you. While in West Germany, Denise Hall found jobs to be scarce. When she looked to crafts to earn some extra money, she also found a way to provide a profitable service to the community. After learning there was no consignment shop in the area, Denise suggested the idea of a craft shop to the manager of the local thrift shop run by Army Community Services. Since there was no shopping center on the army post, she was given some space within the hospital.

To generate interest in The Craft Boutique, Denise ran ads on the local

American radio station and distributed flyers in apartment buildings. The shop began with only six consignors selling off a table in the hospital corridor one day a week. As more consignors brought in merchandise, the Boutique was given longer hours and a room of its own. In time, this idea proved so successful that a second consignment shop was established to serve more than a hundred crafters in the area.

"The volunteer association that runs the shop retains 17 percent of the sales price of merchandise," Denise explains. "This money pays expenses and purchases things for the hospital and the entire military community that cannot be purchased with government funds. The other 83 percent of the sales price goes to consignors, most of whom are military spouses."

Pushcart Merchandising

If you are a prolific crafts producer who yearns for a shop of your own but can't afford the high investment of a retail shop or the time it would take to run it, pushcart merchandising is an idea you might consider.

"Many shopping malls offer attractive pushcarts or other structures on a temporary basis and are willing to strike deals with artists and craftspeople," says Gail Bird of Patchogue, New York, "but this kind of retailing is only for those who can produce in limited volume." Gail has been selling her line of Russian Punchneedle Embroidery and supplies this way since 1980 and she has shared her success secrets in a self-published book titled *Cart Your Way to Success*.

This kind of retailing is an interesting and more profitable alternative to wholesaling because the seller as a part-time shopowner keeps a greater percentage of the profits and can test market the line directly to the consumer. Its advantage over marketing through a craft mall or rent-a-space store is that more merchandise can be moved in a shorter period of time because you're not competing for attention with other sellers, and your customer doesn't have to walk through a door. (Impulse items and demonstrations are very helpful.) The rent on a pushcart is usually higher and is based on the number of daily potential buyers that pass by your business each day. Before you take this kind of financial risk, be certain that your products are appealing to the thousands of people who regularly visit shopping malls. A good track record of sales success at craft fairs, malls or shops is one indication that you might do well with your own pushcart in a busy mall.

The nice thing about pushcarts is that they can be rented for one week, two weeks or a month once or twice a year. How much merchandise would you need to sell this way? Gail suggests that, to sell $3,000 worth of products a week, you would need about $5,000 worth of inventory. She says one of the secrets to success in this kind of retailing is knowing how to negotiate a pushcart lease with the temporary tenant leasing manager. "There is no temporary tenant organization (networking or help) for the pushcart/kiosk industry, so all leasing agencies have different rules and rental fees," she says. "One big problem usually is that the leasing manager is an entry level position of a large leasing organization, and the turnover in this job is rapid because everyone wants to move up the corporate ladder as quickly as possible. You spend time and energy developing a good working relationship with your leasing manager only to find a new one in his or her place the next time you go in."

For this kind of retailing to be profitable, your lease costs (rental) should not be more than 10 to 15 percent of gross sales, Gail advises. Thus, if your goal is to sell $6,000 worth of goods over a two-week period, you should pay no more than $900 total in rent, including percentage. "Avoid renting a pushcart over the Christmas holidays unless you can triple your sales because the rent usually triples at that time," says Gail. "Leasing agents have a standard rental fee, but they are not set in stone. If you have the right product mix they are looking for and you have your facts and figures at hand, you can usually negotiate with them. You'll have some leverage if you act like you know what you're doing."

Craft Cooperatives

Some artists and craftspeople have established craft cooperatives to pool resources for buying supplies at wholesale, but most cooperatives have a marketing goal. Some cooperatives are loosely structured with a simple set of rules established by individual members while others take the form of a nonprofit organization. The following ideas will give you and fellow artisans some guidelines on how to band together for mutual benefit.

■ *Enter Fairs as an Organized Group*. A few years ago, I learned of a group of six craftswomen who formed a cooperative so they could get supplies at lower prices and do craft fairs as a group. They said they never had any problems in gaining entry to a show because each seller presented her work individually. They did as many as eight shows a year, including their own Christmas boutique in December. At shows, they mixed their work to create an old-fashioned store image. A large sign, country painted with the name of their group, was prominently displayed on an artist's easel. Each seller, who offered country items that did not compete with others in the group, wore an apron with the name of her business either embroidered or painted on it.

Here is the strategy these women used to sell to customers at a fair. A designated "catcher," would stand in front of the exhibit to welcome customers and assist them in making a selection. Her job was to emphasize product benefits while providing interesting tidbits of information about the artist or her technique. Of course, customers loved this kind of attention. When a sale was made, the "writer" would take over to write the sales ticket and get the buyer's name and address in a guest book. In the meantime, the "wrapper" was busy packaging the item. Enclosed with each purchase were the business cards of each seller and a flyer about the craft group.

This cooperative idea worked well for four years. When new members were added to the group, personality clashes began to occur, and the six who started this cooperative decided to go back to selling solo.

■ *Open a Cooperative Crafts Shop in a Small Town.* One of the most inspiring stories that ever came my way was the story of how a group of craftspeople in a sleepy little village in the Midwest turned one failing business into twenty-five successful ones. In Holly, Michigan, post-recession years had taken their toll, with many businesses closing. One craft supply shop, "Bobbie's Hobbies," would have become just another sad statistic if not for the fact that when Bobbie hung out a for-sale sign, friends suggested she rent some space to local crafters while waiting for the shop to sell. It seemed like an idea that would at least help cover the shop's overhead for a while. This was in 1987.

There were only six people renting space at first, but by the end of 1988, twenty-five artisans had filled the shop with their arts and crafts and there was a waiting list of others who wanted to rent space. The for-sale sign came down and a new sign, "Bobbie's Shop of Shops," went up.

The group worked up a detailed set of rules and business practices by which the cooperative would operate. Bickering and discontent seems to be the norm in any new organization, and it didn't take long for this group to realize there could be only one boss. As the owner of the shop, Bobbie was appointed. She had the final say regarding approval of incoming sellers and merchandise and she acted as a juror when disputes arose between sellers. She also had complete control over the financial responsibilities and operations of the shop, paying bills, making bank deposits and balancing the register each day. Sellers could pick up their earnings on a weekly or monthly basis. She provided insurance on the building, but individual sellers were responsible for insuring their own merchandise against loss.

In later years, this job has been turned over to a new manager. Today, the cooperative has less than twenty members, but only because some members have rented extra space in the store. New members can't get into the co-op until space opens up in the shop. To serve other crafters looking for a sales outlet, however, a second sales area was opened. Here, crafters pay a flat rental fee to bring in an assortment of merchandise the shop can display as it pleases.

Because the community of Holly has a historic hotel, an old-fashioned soda fountain and a growing number of both antique and craft shops, it attracts its share of tourists. Two annual festivals also draw many visitors. This traffic, added to what the shop draws through its own advertising efforts, has made this cooperative shop a great success.

Perhaps you can become the catalyst to organize a cooperative crafts shop in your town. "The wonderful part of the whole setup," say crafters, "is that we share a camaraderie as crafters and artisans, hoping each of us will succeed. Those with small children have the freedom to work at home while marketing merchandise downtown. Each day brings personal growth and a sense of contribution to society and community."

■ *Open a cooperative crafts shop in a shopping mall.* Here's another example of how one thing leads to another. The Laurel Tree is a craft cooperative located in a shopping mall in Butler, Pennsylvania. "Our shop was born from a craft show in the mall," writes co-op member Rosemary Smith. "After our town was hit by numerous job losses, the mall had a few empty spaces. When the craft show was over, the mall manager approached a few of the crafters and asked them if they would be interested in staying in one of the empty stores for a while longer. As it turned out, 'a while longer' never ended. I joined the group when I heard they were looking for more crafters to share the responsibilities."

Because Pennsylvania doesn't recognize anything but agricultural cooperatives, the group decided to incorporate as an S-Corporation. Stock is sold and each owner puts in $50, an amount that is refunded if they leave the co-op. The number of owners is limited by S-Corporation law, but as long as there are openings in the co-op, an individual can join the corporation. There is a board of directors, a store manager and committees to do everything from screening to cleaning. Co-op members are required to work so many hours a month in the store and they pay back 20% of their sales to the store to provide working capital. Individuals who want to sell in the store but not take an active part in the cooperative are welcome to sell on a 60/40 consignment basis. If they wish to work in the store, however, they can keep up to 75 percent of their sales. The store usually has 15 to 20 consignors.

"We have not been without our problems," Rosemary says. "We had to devise our own forms, a bookkeeping system to handle craft sales, a work schedule for over twenty people, a co-op agreement that would satisfy everyone, a wholesale ordering system and numerous other procedures that needed to be tailor-made to fit an organization with so many people. It took a while for us to think of ourselves as a unit, but because of the desire and commitment of the women we have managed to work out our problems and move on. We have learned to give and take to make the store successful. The name of our store is The Laurel Tree, and a real tree stands in the middle of our store. From the roots of cooperation and the sturdy trunk of hard work, the branches of friendship have grown to produce an opportunity for each of us to achieve what we could not have done alone: own our own craft store."

■ *Crafts on display in a restaurant.* One of the most innovative marketing ideas I've come across was reported to me several years ago by Andrea Warner in Santa Maria, California (mentioned earlier in the clinics section). She conceived the idea of a unique crafts marketing cooperative that helped many talented people in her area realize greater sales. I included the following information in a self-published book that had limited sales and is now out of print. Because the idea is still timely, I want to share it here with a wider audience.

Noticing that a new restaurant had some terrific display space in its window and a lot of blank space on its walls, Andrea contacted the owner and ultimately arranged for changing displays of fine craftwork that could be purchased by restaurant patrons on a custom-order basis. She emphasized that the restaurant owner would not only save money on decorating expenses but make money by renting space to local artisans. No special permit was needed since goods were merely being displayed, not sold. All the restaurant owner had to do was buy insurance to cover the merchandise on display. (Andrea said that when the insurance agent came by to write the policy, he left with $300 worth of crafts.)

Here is how the co-op worked. Co-op members were given a number as they joined, and these numbers were rotated so everyone had an equal chance for space for periods of three months at a time. "Space" included two large windows in the front, walls and some floor space. Twenty people were allowed wall space, and ten were allowed floor space. Each paid a flat monthly fee for each item displayed, paying three months in advance. These fees were taken by the restaurant owner, who used it for extra advertising and insurance on items displayed.

Displays were changed the last Sunday of the third month, and everyone had to come in at a certain specified time to remove their displays so the next group could get set up. Neither the restaurant owner nor his waitresses did any selling. Instead, craftspeople simply hung a framed 3" x 5" card near their work giving price and availability information, telephone and address. Interested buyers jotted down this information during lunch or dinner and dealt directly with the craftsperson thereafter. A deposit of 25 percent was requested on all custom orders with balance due on delivery of merchandise.

This idea was an immediate hit with restaurant patrons. Business boomed as soon as people learned there was a place in town where they could have lunch and shop at the same time. Doctors, lawyers and other business people, to whom time is money, especially appreciated this kind of shopping service.

Local craftspeople saved money by paying a flat fee per month, rather than a commission on every item sold through local consignment shops. They made more sales with less effort, increased their visibility in the community and enjoyed some control in how their work was displayed and sold. Several members of the co-op got enough orders to keep them busy for months after their initial display, and two of them got enough business to enable them to cut down on their outside work and spend more time on craft production.

The co-op was forced to disband a couple of years later when the restaurant was sold to someone who had no interest in this idea, but it had a lasting effect on the community. Before its formation, local consignment shops were taking 45 to 55 percent of sales and charging insurance fees and penalties for too-low monthly sales. The success of the co-op forced them to lower their fee to 25 percent to compete for the quality items they wanted for their shops. In time, most switched to renting display space instead of charging commissions, which resulted in greater profits for the shop and increased sales of crafts whose prices could now be lowered.

I think this idea would work in many communities today, particularly in smaller towns that lack a good gift or handcraft shop. It might even fly in larger, more affluent communities because of the special advantage it offers to busy people who have no time to shop.

Ten Low-Cost Marketing and Promotional Ideas

One of the most common ways to get publicity locally or nationally is through press releases sent to the media, but few artists and craftspeople ever take the time to master this type of marketing. It's a topic worth studying, however, because through publicity it is possible to get advertising that would normally cost thousands of dollars. More important, publicity in the right place can generate hundreds or thousands of dollars' worth of business. When you're ready to explore the art and craft of writing press releases, read one or more of the books on the recommended reading list in this chapter. Meanwhile, here are ten other simple publicity strategies you can use to build word-of-mouth advertising and increase your local visibility.

"Thank You" Sheet Brings Business

Whenever she sells her originally designed paper earrings or holiday ornaments, Alberta S. Johnson always gives customers a special "Thank You" sheet designed to increase word-of-mouth advertising. Specifically, she offers them a 15 percent discount off the next purchase if they will send her the names, addresses and phone numbers of five to ten friends or relatives. Then she gives the customer further incentive to do this by offering an additional 15 percent credit on total sales that may come from these referrals. To further qualify the new leads, Alberta asks her customers to check with their friends first, to make sure they really want to receive such information. She then authorizes the customer to offer her friends a 10 percent discount on their first purchase.

"This sheet not only lets my retail customers know that I appreciate their business, but also rewards them for telling their friends about me," says Alberta. "So far, I've generated nearly 40 related sales this way. One Thank You sheet brought me several hundred dollars' worth of business when a customer passed it on to a friend who booked a home party that led to a second party later."

1. Talk It Up

Talk is not only the cheapest marketing strategy you can use but often the most effective way to advertise a business. You begin by talking and soon others begin to carry the word for you. It's called word-of-mouth advertising and in time the benefits can be enormous. To get this ball rolling, tell your friends, family and small business associates about your crafts business. Give them a couple of business cards, flyers or brochures, one to keep, one to pass along to a friend. (Do not, however, load people down with a big stack of printed materials.)

Your friends will be the first to buy from you, especially when you give them one of your handmade creations as a gift. By including a brochure with your gift, you let them know that you can help them solve their own gift-giving needs in the future. Recently, when I gave a friend one of my tiny teddy bears for Christmas, she said she would love to buy several for Christmas gifts if I had time to make them. I found it amusing that, without even trying, I was back to selling my crafts again.

2. Ask for Referrals

Make it easy for your satisfied customers to help you get more business. Each time they refer you to someone who places an order, you might thank them by sending a 10 to 20 percent discount coupon they can apply to their next order.

Also consider the idea Carol Starr uses for her Starr Gift Basket business. Each time she wants to say "I want your business" or "Thanks for your business," she sends customers a mug imprinted with her company name. It contains a small package of gourmet coffee, tea bags, one wrapped cookie and some chocolate reception sticks. "I wrap it fancy, Starr gift basket style," says Carol. "It's inexpensive and everyone loves receiving a gift. The good will and repetition of business have been outstanding. It also gets your foot back in the door after the first call or order."

3. Work Cooperatively with Other Craftspeople

"Try to get other craftspeople who sell things different from yours to show your projects, and vice versa," says Stewart Madsen. "Keep a supply of each other's business cards on hand. For example, I have two paintings in my workshop by an artist who has one of my larger dolls in his studio. We send each other business all the time."

4. Show and Sell Your Products at Work

A nurse told me she sold hundreds of dollars' worth of jewelry every month to nurses and doctors in the hospital where she worked. Several crafters have told me how they make sales simply by taking samples of their crafts to work with them and showing them to fellow workers during coffee breaks or lunch hours. A friend or family member may also help you sell by taking a sample product to work with them. "Never underestimate the power of family and friends as promoters of your product or service," says Cheri Lynn Gregory. "My dad has sold my gift baskets at his office and several friends now send me customers, earning discount coupons for themselves."

In talking with Susan Young, who worked for a Fortune 500 company for ten years, I learned that so many office workers are selling products on the side these days that it's a wonder any work is getting done. "Somebody was always selling something in my office," she says, from Avon, Shaklee and Tupperware products and Longaberger Baskets to jewelry and handpainted clothing. Everyone with children in school sells things to raise money for special school projects, from wrapping paper and ribbons to oranges and grapefruit to Girl Scout cookies."

Donate Something for a Raffle

When Stephanie Heavey became aware of the Quasquicentennial (125) Celebration in her city, Palatine, Illinois, she designed a special doll named "PalaTINA" and offered it to the centennial committee for promotional purposes. "They were delighted to exhibit her at several events before using her in a raffle," Stephanie reported. "Then the *Daily Herald* picked up on the doll and sent a reporter to do a feature. This generated several calls and letters, which led to sales for both PalaTINA and another doll that was pictured in the article."

—an excerpt from *Homemade Money* by Barbara Brabec

Susan left her high-paying job at the end of 1995 to design and sell crafts full time, and the volume of crafts she sold in her office helped convince her that she didn't have to stay in that job to earn a living. "Four or five times a year, I would take 30 to 50 of what I thought were my most appealing little creations and put them on the credenza behind my desk where everyone could see them," she says. "Within three or four days' time, I could sell $600 worth of crafts without even trying. I began to see that I was really filling a need when my coworkers kept coming to me asking if I could solve a particular gift-giving need and save them a trip to the shopping mall after work." (You may recall reading about Susan's open house sales and little shop in the back yard in Chapter Eight.)

5. *Market to Strangers*

A woman who designs birth announcements always has a supply of brochures with her when she goes out. When she sees a woman who is expecting, she just hands her the brochure, smiles and walks away. This has led to many sales, she says.

Whenever possible, wear the things you make. Some crafters report they have sold jewelry, vests, bags and other items while chatting with strangers as they stood in line at the movies or the bank.

6. *Set up a local display of your work*

Bank lobbies, libraries and other public buildings are a natural for craft displays, especially when they can be tied to a holiday or upcoming community event or are in any way educational. Of course, such a display would include a sign that promotes your business and handcrafts.

7. Donate Something to a Community Event

Having your name mentioned as the one who has donated a special item for a raffle is a good way to get attention in your community and sometimes leads to good orders. A woman who makes personalized towels donated several to a fundraising drive. A child who got one of them happened to have a father in a barbershop quartet. That towel led to $4,000 in sales to a large group of barbershop singers.

8. Donate to a Charity

After reading my advice on how to get publicity, 74-year-old Dessie Durham, who makes sculpted Santas, wrote to tell me how well this strategy has worked for her. Every time she demonstrates her craft at a fair or shop, she draws a crowd by sending press releases to local newspapers and radio stations announcing that she will donate a percentage of her sales to charity. When she donated a portion of her sales to a local shelter for the homeless, the headline on her feature newspaper story read, "Senior helps fulfill kids' holiday wishes."

9. Give a Talk about Your Craft

If you have an unusual craft and the "gift of gab," many groups will be interested in seeing you demonstrate your craft and learning more about what you do. At first, you may not be paid for this kind of speaking, but it's a great way to promote yourself and it generally leads to product sales and other opportunities to speak.

10. Call Your Local Paper

Publicity in the local paper is often as easy as picking up the phone and asking to talk to a reporter. When you do any of the things described in points 6, 7, 8 and 9 above, either send a press release to the paper or telephone them with the news. Because newspapers are always scrambling to get enough news to fill an issue, they welcome human-interest stories and announcements of what people in the community are doing. A mention in your local paper isn't likely to bring you much business, but it sends an important signal to people in your community who may do business with you in the future. It also gives you a great ego boost and a wonderful clipping for your scrapbook.

It pays to read your paper carefully, noting its special columns. A dollmaker who took my suggestion about sending a press release to her local paper got her unusual "Karrott Top Tots" featured in her paper's "Count Down to Christmas" shopping column. She sold many dolls as a result.

How to Get on Television

One year, when rumors began about the possibility of Halloween candy being poisoned, a designer interested in selling her patterns whipped up what she called a "60-Second Crocheted Pumpkin" that held a coin in its mouth. She phoned her local television station to see if they would be interested in announcing this alternative to candy, saying she'd give the pattern free to all those interested. The TV station sent out a video crew and did a 2½ minute tape that aired on the six and ten o'clock news. The station received many calls from people who wanted this clever crocheter's address.

Sometimes the secret to getting local publicity is to get national publicity first in one of the home business or craft marketing periodicals. One of my favorite publicity stories started when I mentioned in my newsletter that one of my subscribers who had a garment business on her farm had found a way to solve her independent contractor problems. A writer for the *Wall Street Journal* noticed my article and contacted the business owner for a few comments he could use in his column. After being recognized nationally in such a prestigious publication, the business owner called her local newspaper to tell them about it. The news that a local business had received national attention prompted them to send a reporter and photographer to her place of business. With a full-page color spread on her business, she became an overnight celebrity in the community and attracted many buyers who never knew about her business before.

Marketing on the Internet

Finally, a few words about the Internet, currently the hottest marketing topic in every business newsletter and magazine in the world. Professional artists and crafters were among the first to explore online marketing opportunities on the Internet's World Wide Web, and you may be surprised to learn that you don't have to have a computer to advertise here. Most of the entrepreneurs who have set up craft sites will design an advertisement for you for a small one-time setup fee and monthly costs of between $20 to $30. Because the cost of electronic advertising is so inexpensive, many individuals and small businesses are now offering fine and contemporary art, handcrafts and related publications and services to the general public. By advertising with toll-free telephone numbers and offering charge card privileges, many crafters may ultimately increase their mail order sales through this type of marketing. As this book goes to press, however,

American Craft Malls - The Professional Crafter (817) 221-1099

Online Service to the Craft Industry

Courtesy of <u>American Craft Malls</u>, published by <u>Phillip Coomer</u>

Check it out!

Now would be a good time to add us to your book mark list, or favorite places!

http://www.procrafter.com/procraft/

This is an example of what a web site looks like on the Internet. When you go to this site and click on the "Sell What You Make" box at the bottom, you'll find Barbara's home page (which is illustrated on the next page).

Barbara's Home Page on The Professional Crafter web site. (Shown in reduced size). Visit this site for detailed information about all of Barbara's home-business books and reports.

few are realizing direct sales. Mostly what product sellers on the Internet are getting is a lot of requests for free catalogs or brochures.

Publisher Renee Chase of Midlothian, Texas, thinks this will change in time. She was the first to simultaneously publish an entire crafts marketing magazine both in print and online, and also the first to establish an ongoing electronic arts and crafts show. She currently manages a 100-page web site called "Neighbors and Friends" that is helping other crafters break into the world of electronic marketing in a comfortable way.

"My move from print publishing to electronic publishing was an accident coupled with serendipity," she says. "In mid-1995, while playing with one of those free disks America Online sends out, I accidentally ended up on the Internet and got very excited by what I found."

Even though she was a computer novice, Renee wasted no time getting her own web site established. She emphasizes that you don't need to be a technical whiz to market on the Internet because there are a lot of people out there who can help you. In fact, Renee is now helping other crafters set up their own home page on her site. In its first three months online, "Neighbors and Friends" (subtitled "The National Arts & Crafts Market Guide"), received thousands of "hits." Here, crafters will find industry news, business and marketing articles, listings of craft malls and up-coming shows and fairs, supplier sources and a bookstore of popular arts and crafts titles.

... s & Friends, The WWW Arts & Crafts Connection

http://www.crafter.com//

Phillip Coomer (whom you met in Chapter Nine), is another Internet entrepreneur in the crafts industry with an interesting web site called "The Professional Crafter." This is an online magazine that features craft business articles by industry experts such as Maria Nerius, editor of *Craft Supply Magazine,* who also contributes articles and a "Tips, Techniques & Tidbits" column for industry pros. You will also find some of my articles here, along with show listing information, craft supply sources and a catalog of products offered by crafters who sell in the American Craft Malls. All crafters, however, can post messages to one another and anyone in the crafts industry can E-mail a press release to the Professional Crafter for inclusion in its "News Wire" department. Other publishers are invited to pick up this information for their own periodicals. In addition, Phillip is currently developing a national directory of E-mail addresses of everyone professionally involved in crafts, from individual sellers, designers and speakers to retailers, manufacturers and publishers. Thus, when you are unable to reach someone by mail and don't have a telephone number, you may be able to get their E-mail address to communicate electronically. Phillip's e-mail address is ProCrafter@aol.com.

As this book goes to press, the public appears to be very interested in browsing online craft fairs, art exhibits, electronic malls and virtual craft shops, but we must wait to see how effective this kind of craft marketing will be in the long run. The fact that hundreds of advertising opportunities exist does not mean that advertisers on those sites are successfully selling products. A study of the Internet in early 1996 revealed that while 85 percent of home shopping network buyers were women, 90 percent of online shoppers were men. Until more women are known to be shopping online, it might be a good idea to advertise products men are likely to purchase as gifts.

The size of the Internet and the number of people using it are increasing every day, and as more Internet advertisers report on their marketing success (or lack of it), I will report on this topic through my "Selling What You Make" column in *Crafts*. Any comments you can share on this topic will be received with great interest.

Recommended Reading

● *Getting Publicity—A Do-It-Yourself Guide for Small Business and Non-Profit Groups* by Tana Fletcher and Julia Rockler (Self-Counsel Press).

● *Homemade Money* by Barbara Brabec (Betterway Books). Includes a lengthy chapter on how to write effective press releases.

● *In Search of Arts and Crafts on the Internet* by Kathleen McMahon (Opportunity Network). Includes online addresses for collectives, exhibits, galleries, museums, publications, resources and retail businesses.

● *Marketing Online—Low-Cost, High-Yield Strategies for Small Businesses & Professionals* by Marcia Yudkin (Plume). Explains how to attract new customers and clients through strategic maneuvering on the Information Highway.

● *Talk Is Cheap: Promoting Your Business through Word of Mouth Advertising* by Godfrey Harris (The Americas Group). Nearly 200 ideas on how to systematically stimulate your customers into talking about your products.

● *Writing Effective News Releases—How to Get FREE Publicity for Yourself, Your Business or Your Organization* by Catherine V. McIntyre (Piccadilly Books).

CHAPTER TWELVE

Your "Potential Opportunity" Box

Offering products by mail is a great way to diversify any homebased crafts business. It's also a near-perfect moneymaker for people who live in rural areas of the country or lack access to the traditional retail outlets discussed in earlier chapters.

What's the most interesting place thousands of people visit every day? I think it's their P.O. Box. Now you may think that "P.O." stands for "post office," but as a mail order marketer, I look at these initials and see "potential opportunity!"

I've been selling my books and reports by mail since 1981, and it still gives me a kick to open our drawer at the post office, see a bunch of envelopes of all sizes, shapes and colors and know that each holds a surprise of one kind or another. On any given day, my mail is likely to include

■ Orders with payment enclosed
■ Requests for information that, when mailed, will bring more orders
■ Inquiries from wholesalers interested in selling my products
■ Personal letters or thank-you notes from satisfied customers who brighten my day
■ Information useful to me as a writer, speaker or publisher
■ Advertising mail loaded with marketing ideas

As I see it, every piece of mail is an opportunity waiting to be explored. Once you begin to advertise and sell by mail, your name and address will be

200

grabbed by companies interested in selling you something. While you may not appreciate all of the mail that will end up in your mailbox, some so-called "junk mail" can be quite valuable. By studying the advertising mail that regularly falls into my P.O. Box, I've given myself a good education in how to write successful advertising copy and design printed materials. I've learned how other sellers like myself market their wares and promote their businesses, and I've gotten ideas for more books than I will ever have time to write.

You may be wondering about whether you can use your home address as your mail order business address, or whether you should get a post office box for your mail. I strongly suggest the latter. If homebased businesses are outlawed in your area by outdated zoning laws, you may avoid problems by conducting your business through a box number. Even when a homebased business is deemed legal, some communities require the owner to secure a "special use permit" to do business. This is something you will have to check out with local officials. A mail order seller once told me, however, that his local licensing bureau advised him to obtain a post office box number for his address "because the post office is in a commercial zone, and that eliminates the need for any special use permit." Zoning matters aside, a post office box address is the best way I know to keep a low profile in the community and discourage drop-in customers.

Analyzing Your Options

According to researchers in the mail order industry, more than half the adult population orders merchandise by mail or phone every year. This suggests that many people would find your mail order offer of interest, too. There are five main ways to break into mail order at the retail level. You can

1. Take custom orders to be delivered later by mail (or another shipping service)
2. Give all retail buyers a copy of your catalog to encourage follow-up mail order sales
3. Place classified ads offering your catalog (or inexpensive products) by mail

In addition to legalities and regulations that apply to any homebased business, mail order marketers must also collect and pay sales tax, something that is no longer simple because of new use tax laws in many states. Mail order marketers must also comply with FTC rules and regulations related to truth-in-advertising and the "30-day Mail Order Rule." (Refer back to Chapter Four for more information on these topics and the address of this government agency.)

4. Offer products direct to consumers through display ads in catalog-magazines
5. Advertise electronically on the Internet's World Wide Web (as discussed in Chapter Eleven)
6. Periodically send catalogs to your customer and prospect list (direct mail)

The kind of printed advertising materials you use will be determined by the number of products you have to sell. If you begin with only one or two, flyers or a brochure should work. Once you have a complete line of products, a multi-page, stapled catalog will enable you to do a better selling job and will also build customer confidence in your company.

As I stress in the following chapter, the quality of your printed materials will have much to do with the kind of response you will receive from mail order buyers. A flyer, brochure or catalog that is poorly designed or printed suggests that the products being offered for sale are not of high quality either. Some handcrafts have to be presented photographically (preferably in color) to sell well by mail, but many common items familiar to consumers can be sold with line drawings if the artwork and overall printing of the catalog are of high quality. Such items include:

- Teddy bears and dolls
- Wooden toys and decorative accessories
- Sweatshirts and bags
- Christmas ornaments
- Gift baskets
- Handmade soap and candles
- Dried items such as grapevine or pine cone wreaths.

If you can offer your art or craft at wholesale prices (a topic I can only touch on in this book), you may find it surprisingly easy to market by mail to out-of-state shops and stores. If you cannot wholesale your crafts or you simply lack ideas for things you might sell, think about related products or services that could be offered to individual buyers by mail, such as:

- Originally designed patterns or design books
- Newsletters, directories or how-to booklets
- Greeting cards, calendars and calligraphy products
- Hard-to-find supplies and materials or kits
- A craft or needlework-related service
- Craft business or marketing information
- Audio or video tapes
- Crafty food items, such as home-grown nuts, jams, candy or seasoning mixes and blends
- Seasonal items, such as holiday decorations or party favors

Mail Order Brainstorming

Now that you have some general mail order guidelines under your belt, it's time to get specific. To brainstorm for products you might offer by mail, answer these questions:

1. **What do you make that is unusual** (not readily available elsewhere) but not so unfamiliar that people would hesitate to buy it? (People won't buy a product by mail if they don't understand what it is or why they need it.) Exclude from your list any product consumers are likely to find at a local crafts fair, boutique or craft mall.

2. **Which of your products "go together"** (made from a common material or themed to a particular style, such as country, Victorian or contemporary)? Focus on offering a coordinated line of products instead of a hodgepodge of crafts.

3. **Which of your products solve a particular consumer need** (gifts, decorative accessories, clothing, toys, etc.)? Also list them in categories under holidays (Valentine's Day, Easter, Mother's Day, Father's Day, Halloween, Thanksgiving, Christmas) and general gifts (birthdays, graduations, baby showers, weddings and anniversaries, etc.). This may help you decide when to make your first mailing or place your first advertisement.

Now look at all the products on your list and delete (1) any that will be difficult to package or are too fragile to travel well through the mail; (2) anything you are unwilling or unable to produce in quantity; and (3) any item whose manufacture is dependent on a single or questionable supply source. (Before you offer any product for sale by mail, you must be confident you can produce enough to fill all orders received, and that you will have no difficulty in buying the necessary materials for their manufacture.)

Building Your Mailing List

Before you spend any money on advertising, pull together a mailing list of every customer you've ever sold anything to, along with the names and addresses of people who have expressed interest in your work but haven't bought anything yet. If you are not already collecting the names and addresses of individuals who see your work at craft fairs and other outlets, you should be. Keep a notebook or tablet in your booth or display area with a small sign that says something like:

> **SIGN HERE . . .**
> **to receive information about**
> **my next craft show and**
> **new products.**

"When you're just getting started in mail order, your main concern is to build your customer base," says John Schulte, Minneapolis-based publisher of *Mail Order Digest*. "Each time you sell something, capture the buyer's name, address and phone number and note what they bought and how much they paid. Then, at regular intervals in the future, send these customers information about your newest products."

Although you can get started in mail order with just one product or service, substantial profits will not be realized until you begin to resell your customer base. As you continue to build your mailing list, your constant goal should be the addition of new products or services so you will always have something different to offer to satisfied customers and others who have expressed interest in your work. If you can't come up with new products and services, try to think of new ways to offer the same old merchandise.

Classified vs. Display Ads

Janet Brewer began selling crochet patterns through classified ads in magazines. Her first ad cost $20, the second $120. For a total cost of $140, she got over $3,000 worth of business in six months. Then she took what she felt was a logical next step. She began to run ads in bigger magazines with higher advertising rates. It didn't work. "I never lost money, but I also didn't run to the bank," she reported. "After spending a fortune on one ad in a national magazine, I barely broke even. The lesson I learned was that higher advertising rates and larger circulation numbers mean nothing if my product isn't right for that publication's audience. I'm back to $20 ads in crochet magazines, and they're still pulling."

Classified Advertising

To attract new prospects for your mailing list, try some of the publicity strategies mentioned in Chapter Eleven, plus a few classified ads. Begin by selecting two or three magazines that carry advertisements for products similar to what you want to sell, then use the "two-step advertising method" to hook prospects. The idea here is not to catch fish, but merely to go fishin'. When you get a nibble (a written request or phone call for more information), send an appropriate response (sales letter and flyer, brochure, catalog, etc.). Answer inquiries immediately before prospects forget why they were interested in your offer.

There is a limit on what you can successfully sell directly through publicity or a classified ad because people won't buy "a pig in a poke." But they may buy from you once you've given them your best sales presentation. Each year for over twenty-five years, I've generated thousands of new prospect names for my mailing list and sold thousands of books and reports in the process. To keep my list to a manageable size, I periodically drop older prospect names that have not responded to earlier mailings. Once you've got a good mail list going, the most important thing is to keep it up to date because constant remailings to your entire list are yet another secret to success in direct mail marketing.

Clean Your List with Postcard Mailings

If your mailing list is even slightly out of date, you can "clean" it (get address updates from the post office) at no cost with a postcard that includes an "Address Correction Requested" line beneath your return address. (If you request address changes on a third-class bulk mailing, you will have to pay extra for these corrections.) If you already have a bulk-mail permit number, you can get a first-class permit at no extra charge. The same number can be used for both kinds of mail. Ask your postmaster for details.

In one day's mail, I happened to receive two postcards from small homebased businesses that had previously sent me catalogs. Both mailers said I must respond if a new catalog was wanted. One company asked that I return the postcard. The other asked me to return the postcard with an SASE with 52 cents postage. Although this is an inexpensive way to weed out disinterested people on your mailing list, be prepared to lose some potentially good customers who may simply be too busy to respond to your postcard reminder or annoyed about sending an SASE.

Before automatically deleting the names of people who do not respond, however, try another postcard mailing about six weeks later. This time, instead of offering your catalog again, feature a hot item from the catalog and emphasize new products. Offer a free catalog with purchase or sell it singly.

Seven Classified Ad Copywriting Tips

If you've never written a classified ad before, or if your present ads aren't pulling well, the following copywriting tips will save you money and help you generate a greater response.

1. *Keep your ad short* (20 to 30 words at most). Eliminate unnecessary words. Instead of writing, "Here's a wonderful way to store and carry all your needlecraft supplies," say instead: "Stores and carries needlecraft supplies efficiently." (Without changing the meaning, you've cut the ad cost in half while strengthening your product's benefit to the customer.)

2. *Offer only one product per ad.* Don't try to sell six kinds of potpourri, each at a different price, then ask customers to specify order numbers, add sales tax, or include $3 for postage and handling. Any reader who made it this far would probably be too confused to order. However, anyone interested in potpourri would probably respond to a simple ad that states: POTPOURRI "Scentsational" sample and catalog, $1.

SASEs: Good Idea or Not?

"SASE" stands for "Self-Addressed Stamped Envelope." While an SASE or small handling charge will help offset the cost of advertising, it also diminishes ad response. Some people won't respond if they have to bother with taping coins to a card or enclosing an SASE. Yet the advantage to the seller in asking for an SASE or some money is that it qualifies prospects and eliminates many curiosity seekers who send for things just because they're free. The person who does take the time to send an SASE or a dollar for information is at least truly interested and more likely to buy. Some mail order novices ask for both an SASE and a sum of money, but if you do this you could cut your total response by 35 percent or more.

Many businesses now charge from $1 to $3 to mail a descriptive brochure or catalog, and most consumers see this as a reasonable postage and handling cost for information. To increase the number of orders for a more expensive catalog, try advertising it together with something else, perhaps a sample pattern, swatch of material or yarn, a tip sheet about your craft, a list of recommended supply sources or a reprint of an informative article you've written. I recall the dollmaker who created a wonderful full-color poster of her product line, then advertised and publicized it for $3. The orders she received for the poster covered her printing and advertising costs and enabled her to get her catalog into the hands of hundreds of interested consumers and wholesalers.

3. *Offer more information*. Don't try to sell a high-priced item directly in an ad. The higher the price of your product, the lower your response rate, unless you also offer additional information. If you can't afford to send free information, experiment with one of these closing lines: (1) For details, send SASE (which stands for self-addressed stamped envelope); (2) Brochure, $1; or (3) Catalog, $2 ($1 refundable).

If you decide to offer a product direct to customers, keep the price under $10 and don't waste ad money on useless words. "Please send check or money order for $6.00 plus $2.50 postage and handling" is a thirteen-word statement that can also be stated in just three words: "$8.50 ppd. from . . . ." With some classified ads costing $3 a word or more, this kind of tight copywriting could save you hundreds of dollars a year.)

4. *Stress customer benefits*. An ad that offers a "Summer Special—Two-for-One Sale" suggests the benefit of ordering now to save money. "Bonus pattern with first order" promises a reward to someone who requests your catalog and

then orders something. "A catalog that solves gift-giving needs" will appeal to people who are too busy to shop, or who lack ideas on what to give as gifts.

In writing ad copy, avoid the use of opinionated words and phrases such as "beautiful" or "You'll love it." Instead, stress words that imply customer benefits, such as "comfortable," "practical" or "lasting." The use of such persuasive words as "save," "new" and "guaranteed" may also increase your ad response. (Note that Federal Trade Commission restricts use of the word "new" in advertising. Generally, a "new" product can only be advertised as such for six months.)

5. *Remember the AIDA formula.* It stands for Attract, Interest, Desire, and Action. ATTRACT readers with an appropriate two- or three-word heading, then INTEREST them by appealing to one of their needs or wants. Stimulate DESIRE for your product by listing benefits to be derived from it, then demand ACTION by telling readers to write, call, send for, order, etc.

6. *Test a special offer.* Try "Free gift for ordering within 30 days," or offer a sample or sampler package for a special price. A spinner who breeds Angora rabbits to make a line of handspun yarns offers her brochure and a dozen samples of lush yarns for a dollar. To emphasize the benefits of her product in her brochure and publicity promotions, she points out that handplucked/handspun Angora does not shed like the commercial Angora imported from China. Sheared from rabbits, the China Angora gives short fibers and flat ends that work their way out of the yarn, she explains. (This is a great example of how to make a product stand out from the competition.)

7. *Analyze the ads of others.* Here is a homework assignment you can give yourself to learn how to write more effective ad copy. Pick a magazine that carries advertising similar to what you'd like to place. Analyze each ad in the magazine, noting things that grab your attention, pique your interest or make you want to reach for your checkbook. Apply to your own advertising copy the same techniques these advertisers are using.

Selling Nationally through "Catalog-Magazines"

If you offer handcrafted items not commonly found at craft fairs and want to break into mail order and possibly wholesaling, try a display ad in one of the consumer catalog-magazines (also called "magalogues") that now showcase American handcrafts. Check your newsstand periodically for such magazines as *Country Sampler, Country Folk Art, Folkart Treasures* and *Better Homes and*

Gardens' Crafts Showcase, which premiered in the fall of 1995. Advertising rates are affordable to serious artists and craft sellers and distribution on newsstands and to paid subscribers guarantees a large national audience. A great benefit of working with such magazines is that you don't have to create your own display ads. Each publisher will photograph your products and create an ad for you based on information you provide. While such ads are designed to generate retail sales up front, many people will want to see your catalog before they order. You may also receive interest from gift shops and other wholesalers, so plan accordingly.

After seeing the premier issue of *Crafts Showcase,* I thought it would be interesting to call a few of the advertisers in that issue to see what kind of sales they had received from their ad five months after it was published. Picking craftspeople at random, I was delighted to find all of them eager to share information that would be helpful to fellow artists and crafters. I was totally fascinated by what I learned from these calls, as I am sure you will be. I believe the information that follows will help you avoid disappointing and costly advertising and give you an entirely new perspective on wholesaling by mail. (Many readers will find this section alone worth the price of the book.)

Hand-Painted Santas

Charlene Cooper had a one-third-page ad that pictured three limited-edition, handpainted Santas for $100 each. Carved from cypress knees, no two were alike, and buyers could obtain them in seven colors and varying sizes. A color brochure was offered for $2.50.

Charlene's product is clearly aimed at the collector market, so she was satisfied to get eight orders, which covered her ad cost. "My ads in *Country Sampler* have drawn better," she said, "perhaps because this is an older publication with a larger following. I am nonetheless satisfied with the results of this advertising, however. People tend to keep magazines like this and may order up to a year and a half later, so I expect my ad to generate additional orders next Christmas."

Tip

If you can afford only one ad to begin with, you might consider offering a unique product in the fall that's perfect for the Christmas season, priced between $30 and $50. If you try to sell anything priced lower than this, you will have a difficult time getting the cost of your ad back. By offering a product priced higher than $50, you may cut your order response in half.

Bargello Pillow and Pottery

Selecting another ad at random, I called Susan Kehr, who had offered a Bargello needlework pillow for $195. Although she also offered kits, she didn't receive a single response to her ad and questioned whether the magazine actually had the distribution it claimed.

To find out, I called Corina Neher, whose ad appeared on the same page immediately above Susan's ad. Corina had advertised a selection of Crimson Apple pottery pieces priced from $10.50 to $29.50. She said the ad had generated more than enough orders to pay for itself, which indicates that many people did stop to read that page of the magazine. "At first sales were slow, but we've received a lot of wholesale inquiries and now the retail end has really picked up," Corina says. "Most people who read the ad and requested a brochure placed good-sized orders. We've found that you have to keep running an ad to make it pay off. We're now in our third year of advertising in the *Country Sampler* catalog, running six ads a year."

Tip

Corina's order response suggests that Susan's failure to get orders was not due to lack of distribution of the magazine, but the fact that the average consumer reading this kind of publication is unlikely to be interested in buying $200 products by mail, especially when many prospective buyers are probably women who needlepoint as a hobby. I can't help but wonder how many needlepointers saw Susan's ad and thought, "Wow! Look what I could get for *my* needlepoint if I offered it for sale." This kind of logic may be one reason why so many display ads fail. The fact that someone has advertised a product at a certain price doesn't mean it is actually selling at that price.

Angel Jewelry

At this point in my investigation, I was curious to know how others had done with ads for lower-priced handcrafts, patterns and kits. When I spotted Carolyn Choate's ad for angel jewelry, I figured that if anyone had done well, it would be her because angel products are really hot now. Surprisingly, Carolyn reported that she had received just enough orders to break even on the ad. She offered four pins with matching earrings priced from $6 to $12 each, and a catalog for $2 (refundable with order). She got more requests for the catalog than sales, but one out of three of these prospects eventually ordered something.

"More important than these retail sales were the new wholesale doors this ad opened for me," says Carolyn. "It led me directly to other people who are now showing my line in wholesale markets in Dallas, Atlanta, Chicago, New York and Los Angeles. The color flyers I use have made all the difference in getting my products into shops across the country."

Tip

Carolyn believes that if you're going to sell to consumers by mail you need an 800-number and the ability to take Visa or MasterCard orders. I agree that your ability to take charge card orders will attract business you wouldn't get otherwise, but the success stories in this section prove that an 800-number is not essential to mail order sales success. Of the nine mail-order sellers interviewed here, Carolyn was the only one using an 800-number, and only Randall Barr and Corina Neher offered Visa and MasterCard privileges. The sales enjoyed by other advertisers prove that if people really want what you offer, they will gladly pay the cost of a telephone call to place a credit card order, or send you a check if you don't take credit cards.

Country Dolls and Doll Patterns

My next call was to Donna Fuller, who has been selling country dolls and doll patterns for five years. She began selling as a hobby, but now wholesales her dolls through a sales rep and continues to offer doll patterns to consumers. In her *Crafts Showcase* ad, she offered an "Apple a Day" pattern for two 14" boy/girl dolls at $6.50 and a brochure ($1 or free with order.) The orders she received did not begin to pay for the cost of the ad.

"I've run ads in other magazine-catalogs and have decided that the pattern market is much harder to break into than the product market," says Donna. "But at least my earlier ads in other magazines of this nature have generated

The Odds Aren't With You

The biggest mistake the beginner in mail order makes is expecting too great a response to their advertising. An experienced dollmaker once asked the readers of a doll magazine to estimate the number of responses they thought they might get from a color display ad in a consumer magazine with a circulation of 700,000. Some thought that one person out of a hundred would respond (or 7,000) while others guessed at least one out of a thousand (700) would order. The advertiser who posed this question went on to explain that when she offered a tested product with a color ad, her response rate was actually about one in ten thousand, or just 70 responses. The three-month run of her ad cost $2,500 and netted $350 worth of orders. "My biggest mistake was to believe that the odds were with me," she said.

inquiries from wholesalers, and this has helped me move into a more profitable area. I've learned that the time of year you advertise makes a big difference in the response you will get. Summer is a bad time for most mail order sellers, but fall is usually good because people are then starting to think about Christmas gift needs."

Tip

With a guaranteed circulation of 400,000 or more, you might think it would be easy to get 100 orders, but it's not. What you must remember is that five hundred advertisers or more may be competing for attention in the same issue. It would take a very unusual product to get back the cost of a $500 ad from a single item retailing for less than $10. Offering a selection of several items in this price range, however, has worked for some advertisers.

Sewing Patterns

The next pattern seller I reached was Diane Williams. She got her start as a pattern seller by advertising in *Folkart Treasures*. In evaluating advertising costs in *Crafts Showcase*, she figured that if she offered a pattern for $8.75, she would need to sell 70 patterns to break even on her ad. "And this covered every penny of the expense of putting the pattern package together," she emphasized. "Response was slow in the first month, but it picked up in the second month, and I ended up with 150 orders, plus some new wholesale contacts."

Tip

Diane's ad worked because she offered consumers a good buy on an unusual set of patterns that were perfect for the season. I've noticed that most craft and sewing patterns today are selling for around $6, with some as high as $7.50. What Diane offered for $8.75 ppd. was a "Little Sweeties Holiday Collection" of three full-size patterns for a 17" sugarplum doll holding a mitten bunny, a 9" gingerbread girl, and a 17" × 20" gingerbread wall quilt.

Country Crafts

Deena Nixon has been selling her crafts for five years at fairs and through open house sales. Because it's difficult for her to do weekend shows, she tried an ad hoping she could expand her business by mail. In her first ad for *Crafts Showcase,* she offered a hand-painted signboard, a paper ribbon/dried flowers heart, and a couple of country wall hangings in three different forms: finished, as a kit, and as a pattern. Initially, sales were disappointing. She sold only a couple of kits, half a dozen patterns and a few finished products, earning back less than half the cost of her ad. Six months later, however, the ad finally paid for itself when Deena got orders from a couple of new wholesale accounts. Twenty people requested Deena's brochure (offered for $1, refundable with order), but six of them "forgot" to send the dollar, which is about par for the course in my own experience.

"Only one out of twenty ordered anything," Deena says. "I think one of the main problems with magazines like this is that many people who are reading them are other crafters like myself who are looking for new ideas for things they can make and sell at fairs."

Tip

Earlier, when Deena tried a similar ad in *Folkart Treasures,* it fared no better. I believe many crafters do buy such magazines to get ideas, but I think the main reason Deena's products haven't sold well by mail is because too many people are offering similar country items at fairs. To succeed in mail order, you must offer products that are not readily available from any other source.

Fabric-Doll Patterns

Rhonda Reichle sold handmade dolls at craft fairs
for ten years before breaking away from this labor-
intensive work to design and sell patterns of her
creations. After two years as a designer, she has 40
patterns in her line and a very profitable mail order
business.

"I felt confident about placing a half-page ad in
the premier issue of *Crafts Showcase* because earlier ads in this type of magazine have proven profitable," she told me. Her half-page ad paid for
itself in less than a month. It featured four whimsical fabric-doll patterns including Herkimer Toad,
Merrie Mothwing (a woodland faerie) and Celeste (the
homeliest and most amusing faerie godmother I've ever
seen). Each pattern was offered at $7.50 each with a
color brochure priced at $2, free with order.

> NOTE: Some ads say "Catalog, $2, refundable," meaning you can deduct $2
> from the total of your first order. You might want to experiment with "free
> with order" and see if it works any better. Rhonda's logic is sound: "Only a
> small number of people requested my catalog," she says. "I think they figure
> that if a catalog costs $2 and a pattern costs $7.50 and includes a catalog, it
> makes sense to just order a pattern to begin with."

In talking with Rhonda, I found it interesting to note that while she offered
patterns only, about 20 percent of the people who called her wanted finished
dolls instead of patterns. She agreed to make them provided she could deliver
them on her own time schedule. (Her dolls retail for around $50 each.) Like
other advertisers, Rhonda got several new wholesale accounts from her ad, making it extremely profitable. By the time her second ad had appeared in the magazine (featuring new patterns), she was getting reorders from many individuals
and quilt shops who had ordered from her first ad. "Once you connect with a
new shop, you can usually count on getting repeat orders on a regular basis."

Birdhouse Clocks

A good example of a product that is different and not readily available at craft
fairs, or anywhere else for that matter, is the clever product Randall Barr has
designed. It is a crackle-finish "Time Flies" Birdhouse Clock that features all-
natural materials that include dried flowers, foliage and mushroom birds. In a

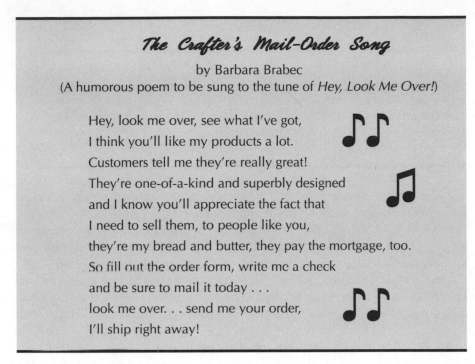

The Crafter's Mail-Order Song

by Barbara Brabec
(A humorous poem to be sung to the tune of *Hey, Look Me Over!*)

Hey, look me over, see what I've got,
I think you'll like my products a lot.
Customers tell me they're really great!
They're one-of-a-kind and superbly designed
and I know you'll appreciate the fact that
I need to sell them, to people like you,
they're my bread and butter, they pay the mortgage, too.
So fill out the order form, write me a check
and be sure to mail it today . . .
look me over. . . send me your order,
I'll ship right away!

quarter-page ad, he advertised this product in three sizes and four different color accents priced from $25 to $54.

"I got my money back from the *Crafts Showcase* ad within ten days after the magazine hit the newsstands," he said, "and I am still receiving orders from this ad five months later. Some of them are repeat orders from satisfied customers."

Of the 75 orders Randall got from the ad, most were not for the lowest-priced item as one might think, but for the two larger and more expensive clocks priced between $48 and $54 (prices that included shipping costs). What I found most interesting about Randall's story was that, like other advertisers mentioned above, the real benefit of his ad in a consumer magazine came in the form of wholesale business. "I would have gotten my money back from this ad from just the retail sales," Randall says, "but the fifteen new wholesale accounts I've gained have made this ad extremely profitable. Many of these accounts placed repeat orders right after Christmas."

In years past, Randall's idea of a big order was a dozen clocks. Last year he had orders for 10,000 clocks, but could only produce 6,000. "We're going crazy trying to keep up with production. Everyone in the family is helping out and we're all working very long hours. It's kind of funny when you think that all of this started because I wanted a little something to do in my spare time."

Tip

If you suddenly find yourself with more wholesale business than you can handle, you may need to hire outside help. To increase his production capabilities, Randall signed a contract with Veterans Industries, a program of the Veterans Administration. In the future, the wood portion of all birdhouse clocks will be assembled by disabled vets, an idea that is very satisfying to him.

In Summary: You may think that advertising in a magazine such as *Better Homes and Gardens* will practically guarantee sales, but it doesn't work like that. While your association with a prestigious magazine will always be good for your professional image, your sales success will depend on how well you have matched your products and prices to that particular marketplace.

One secret to selling successfully by mail is not to follow the trends so closely. Be more creative. Set your prices high enough to yield a true profit but don't overprice them in an attempt to get your ad costs back. If mail order shoppers find an item that is truly unique, they may be willing to pay anything to get it. If what you are advertising is something the average consumer can find at a local crafts fair or shop, however, they won't pay an inflated price merely for the convenience of buying it by mail.

Telephone Tips

Don't advertise your phone number in a national magazine unless you're going to be available to answer the phone. I was unable to reach several advertisers who had placed ads in *Craft Showcase*. In some cases, the phone rang off the wall, and no answering machine clicked in. Once, a young child answered the phone. (Not a good way to impress prospective buyers.) I left two detailed messages with a couple of craftspeople saying I wanted to interview them for this book, but they never called back.

It is commonly known that many home-business owners run a business off their personal telephone line. This is not only unprofessional but likely to be in violation of local telephone regulations. Generally, a personal phone number may not legally be advertised anywhere. Even when you have an answering machine, many callers will hang up rather than leave a message, particularly if your recording isn't professionally done.

Tip

When you prepare a message for callers, don't say "Hi, we're not here. You've reached (telephone number) . . . leave a message," but answer with your personal or company name so callers will know they've reached the right number. Tell them what they need to do to place an order (leave charge card information or their number so you can call them back). Voice mail is more professional than an answering machine, and its great benefit is that messages from several people can be received at the same time.

Prospecting for New Business

Once you have developed a mailing list of interested prospects and satisfied buyers, you should constantly mine it for new business. Many inexperienced mail-order sellers figure if someone doesn't order the first time information is sent to them they will never order. This is not true. You might have to mail a consumer or wholesale buyer half a dozen times before you hit that prospect's hot button. At any given time, only a certain percentage of a percentage of those on your mailing list will be in the "right mood" to consider your advertising offer. Think about how often you have received and discarded advertising mail and catalogs. When it arrived, you may have been at the end of your income for the month, down with a cold or busy trying to get ready for weekend guests. If the same mailing were to arrive at a different time a few months later, your situation would have changed, and now you might be interested in the advertiser's offer.

One mail order advertiser once reported that she never runs ads in December issues because she has found that what is happening in people's lives is directly reflected in her business. "April (income tax), June (school graduations and weddings) and September (school beginnings) have always been slow mail order months for me," she says.

While there are some general guidelines on the kind of response you might expect to your direct mailings, there are no guarantees. Each seller has to do a lot of testing to figure out an average response. So much depends upon how prospective customers perceive your products and how good your follow-up printed materials are.

Industry research suggests that the average mailer may get an order response of only one or two percent, but your response will always be greater from mail lists you develop yourself (as opposed to mail lists you might rent or trade with other businesses). Again, I stress the importance of under-standing basic advertising concepts when you get into direct response marketing. Having a good product or service is not enough. You must also learn what motivates people to buy, then incorporate this knowledge into all your advertising, publicity and mailing programs.

 *Recommended Reading*

● *How to Start and Operate a Mail Order Business* by Julian L. Simon (McGraw-Hill).

● *Mail Order Selling Made Easier* by John Kremer (Open Horizons Pub. Co.).

● *Mail Order Moonlighting* by Cecil C. Hoge, Sr. (Ten Speed Press).

● *Money in Your Mailbox: How to Start and Operate a Mail-Order Business* by L. Perry Wilbur (John Wiley & Sons).

● *Starting and Building Your Catalog Sales Business* by Herman Holtz (John Wiley & Sons).

CHAPTER THIRTEEN

Your Printed Professional Image

Good printed materials make a difference to buyers, but few crafters realize the direct connection between sales and the type and quality of their printed materials.

If you have no printed materials at all, you are telling the world that you're an amateur seller. If your printed materials are of poor design or print quality, prospective buyers may question the quality of your products. For maximum success in selling directly to consumers in person or by mail, you need high-quality printed materials. Besides bringing in more orders, attractive printed materials enhance your professional image, make you feel good about your business and enable you to charge higher prices than the competition.

Since any printer or copy shop can help you prepare materials for printing, my focus in this chapter is on when and how to use printed materials to make sales, get reorders, attract a following and impress buyers. The specific printed materials under discussion are stationery, business cards, hang tags, designer labels, flyers, brochures, postcards and mail order catalogs.

Stationery: What It Says about You

A well-typed letter on business stationery suggests a degree of professionalism and stability no handwritten note on tablet paper can convey. No matter how small your crafts enterprise, one of your first expenditures should be for stationery and matching envelopes. Besides helping you in business, printed stationery

A. *Beverly Durant's stationery is printed in burgundy ink on pale pink paper, just right for her line of angel products.*

B. *Teddy bear maker Jan Bonner uses an original "bear logo" on her stationery, business cards, hang tags and greeting cards, all of which are printed in brown ink on ivory stock.*

C. *Elizabeth Bishop uses her "Seams Sew Creative" trademark on gray stationery printed in black, and indicates her membership in The Society of Craft Designers by adding the organization's logo in the bottom right-hand corner.*

D.

E.

F.

D. Notice how Stephanie Heavey has created a word logo by arranging the word "DOLLS" in an artistic way. She uses light gray paper printed in rose-colored ink.

E. Sue Brown's stationery is a good example of how to combine hand lettering and original art to create a distinctive letterhead. It's printed in black ink on white paper.

F. Barbara Pillsbury also uses black ink and white paper, but has used calligraphy instead of hand printing or typesetting to give her letterhead special appeal.

will make you feel less like a hobbyist and more like the professional craft seller I know you want to be.

Once, when I emphasized in my "Selling What You Make" column that professional crafters should type all letters on business stationery, a reader complained that not everyone could afford business letterheads or typewriters. "Perhaps concentrating not so much on the professional look but on the legibility and correctness of handwriting and grammar would have been more kind and gotten your point across just as well," she said.

While I try never to be unkind, I do have a responsibility to my readers to be truthful, even if the truth sometimes stings a little. I do not see it as kind to let people think that legible handwriting and good grammar are enough when a letter's purpose is to secure supplies at wholesale prices or get one's foot in the door of a prospective buyer. If you're trying to get the attention of buyers and suppliers, you must present yourself as a businessperson, and typed letters on business stationery help achieve that image.

By "typed," I do not necessarily mean "on a typewriter." In fact, typewriters are now considered archaic equipment in most offices, having been replaced by inexpensive computer technology. If you have a home computer with word processing software that corrects spelling and grammatical errors, all you really need are a couple of fingers to hunt-and-peck great-looking letters. Space in this book does not allow for a discussion of why homebased businesses should embrace computer technology, but this topic has been discussed at length in my *Homemade Money* book.

Business Cards: How They Boost Business

The primary purpose of a business card is to help people remember who you are and how they can find you when they want you. Most business cards are rectangular and measure 3½" x 2", but cards used by artists and craftspeople come in all sizes, shapes and colors. Like hang tags (see below), they are sometimes folded. If you want to stand out in a crowd, one way to do it is with a clever or unusual business card. But before you decide on the design details of your card, ask first what you really want a business card to do for you (or *not* do for you).

Because every business book advises new business owners to order business cards, this is often the first printed item an artist or crafter buys. But if your printing budget is severely limited, invest first in hang tags, flyers and price lists. Handing out business cards to everyone who stops by your craft fair display is not only costly but unlikely to generate follow-up orders, says author and fiber artist James Dillehay. In his book, *The Basic Guide to Selling Arts & Crafts,* James reports that in his first two years of selling, he handed out

Business Card Ideas

◆ Want business cards in color, but can't afford them? Diane Molaro's "Country Cozies" business includes dolls, quilts, teddy bears and other handcrafted fabric items. "My card is printed in black ink on tan stock," she says. "During slow periods at craft shows, I use colored markers to fill in the doll drawing to brighten up the card. It's less expensive than four-color printing and keeps me busy when I need a break from crafting."

◆ Here's how to turn a business card into a promotional item. A mail order book seller offers titles of interest to home sewers. She created an interesting freebie by printing a handy Fabric Conversion Chart on the back of her regular business card and laminating the card to make it a practical purse or wallet reference when shopping. She later turned the card into a promotional item by sending out press releases that offered her catalog and the "conversion card" for $1. This brought her many new prospects for her mail order catalog.

◆ Artist Ruby Tobey uses a small yearly calendar as her business card. She has them printed in October when she prints her annual calendar with sketches, then tucks them into all the bags during Christmas sales and gives them away afterward. She says people have commented that they like them because they are handy to stick on the refrigerator.

◆ Stewart Madsen makes custom designed Halloween costumes. When he began to sell, he had his name and phone number printed on actual vinyl black half-masks. He included a couple with each completed costume and told the kids to give them to their friends. That way their parents would know where Johnny got his costume made and could call.

nearly 1,000 cards to craft fair buyers and got no sales, phone calls or leads from any of them. Now he hands out cards only to store owners who give him their card in exchange, and he suggests that craft fair sellers could save money and accomplish as much by making their own business cards using rubber stamps. "There is small expense in the self-made card and a card with an old-fashioned, hand done look is a sales plus, especially at craft shows," he says.

Content Suggestions

Shirley E. Basile agrees with James that business cards are more effective when distributed personally. "People who pick up cards at a fair may look at them when they get home, but forget where the card came from or why they were interested in it in the first place," she says. "For that reason, I no longer put my business cards on my table at craft shows. Instead, if someone asks for a

A — "The Quilted Bear"
Yvonne M. Deshayes
601 Salty Alley
Mt. Pleasant, SC 29464
(803) 856-0889
Tole Painting, Custom Sewing, Crafts, Lessons Available.

B — Wee Folk Creations™
18476 Natchez Avenue
Prior Lake, MN 55372
(612) 447-3828

Dan Carlson	Maureen Carlson
Sales	Clay Artist
Marketing	Designer
Instructional	Teacher
Videos	Storyteller

C — JERI WHITE
Jeri's Soft Sculpture
619-263-4950
Handmade Gifts
Specializing in Unicorns, Rocking Horses & Holiday Decorations

D — Trudy Jacobson
7801 Wade School Rd.
Columbia, MO
65202-9665
(314) 442-5044
Tea Berries ©1992
These cast wood resin designs are each hand painted,
signed and dated by the sculptor, Trudy Jacobson

E — Peach Kitty Studio
by Susan Young, SDP–SCD
The Peach Kitty and Me
We welcome Thee
To Painted Pleasures
and Tiny Treasures
And to Share a Cup of Tea.
Decorative Painting
Exclusively Designed Accents & Gifts
By Appointment
P. O. Box 1202 Madison, AL 35758
(205) 895-0656

F — A. Bean Production
Miniature Clay Creations
by
Anita Behnen
(513) 293-5963

G — Vickie Canham
Creating Classic Beauty
Custom Ceramic Tile &
Fine Porcelain
4445 Roemer Rd.
Columbia, MO 65202
573 442-8033

H — JUST SCARECROWS
By
Phyllis R. Johnson
445 So. Lake
Phillips, WI 54555
715-339-3312

An originally designed business card will speak volumes about you and the quality of your handcrafts. These sample cards will give you ideas on how to lay out copy, incorporate a business logo, interesting border design or hand lettering in your overall design. To give your card extra appeal, select a colored or textured card stock or print in some color other than black.

A. *Yvonne M. Deshayes' card is slightly larger than standard business cards, nicely printed with black ink on light blue stock.*

B. *Dan and Maureen Carlson's card features their trademarked Wee Folk Creations logo and has raised lettering printed in dark brown ink on a textured, tan-colored stock.*

C. *Jeri White's card is simple, but effective, printed in black ink on white stock.*

D. *Trudy Jacobson has illustrated her card with a picture of two of her products. It's printed in black ink on ivory stock.*

E. *Susan Young uses her Peach Kitty Studio cat design on all her printed materials. Her card has raised lettering and is printed in brown and black ink on tan-colored stock.*

F. *Anita Behnen couldn't find the look she wanted for her cards, so she designed a motif that she could also use on other printed materials, such as hang tags and show announcements. Her card is printed in raised black ink on white stock. During slow periods, she hand-colors the flowers on a batch of cards using red, gold and green felt-tip pens.*

G. *Vickie Canham's card is printed on a pumice-colored stock that has flecks of green and lavender in it. The border artwork is printed in a pale green and the center text is printed in lavender.*

H. *Phyllis Johnson has sketched two of her scarecrow dolls to illustrate her card, which is printed in brown ink on tan paper.*

---

card or shows real interest in an item but may not buy that day, I offer them a card. On the back I write the show or location and the item and price (when I'm sure the price will not be changing). This has been very successful for me, and I get a high call-back rate this way."

One crafter told me that she omitted the address from her business card because many people thought nothing of just dropping by her home to see if she would let them in to see what she had for sale. "This interfered with my work schedule and all that visiting proved to be very wearing," she said. Artists who work with gold, silver and other precious materials rarely put their home address on a card because they don't want to invite thieves to their home. It's a mistake, however, to print your telephone number without an area code. You may exhibit only at local shows, but many people outside your area may attend such shows.

If you invite wholesale inquiries when you do a retail crafts fair, you might consider using a photo business card. A homebased photographer told me about her friend who scouts for new mail order products at shows and fairs, saying: "She complains that she has to write product descriptions on the backs of business cards, but even then she can't always remember the products. Business photo cards would be an excellent visual marketing tool for wholesale buyers like her."

Hang Tags: Great Image Tools

As consumers, we have all been educated to read hang tags and labels on commercial merchandise because it is here that we find the designer's or manufacturer's name, guarantee, care instructions and other special features of a product. It makes sense, then, that handcraft buyers also look for and appreciate the special tags and labels on handmade products. Many buyers think a product is worth more simply because it carries this professional touch, so a tag that costs only a few cents could enable you to raise the price of your handcrafted items by several dollars.

One craft seller told me her sales increased 15 percent after she added hang tags to her products. Other crafters have reported an increase in sales simply because products displayed in craft shops bore an attractive hang tag. You would be surprised at the number of shop owners who browse competitor shops in search of suppliers. When they spot an item they'd like to sell, they look for a hang tag so they can call for wholesale information. Johnnie Kearney of Richlou Crafts told me that her first $99 investment in professionally printed hang tags for music boxes and ornaments displayed in one shop quickly led to $2,000 in orders from other retailers.

Tip

Some shop owners automatically remove tags that include a seller's complete address. That's because they want to encourage customers to buy additional products in their shop, not by mail directly from their suppliers. Thus, on merchandise wholesaled to shops, many professional crafters use tags containing only their copyright information, crafts business name, city and state. Because they have a business telephone number anyone can obtain through Information, this is all that's needed to get additional sales from other wholesale buyers. (The next time you visit a gift shop, check product hang tags to see how other sellers handle this problem.)

Copywriting and Design Tips

First decide whether you will use a simple two-sided tag or one that is folded to reveal four separate areas where art or messages can be printed. Select a size that is appropriate to the size of a product. While miniature items may call for a tiny, one-inch tag, larger items could use a larger, folded tag. (Tags need not be square or rectangular, but other shapes will require hand cutting or extra print shop costs.)

Since a hang tag is an image product, you should incorporate your logo if you have one or use the same special design or typeface used on your business cards or stationery. Use calligraphy, artistic hand-drawn letters or computer-generated typesetting to create a tag that looks as professional as those found on commercial gift items. The copy you put on a hang tag depends on who you are, what you do, what kind of products you make, what's special about them and how they should be cared for. Some products need their own special tags while other products can share a common hang tag. When writing copy for the inside and back of the tag, ask yourself what you would like to know about each of your craft products if you were in the buyer's shoes. Consider such information as colorful details about your business, traditions involved with your craft, special materials used and other things that make you or your products unique.

For example, the weaver who spins and dyes her own wool could mention this fact on her hang tag while the potter who digs his own clay would use that as a selling point. The woodworker who carves only the burls from trees on his property in Missouri would pass such interesting information along to buyers. The dollmaker whose dolls are perfect replicas of antiques . . . the toymaker who sells unfinished products for safety's sake . . . all would use such information to their advantage on a tag.

Printing Tags

Many crafters use rubber stamps to imprint a tag with their logo or address, and when neatly done, this can look professional. (See nearby illustration.) Others make copies on inferior photocopy machines at the local drug store, which looks unprofessional. While such tags may be better than nothing if you're selling directly to consumers at fairs, they are not suitable for merchandise sold through shops. Here is information on how to print professional-looking hang tags economically.

After you have designed a tag, reproduce it several times to fill a page that can be copied. Take this "master artwork" to any quickprint shop or copy center and have tags printed on a lightweight card stock. Choose stock that looks appropriate for the kind of products you make. If you already have your

Hang Tag Tricks

◆ Prior to exhibiting in an art fair, porcelain painter Gaby M. Olson sends a notice to all customers in that area, inviting them to her home for a preview prior to the fair. "My pieces sell very quickly," she says, "and this fact encourages my customers to come and buy before I open to the general public." All of Gaby's pieces bear a gold sticker that says "An Original by Gaby," and when she sells at a fair, she also adds a hang tag (see illustration). But she deliberately leaves the hang tags off the items sold from her home. "After my customers have made their purchases, I send them a thank-you note on classy embossed stationery, enclosing some hang tags they can add to items they plan to give as gifts. I also use this second contact to let my customers know that I will contact them about my next show and when my new line will be available for viewing and private purchase, before taking them to my town's finest gift stores. My customers love this personal contact and I get many repeat orders as a result."

This piece of exquisite porcelain has been individually designed and hand painted. Gaby, an award-winning artist of porcelain painting, tastefully, hand paints each piece with the finest mineral colors available. The paint is fired into the ware needing no special care to guarantee lasting usefulness and beauty.

This piece assures you a unique gift, to be appreciated now and in the years to come.

An Original by Gaby Olson

◆ As soon as Suzi Fox began to attach a hang tag to every item she sold, she began to get reorders from people who had purchased one item at a show and wanted more. Suzi's punched and perforated tag serves a dual purpose. "Although I've included my telephone number, city and state on the front of the hang tag," she says, "I purposely omitted my street address so people wouldn't be tempted to stop by our home. When folded, the inside left side reads 'Thank You,' and the right side is blank. This is where I write a brief description of the product and its price. When the item sells, I tear off this part of the card and keep it for my sales records. My customers go home with the part of the tag that bears my telephone number."

FOX CREATIONS

created by
SUZI FOX

Brookville, Ohio
854-1553

◆ Diana Bush uses her business card as a hang tag. She has designed it so that the left side contains her name, address and phone with the right side reading "Handcrafted by Diana." When folded in half, the card doubles as a tag with blank space inside for writing washing instructions. "I use removable price stickers so the card can remain on the item if it is given as a gift," she says.

◆ A special message on a hang tag can clinch a sale. Beverly Durant, known in craft mall circles as "The Angel Lady," attaches tags to her soft sculpture angel creations that include a little verse on the front and her name and address on the back. The tag on her amusing "Holy Cow" angel reads: "Hi, my name is Sunshine. Sit me in your windowsill. I'll be a gentle reminder to pray. Have you stopped to give thanks for God's Love today?" On a companion item, she uses a tag that says "I'm a little angel from Hog Heaven. God sent me here to root just for you." After buyers discover Beverly's products in a crafts mall, they often order additional items by mail.

stationery and cards, use the same colors and type styles on your hang tags so all your printed materials have a coordinated look. If copies are printed on a commercial photocopy machine rather than by the offset process, cost may run no more than five to twenty cents a sheet depending on type of stock selected. To save money, buy an inexpensive paper cutter and cut the hang tags yourself. Punch holes, add a nice cord, and you've got a great selling tool for just pennies apiece.

Designer Labels: An Impressive Sales Aid

I have previously discussed labels that are required by law on textile products and items made of wool (see Chapter Four). Designer labels are something extra you can add to impress buyers of such handmade items as garments, toys, teddy bears and decorative accessories. They convey a professional message that a product has been exclusively designed, is one-of-a-kind, one in a

ID # LC
Item # 92
Description:
Scented Country Doll

Price **$6.95**

**Country
COLEction**
LINDA COLE

Phone 507/223-5946
**Route 3, Box 133
Canby, MN 56220**

Linda Cole's hang tag is perforated. When she sells an item, she tears off the price section (left side) for herself and the address section is included with customer's purchase. "The left side of the tag provides an inventory record for me when I get home from a show," she says. "I use a pricing fabric gun to attach tags, and the needle on that puts a hole in the tag itself. By using these tags I don't have to take the time at a show to write out a sales slip."

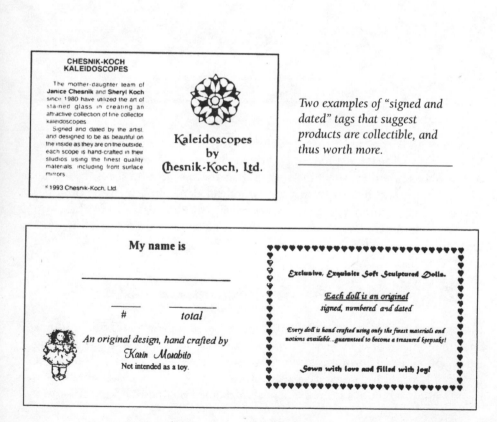

**CHESNIK-KOCH
KALEIDOSCOPES**

The mother-daughter team of **Janice Chesnik** and **Sheryl Koch** since 1980 have utilized the art of stained glass in creating an attractive collection of fine collector kaleidoscopes.

Signed and dated by the artist and designed to be as beautiful on the inside as they are on the outside, each scope is hand-crafted in their studios using the finest quality materials, including front surface mirrors.

© 1993 Chesnik-Koch, Ltd.

**Kaleidoscopes
by
Chesnik-Koch, Ltd.**

Two examples of "signed and dated" tags that suggest products are collectible, and thus worth more.

My name is

_____

*total*

An original design, hand crafted by
Karin Morabito
Not intended as a toy.

Exclusive, Exquisite Soft Sculptured Dolls.

Each doll is an original
signed, numbered and dated

Every doll is hand crafted using only the finest materials and notions available ...guaranteed to become a treasured keepsake!

Sewn with love and filled with joy!

Above: Examples of hang tags that can be created using rubber stamps. The above designs by Sue Brown are from her Wood Cellar Graphics catalog. (For address, see illustration of business letterheads elsewhere in this chapter.)

Right: Sample tags from E & S Creations "Cranberry Junction Designs" catalog.

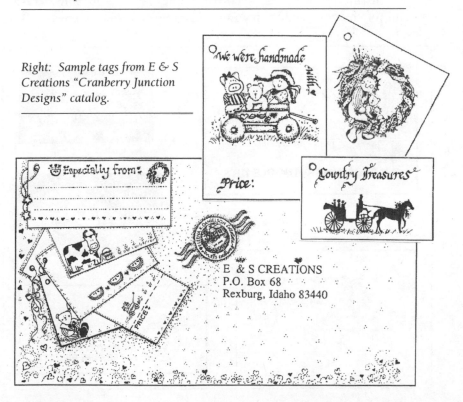

E & S CREATIONS
P.O. Box 68
Rexburg, Idaho 83440

series of collectibles, handcrafted or fashioned by a specific individual. Since consumers have been educated to the value of originally designed items, they expect to pay more for them. Thus, the crafter who uses designer labels can get higher prices than the average seller. As you look for certain brand names when you shop, so, too, do craft consumers look for designer labels they recognize.

"The public loves to see new things, and to compete with the shops, I do things a little differently," says Marla King, who owns Stencil It! and sells designer sweatshirts signed with her MK initial logo. "Satisfied customers often make a point to look for this mark when they return to my booth. To encourage custom orders, I take pictures of all my designs and put them in a photo album that goes everywhere with me."

Several companies will create designer labels at modest cost and in small quantities any crafter can afford. Stock designs are offered, but for a small extra charge, you can design your own label, incorporating whatever images and words you want. (Check craft magazines to find advertisements from label suppliers such as Charm Woven Labels in Portland, Oregon; GraphComm Services in Freeland, Washington; and Widby Enterprises in Knoxville, Tennessee.)

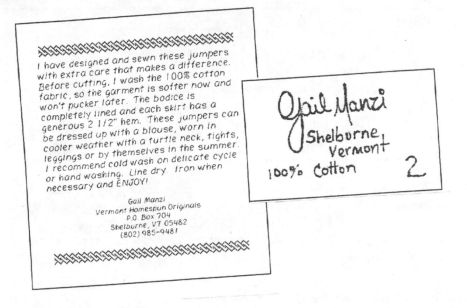

Examples of a hang tag (inside copy) and care label used by Gail Manzi.
The front of the folded hang tag has a rubber-stamp design, and is punched
so a ribbon tie can be added.

If you can't afford to buy designer labels right now, try what works for Gail.
"I cut freezer paper the size I want the label to be and iron it onto muslin,
turning under the edges and zigzagging it all the way around," she says.
"Initially, I created each label by hand using a micron pigma pen (which can
be found at art supply or quilter's supply stores). When this got too time-
consuming, I had a rubber stamp made. I use a stamp pad with indelible ink
that matches the pigma pen so I can write in the size of the garment by hand.
Besides the time and cost advantages, when you do it yourself you can make
only the quantity you need and easily change things when necessary."

Flyers: How to Use Them Effectively

Flyers are not the greatest selling tool, but they are an inexpensive form of
advertising that may work for you. I use flyers when I don't want to waste
expensive printing on a mass audience that may or may not be interested in
what I have to offer. At home-business conferences I have often distributed
hundreds of flyers to individuals without receiving a single mail order in response. What I never know, however, is how many of those people were influ-
enced by my flyer to purchase one of my books in a bookstore.

Flyer Strategy

Karen Willard uses flyers in her direct mail promotions to previous craft fair buyers. "When people ask me where I will be exhibiting next, I add their name to my mailing list," she says. "Every two months, I let my buyers know where I will be selling in the next eight weeks. I always include a flyer and order blank for some special new item or sale item that can be preordered and picked up at a show (or shipped, if they prefer)."

Initially, everyone who inquires by mail or phone about my publications receives my best brochure or catalog (whatever I happen to be offering at the time). When they order something, I acknowledge their order, including a different brochure or individual flyers on specific publications I want them to notice again. This often results in a bounce-back order from satisfied customers.

Flyer Content and Distribution

If you're aiming for follow-up sales, select one of your most popular items, something that is easy to pack and ship by mail or UPS. Make a flyer for that product, including a picture or illustration of it. Also create a descriptive price list that can be tucked into packages along with your special promotional flyer. After returning home, some shoppers may regret that they didn't purchase a particular item, or maybe they now wish they had purchased two instead of one. By including a flyer and order form with every item you sell, you will be encouraging mail order sales.

Tip

Each flyer you create should focus on one or two related items. If you try to sell more than one thing on a flyer, you're asking people to make two decisions instead of one: whether to buy at all, and which one to buy. Make it easy by telling them what to do: "To order, clip and mail the handy order form below." Place the order form either in the bottom right-hand corner of the flyer or run it clear across the bottom. (If you need to include a lot of "sell copy," print on both sides of the flyer and put the order form on the back.)

The right color or paper can increase response. Studies have shown that advertising messages printed on yellow paper generate a greater response than white paper. To convey business messages, a better response may be gained by using subtle colors such as tan, gray or ivory. If you're promoting a holiday boutique, however, try bright yellow, green or pink paper to attract attention. Avoid the use of red paper because black ink on red is very hard to read. Experiment with colors to see if one is more effective than another. Instead of the standard paper colors, try some of the "hot" paper colors that are currently popular.

Tip

There is no sense in advertising if you're not going to monitor the effectiveness of each promotion. To monitor sales results of flyers you distribute, either code individual batches of printing or use different colors for different events. You might also stamp something on the back or corner of the order form that tells you where a flyer was distributed.

To promote an event, post flyers on community bulletin boards, distribute them to groups or tuck them into door handles, but never place them in mailboxes, because this is a violation of postal rules. It is generally a waste of time and money to stick flyers under the windshield wipers of cars in parking lots because nothing you're promoting is going to be of interest to everyone.

Brochures: Good for Your Business

Many craftspeople use flyers with success, but a brochure is more professional, and it will do a better selling job for you. Because brochures are more expensive to print than flyers (estimate 20 to 50 cents each), they should be distributed on a selective basis. When you make a sale, include a brochure to encourage a follow-up sale by mail. Give copies to friends who offer to tell others about what you do. Include them with promotional mailings to the media. When sending a brochure by mail, either to an individual or wholesale buyer, always include a sales letter that focuses on the benefits of ordering from you now. If you have a mailing list of satisfied customers from craft fairs, send them your brochure with a note telling them when you'll be in their area again, reminding them that you have several new items in your line.

Content and Printing

Like flyers, brochures should focus on only one or two related products or services. (To market a complete line, use a catalog.) Brochures come in all

A

B

C

D

These well-designed brochures have been printed on 8½ x 11 inch paper and folded in thirds for mailing in a business-size envelope. If you prefer a brochure that can be mailed without an envelope, print on a sturdy card stock and turn one section of the brochure into a to/from address area.

For her "Gramma's Graphics" brochure (A), Sue Johnson has used glossy yellow paper. The Country Blessing Collectables brochure (B) is printed on ivory stock. Ruby Tobey's brochure (C) is printed on light green paper, and the Quiltworks brochure (D) is printed in brown ink on ivory paper.

sizes, shapes, textures and colors, but the simplest brochure begins with a piece of heavyweight paper or lightweight card stock that measures 8½" x 11" inches or 8½" x 13." The first folds nicely in thirds, while legal-sized paper allows for folding in fourths. Any printer will provide paper samples and show you other ways to fold a brochure.

Always get more than one printer's estimate since prices can vary dramatically depending on a printer's specialty or the type of equipment used. For your first brochure, print as few copies as possible because you will want to make changes to it long before your supply is exhausted. Printers will encourage larger press runs for economy's sake, but beginners who follow this advice are often stuck with thousands of pretty brochures that don't produce sales. By starting with a small run of 500 brochures, you will automatically limit your loss in case the new brochure doesn't pull orders or has to be changed because of a mistake.

Insert sheets can always be added to a brochure to announce new items, but it doesn't look professional to start writing in price changes and other corrections. One way to avoid this problem is to include only descriptive information in the brochure and print a separate price list that will fit inside the brochure (the size of one brochure panel). Then, if prices change, all you have to do is reprint the insert. You'll know it's time to design and print a new brochure when you begin to feel embarrassed about your current one. Since many buyers base their buying decisions on the quality of a seller's printed materials, it's far more expensive (in terms of lost business) to use old materials than to print new ones.

Copywriting Tip

In describing your handcrafts in printed materials, you may sell more if you suggest ways in which your products can be used as gifts. Instead of simply saying, "A great gift idea!" be more specific by suggesting, "A great gift for . . ." (a friend's birthday . . . stocking stuffer . . . housewarming party . . . anniversary or wedding . . . baby or bridal shower . . . new mother or grandmother . . . a crafts collector, etc.).

Paper Suppliers

If you own a computer and a laser printer, you can print your own promotional materials by adding copy to colorful preprinted papers. In the catalogs listed below, you will find a wide variety of papers for stationery, flyers, business cards, postcards, presentation folders, labels, and much more. Call the following toll-free numbers to receive a free catalog from

- ❏ Paper Direct: 1-800-A-PAPERS
- ❏ Queblo: 1-800-523-9080
- ❏ Quill Corporation: 1-800-789-1331

Postcards: A Powerful Marketing Tool

Postcards are inexpensive yet powerful marketing tools that can be used in many ways to publicize or sell products and services. Currently, to receive the lowest rate, postcards must be at least 3½" inches high and 5" long, but no more than 4¼" high and 6" long. If you have a laser printer and occasionally need special postcards, check out the colorful postcard papers offered by the companies listed above. Here are five ways to use postcards as a selling tool:

1. Announce upcoming appearances at craft shows and fairs or new shops and malls that now feature your products.
2. Announce a new product, slanting your message to people who may have special gift-giving problems at the time (i.e., graduation gifts, weddings, baby showers, teachers, Mother's Day, etc.).
3. Announce a holiday special—your best offer for Valentine's Day, Easter, Halloween, Christmas, St. Patrick's Day, etc.
4. Invite people to your open house, boutique or home party.
5. Send a thank you to a valued customer—good image advertising for small businesses. You might remind people that you offer custom design services and can help them solve special gift-giving needs.

Catalogs: Building a Mail Order Business

Once you have a growing line of products, a catalog will make your selling job easier. One advantage of a catalog is that it is a self-mailer that does not require an envelope. Although it will cost more per unit to print only 500 catalogs instead of a thousand, you might want to keep your first print run

A

A. Jan Bonner used this photographic postcard to promote a new line of limited edition "Snow Bears." The back of the postcard described the bears and included her address.

B

B. Randall Barr's photo card includes this message on the back: "The Gift of Time, Handcrafted in USA from all natural materials."

C

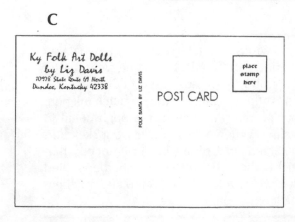

Ky Folk Art Dolls
by Liz Davis
10978 State Route 69 North
Dundee, Kentucky 42338

FOLK SANTA BY LIZ DAVIS

POST CARD

place stamp here

C. Postcards do not have to be in full color to be effective. Liz Davis uses this simple card, which features one of her dolls on the other side. It's printed in brown ink for a softer look.

short. As soon as it comes off press, you're likely to find yourself wishing you had "done this instead of that." Most small businesses use a 5½" x 8½" stapled catalog with 10 to 12 pages, including the cover (five or six sheets of 8½" x 11" paper folded in half). Use a sturdy paper for the cover so your catalog will travel well through the mail.

Tip

Make sure your printer gives you a dummy copy to weigh before you print it so you can keep the weight under one ounce. More than one business novice has printed a thousand catalogs only to find they couldn't be mailed without the addition of extra postage. Also check with the post office to make sure that the size and style of your catalog are acceptable for mailing. In particular, ask which direction the address area must run to meet postal requirements.

On the inside front cover of your catalog, you might write a personal note to your customers about who you are, what you do, and why you can serve them well by mail. A photograph of you working at your craft or selling at a fair would build confidence and probably increase sales. For added customer confidence, offer satisfaction or money back.

Professional photos of your products will also increase sales, but many crafters just beginning in mail order don't feel they can afford the extra cost of photographs, so they use line drawings and artistic hand-lettering instead. To make your catalog less "folksy," use computer typesetting instead of hand lettering. (Most communities now have "quick printers" who offer inexpensive computer typesetting. Just take a dummy of your catalog to them and they'll do the rest.)

Tip

To make your own line drawings, first take snapshots of what you want to picture in your printed materials. Buy some clear plastic sheets (the kind used for photos or business documents) and place your snapshots under them. Using a fine tip black ink pen, trace the outline of your product, adding just enough detail to make the picture interesting. When satisfied with your sketches, use the reduction or enlargement options on a photocopy machine to make illustrations in the sizes desired. For sharper printed copies, take your "plastic art" to a local copy shop and ask them to give you prints on slick white paper.

These catalogs illustrate how to use original drawings and designs for cover appeal. Tim and Connie Long created an interesting self-mailing brochure/catalog by imprinting the back side of a large full-color product sheet with some of their drawings. The Animal Crackers ivory-colored catalog is impressive with a touch of red and blue ink in the bear's ribbons and in the diamond design behind the company name. The Folkart Dolls catalog is appropriately printed in dark brown ink on tan paper.

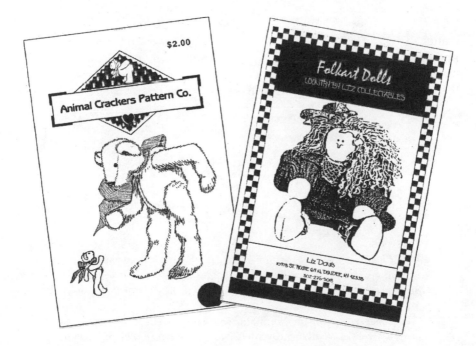

Dear Friends,

In the world of play there is much learning and laughing and loving taking place. These are the nurturing experiences we hope to encourage with the creative designs of our toys.

Since 1979 North Star Toys have been handmade and non-toxic. Mineral oil enhances the lovely color of the woods and allows their natural beauty to shine. We seek to offer you quality materials and craftsmanship at affordable prices.

We are a family business and thoroughly enjoy our work. We hope the toys reflect this warmth and bring pleasure to you and your children.

The opportunity of meeting some of you personally and corresponding with others has been a privilege.

Thank you for your interest and best wishes,

The North Star Elves

Timothy, Connie, Claire and Joan Long

P.S. Please keep our catalog for shopping and gift giving throughout the year or pass it along to a friend. Fewer catalog mailings help Mother Earth and keep our costs low.

617 North Star Route, Questa, NM 87556   (505) 586-0112

The best handcraft catalogs feature a letter on the inside front cover or first page that gives a little story about the company and the people behind it. Often, business owners include a photograph of themselves or their family at work on the business.

This cover letter from the North Star Toys catalog will give you ideas on how to write a trust-building cover letter for your own catalog or brochure.

Christmas in July

Carol Zoffman purchases Christmas cards on sale in the off season and mails them to selected gift shops in early July with a special insert. "On my business stationery, I attach (with gold photo mounting corners) a snapshot of a new product I'm promoting," she explains. "Beneath the picture is a typed description of the product, with dealer price and other pertinent ordering details. New customers have mentioned their surprise in receiving a Christmas card in July, and it reminds them to place their Christmas order."

Make the last page of your catalog an order form the customer can tear out and mail back to you with payment. You will get a larger order response if you can take charge card orders. If you plan to mail more than 200 catalogs at a time, save money by mailing at bulk rates. (Your postmaster will tell you what you have to do to get this savings.)

Finally, will you be selling at retail to individuals only or wholesale to shops and stores? A single catalog can do double duty if you print a separate wholesale price list to tuck into the catalog before it's mailed to a shop owner. In approaching shops, however, it would be more professional to send the catalog in an envelope with a cover letter and a color photograph of some of your best items. If you don't hear from a shop you are particularly interested in selling to, follow up with a telephone call three or four weeks later to determine level of interest.

 **Recommended Reading**

● *The Basic Guide to Selling Arts & Crafts* by James Dillehay (Warm Snow Publishers).

● *Better Brochures, Catalogs and Mailing Pieces* by Jane Maas (St. Martin's Press).

● *Creating Brochures & Booklets—A Hands-on Guide to Planning, Designing and Producing Every Kind of Project* by Val Adkins (North Light Books).

● *Great Promo Pieces—Create Your Own Brochures, Broadsides, Ads, Flyers, and Newsletters That Get Results* by Herman Holtz (John Wiley & Sons).

● *Homemade Money* by Barbara Brabec (Betterway Books).

CHAPTER FOURTEEN

From time to time, we all need to ask ourselves if we are living life the way we really want to, and when that life includes a business at home, the questions become more pointed.

Crafters have much in common with writers. To be a good writer, you must be able to express thoughts clearly, arrange sentences into paragraphs, then smoothly link those paragraphs to create an article, story or book.

This linking process is called "making transitions," and it's like shifting gears on an automobile. Writers who do not take the time to learn how to make good transitions will probably remain amateurs forever, while those who study their craft and learn how to put everything together properly will have the elements of success at their fingertips.

Like writers, crafters must learn to make regular transitions if they are to grow as part-time craft sellers or full-time craft professionals. Sometimes this means arming yourself with new information, other times it means taking a step into unknown territory. Often, it requires a bit of courage that seems hard to muster at the time. One of my jobs as a crafts writer is to help people shift gears at the right time. I try to point them in new directions while offering encouragement, ideas, information and resources.

Shifting gears does not always mean going forward, of course. Sometimes we have to back up before we can go on, and sometimes we just need to idle in neutral for a while. This chapter is designed to make you think twice about whether you want to go forward, backward, or just stay where you are for the time being. Now is a good time to pour a cup of tea or coffee and relax a bit.

Moving From Hobbyist to Professional

I've tried for years to figure out just what it is that motivates some people to move from the hobbycraft stage into the professional world of business, but it's not easy to pinpoint. Mostly it seems to be a matter of things falling into place at the right time or getting the right information at the right time.

"After reading about the successes of others, I'm going to try my luck at my own home business," one of my readers told me. "It doesn't seem such a far-fetched idea to me anymore." Another wrote to thank me for the encouragement and information I had provided, adding: "I'm jumping into the craft business with both feet, going from a hobby seller to a full-fledged home business owner."

Perhaps the biggest mistake beginners make is their failure to buy specific information that could benefit them. They often look at the cost of a book or subscription as an expense they cannot afford. The purchase of business information, however, is not an expense but an investment. True, it's an expense because it is tax-deductible if you're presently making money from your craft, but in truth, information is always an investment in your future. Everything you learn about business today can help you earn more money tomorrow.

If you want to get ahead in life, I cannot emphasize enough the importance of reading and self-study. Reading makes us aware of things we did not know before, giving us a broader perspective on a wealth of topics. Reading is especially beneficial when it forces us to ask questions. Only by asking new questions and seeking answers to them can we hope to keep growing. Phil Jackson, coach of the Chicago Bulls and a bookworm and spokesperson for the Literacy Foundation, puts it this way: "You have to assimilate. If you read, you're letting someone else say something to you. And you have to refute it, assimilate or dispute what the person has brought to your consciousness."

The Secret to Big Profits

Based on surveys I've taken of my newsletter and column readers through the years, I've learned that the average *hobbyist* who sells at fairs and boutiques on a part-time basis makes about $1,000 a year. More aggressive sellers in this category may generate sales of $2,500 to $5,000 a year. While the average part-time *craft business* may gross between $20,000 to $30,000 a year, full-time craft businesses may quickly reach the

$50,000 to $100,000 level. Some of my readers have reported gross incomes of half a million dollars from a craft business based at home.

As I've explained in earlier chapters, people who want to make big money from crafts soon realize that the greatest profits are not in one-of-a-kind craft, but in fashionable lines that can be wholesaled or sold through multiple retail outlets, such as rent-a-space shops and craft malls. Professional crafters must step into the world of serious manufacturing and marketing if they want their business to grow. They will arm themselves with computers and sales reps, advertise with high-quality printed materials and make a concerted effort to learn more about business practices. They will read business periodicals, attend conferences and business workshops, network with other business owners and work hard to stay ahead of the competition. They will stay in tune with the times and check out new methods of marketing. In addition to selling products, many craft professionals ultimately branch out into writing, designing, speaking, teaching, consulting or publishing.

On second thought . . . maybe you've just decided that you don't want to get *that* serious about a craft business. If so, let me give you a gracious "out." You may identify with the crafter who told me that my comments had made her realize the importance of reevaluating herself and her craft ambitions.

"I now realize that I am not cut out to be a producing, selling craftsperson," she said. "Actually, I really never wanted to be one, but my friends and acquaintances sort of pressured me into it. To be absolutely truthful, I hate to part with the things I make, and maybe subconsciously that is why I price everything so high. Everything I make, I love fiercely. Sometimes after finishing a project I can't keep away from it. In the middle of the night I get up and have to look at it to see if it's still there to reassure myself that I really did make it and not imagine that I did."

I've had similar feelings myself, and if you also identify with this crafter, maybe you're not cut out to be a professional craft seller either. There is an easy way to find out for sure. Ask yourself this question: "Do I view my finished craft objects as an expression of my inner self, and therefore find them magnificent?" If you answered yes, that's wonderful! But it also means you're going to have trouble when it comes to selling your work.

Individuals who work at their craft full-time cannot afford to be emotionally attached to the things they make. As craft professionals, they must view their work impersonally, look at it from a commercial standpoint and be able to say that perhaps it isn't perfect after all, that it needs a bit of redoing before it will be a good, marketable item. Until you can do that with your work, you won't be thinking like a professional, and this is important because professionals are the only ones who make sizable amounts of money from crafts.

I hasten to add that you do not have to sell full-time to be seen as a professional. In fact, that is really the whole point of this book. My wish is that even

A New Career at 62

After a 38-year career in retailing with 28 of those years in top-management positions, Gaby Olson retired at 62 and began to look for something interesting to do with the rest of her life. Although she had never painted before, nor even had time for a creative hobby of any kind, she had always been attracted to china painting. When a friend told her about a porcelain fair, she went and was thoroughly hooked on the idea of learning how to do this art.

She began by taking painting classes, then joined organizations and attended seminars to meet other artists, all the while steadily building an extensive library of books on her favorite topic. Within four years, she was buying blank china pieces from all over the world, painting them with her own designs, and selling her work as fast as she could turn it out. Now her art is found in museums and sold at art fairs and to private customers. Some of her specialty items have sold for as much as $280.

Could anyone do what Gaby has done? Yes and no. Not everyone is gifted with Gaby's God-given artistic talents, but anyone can learn art and craft techniques, and I know from personal experience that the process of creating original designs is also something that can be learned by many. Or, as Gaby explains her success: "I believe there is nothing we cannot do if we put our mind to it."

part-time hobby sellers will strive for professionalism in the way they approach their moneymaking activity, make products, keep records, and display, package and sell what they make.

A Little Retirement Business

Maybe all you really had in mind when you bought this book was a little retirement business that would add some fun and extra profit to your life. Great! Let's talk about that.

You may be years away from retirement right now, but it is never too early to start thinking about what you will do when you reach the "autumn of your life." Many older people are interested in starting, or have already started, part-time craft businesses they expect to operate full-time once they retire from the work force. If you're already at this point in life, you may find yourself wishing for additional income to supplement Social Security. Senior crafters who do not need extra income may want a deeper involvement with crafts because they know it will add interest and enjoyment to their later years. Instead of rocking away time in front of the television set, thousands of energetic seniors across the country have something special to get up for every morning, thanks to a beloved crafts hobby.

In summarizing the benefits gained from crafts, a senior crafter explained, "Crafting is therapeutic and builds confidence. It provides supplemental income, keeps my thought processes active and enables me to make new friends." This woman told me she was selling Valentine wreaths, flower arrangements for weddings and special calligraphy documents. She was also teaching a crafts class at a local community service facility, regularly donating small items to a local nursing home for Bingo prizes and making gifts for friends and family.

"I'm slowing down," says a woman in her sixties, "but I hope to leave a few dolls, signed and dated, that might end up in someone's collection. At least I'm not one of those bored people who sit in front of a television set all day. I'm having fun!" Another dollmaker who didn't start selling until the age of seventy-two reported to me three years later that she had her dolls and crafts in eleven states and had just sent $1,000 worth of crafts to a friend who sold them in schools. Stories like this are inspiring to all!

Self-publishing guru Jerry Buchanan once shared this interesting view of ego, creativity and enthusiasm in his TOWERS Club USA, Inc., newsletter:

Gerontologists aren't exactly sure why, but they know that those of us who are artistically inclined . . . driven to create new and original concepts in music, art and literature past the age when the rest of us retire to rest on our oars . . . live decades longer. Perhaps this was the fountain of youth Ponce DeLeon was searching for. To create beautiful and original works is to earn the praise of the multitudes. Praise feeds the ego. An ego that is continually fed is one that generates enthusiasm for the next project. And so, it seems to me that the three form a magic ring of longevity. Ego, creativity, and enthusiasm feed upon each other to form a kind of perpetual motion of the Life Force.

Ten Other Ways to Profit from Your Creativity

Many people with skill in an art form or craft have narrow vision when it comes to making money. Instead of exploring other ways to profit from years of creative experience and know-how, they limit themselves to making products for sale. While this can be great fun for a long time, it can also be physically exhausting. In the life of every serious craft seller there will come a day when he or she says, "Whew! I'm tired of this. There has to be an easier way to make money than this!"

In addition to—or instead of—selling handmade products only, give some thought to the following crafty income suggestions. One or more of them may put you on a new road of discovery, and all of them are less physically stressful than making and hauling carloads of craft merchandise from one show or craft mall to another. Due to space limitations, my discussion of these moneymaking ideas must be brief, but I am now planning a whole book on these topics. Meanwhile, you can get additional information from the books I've mentioned in the recommended reading list at the end of this chapter.

1. *Sell how-to projects to magazines.* Not everyone can write well or design original how-to projects, but history has shown this to be a profitable possibility for many. In fact, most of the how-to projects in leading craft consumer magazines today are created by individuals (mostly women) who were once hobbyists themselves. The editors of craft, needlecraft, hobby and handyman magazines buy how-to craft and needlework projects every month, paying from $25 to $350 per design or project, depending on the design, one's reputation as a designer and the magazine's budget.

After years of stitching needlework pieces for herself, friends and relatives, Lois Winston finally found the courage to present her needlework designs to a publisher. She walked out of that interview with seven assignments in counted cross stitch and was on her way to a successful career. Now well-known in her field, she has sold countless designs to magazines and has published several books and design leaflets. (See sidebar, "Selling Original Designs.")

2. *Design for craft manufacturers or publishers.* Besides selling project ideas to magazine editors, professional designers often work with manufacturers or publishers in the crafts and needlework industry doing pattern leaflets or design books. Some earn extra income by demonstrating at industry trade shows or doing project sheets.

Manufacturers in the crafts industry often use one-page idea or project sheets to help them move their products in shops. These sheets are either offered free to dealers or sold at very low cost. Shops then give or sell these sheets to consumers. If you've done an original project using a particular raw material or commercial art/craft supply item, contact the company that manufactures this merchandise and ask if they'd be interested in buying project sheets from you. Payment for such ideas is usually on an outright basis and may range from $25 to $200, depending on the designer's experience and the manufacturer's budget.

At one time, professional designer Joan Green published thirty-two cross-stitch pattern booklets. As the needlework industry changed and it became difficult for small homebased publishers to get distribution in stores, Joan began to design for larger publishers. Today, she specializes in designing plas-

Selling Original Designs

You don't need to copyright a design before you sell it to a magazine editor, but you need to understand the rights you are selling when you offer one of your designs for publication. Basically, if you sell "all rights" to a magazine editor, you are literally giving them the right to profit from your design in the future, and you can never turn it into a kit or put it in a book of collected designs or anything. Many magazines insist on buying all rights because they want to protect their readers who are likely to make a project and sell it at craft fairs. This may limit your opportunities, but if you're a prolific designer, you might sell only selected designs outright and keep the best ones for your own special uses.

Browse local magazine racks or the library to find specific magazines that feature how-to projects. To learn what individual editors want, request a "Writer/Designer's Guidelines" sheet from each magazine of interest. Rank beginners need not be afraid to submit an idea because craft editors do buy from beginners if they are professional in their approach and offer original designs and projects of the right type. (This means sending typed query letters and project instructions.) Do not send a sample of your work unless it is requested, but do include a couple of photographs with your initial letter.

Editors rarely explain why they don't want a particular design because you're expected to know this through a study of a magazine's contents. Read several issues before contacting an editor to make sure you understand the type of projects they buy, and pay particular attention to the type of supplies and raw materials used in each project. Many editors want projects that use the kind of supplies the average reader can buy in a local craft supply shop, while others may want scrap craft projects or things that can be made from nature's bounty.

Remember that designs submitted for publication must be truly original, not adapted from, inspired by or "lifted" from another source. Although an editor might not realize that your design isn't original, upon publication the original designer might see elements of her copyrighted work in your published project and bring a copyright suit against both you and the magazine.

tic canvas needlepoint projects, working with a dozen magazine editors and eight publishers.

3. *Write a book.* If you've ever browsed the book rack in a shop that sells fabric, needlework or craft supplies, you've noticed the many colorful booklets and leaflets that offer patterns and designs. Other design and pattern books will be found in any bookstore. If you've ever opened one of these books and

thought, "Why, I could have done this," then you ought to contact the publisher to see if they would be interested in publishing your designs.

Your profit potential here will vary dramatically, depending on the kind of publisher you work with (craft industry or trade book publisher), how the book will be marketed (craft and needlework shops or bookstores) and your degree of skill, reputation and ability to negotiate a contract. For "floppy books" normally found in craft and needlework shops, a beginner might be offered a flat fee of as little as $250 for a single design, or as much as $2,000 for a collection of designs. Royalties might range from 5 to 15 percent of the wholesale price of a booklet or leaflet. Trade book publishers who sell mostly to bookstores work with writers and designers on a royalty basis that varies considerably from publisher to publisher.

After reading *Creative Cash,* Starr Steil wrote to thank me for encouraging her to write a how-to book about her hobby, beading earrings. "On my first attempt, and with my first submission, I was offered a contract," she reported. "It is so exciting to have a book of my own! I am now planning to write many others, and possibly produce my own beading kits as well."

After twenty years of designing and making baskets, Flo Hoppe wove her lifetime of experience into the pages of a book titled *Wicker Basketry*. It took two and a half years to write, but its sales success led her to write other books, and now she travels and teaches all year long. Her craft has taken her across America and to foreign countries as well.

4. *Sell your own kits*. Manufacturers have their own in-house designers so they are rarely interested in working with unknown designers off the street. For that reason, don't expect anyone to buy your craft kit idea on a royalty basis. If kits are of interest to you, begin with the idea that you will sell them yourself, either by mail or as a sideline product at craft fairs and other retail outlets.

Over time, this can be extremely profitable. In 1970, when Sue Johnson's "gramma" reached her hundredth birthday, Sue turned to her quilting and the new use of an antique process known as blueprinting to create a "Centennial Quilt." The resulting one-of-a-kind gift featured family photographs printed onto squares. Everyone who saw the quilt wanted to know how to make one like it, so Sue started a mail order business called Gramma's Graphics, offering her now-popular "Sun Print Kits" and related items. (Her brochure is illustrated in Chapter Thirteen.)

5. *Sell your own patterns and designs*. If you have a collection of your own original craft patterns or designs that you're ready to retire (no longer interested in making and selling them as finished crafts), offer them to other crafters who aren't creative enough to design their own projects. This is as easy as

drawing them neatly on sheets of paper and having them copied at a local quick-print shop or photocopy center.

Quiltmaker Lil Golston uses her Macintosh Plus and Macdraw software to design quilts and do drawings for the pattern packages she sells by mail. After printing designs and text on a laser printer, she delivers camera-ready copy to a local printer who reproduces patterns in quantity. When she last wrote to me, her patterns were selling in 87 shops in 32 states and Canada.

Most crafters package patterns in Zip-loc bags, adding an attractive, lightweight cardboard header or cover sheet with a color photograph to give the package a professional look. Such pattern packs make good mail order items and are also the perfect solution for craft fair shoppers who say they'd rather make it themselves. A pattern kit might cost only a dollar to produce, but could retail for between $4 to $8. Check local craft and needlework shops for ideas on how others are packaging patterns.

One of the most convincing reasons to think seriously about selling patterns instead of finished handcrafts can be illustrated in this remark from Rhonda Reichle, whom you may recall reading about in Chapter Twelve: "When I was selling my $34 dolls at fairs, I figured the most I could earn a day was a hundred dollars because I couldn't make more than three dolls in one day. Now that I have a pattern business, however, I sometimes get orders for $300 worth of patterns in a single day, and I spend only two or three hours filling the orders."

Susan Brown doesn't sell patterns, but she has turned her design abilities and love of crafts into a very successful rubber stamp business called Wood Cellar Graphics. Susan has a good mail order business, but most of her stamps are wholesaled to country gift shops and rubber stamp shops. Now ten years old, this full-time business in rural Coleridge, Nebraska, is expanding with a crafts shop and a line of stationery, recipe cards, note pads and hang tags. (See Chapter Thirteen for an illustration of Susan's rubber-stamp hang tag designs.)

6. *Speak professionally*. Individuals with business and craft marketing skills can earn extra income by speaking at art or craft business conferences. Small groups might pay a beginner only $50 to $100 for a short talk, but experienced speakers can command $1,000 or more, so this is worth working for. In my experience, one speaking engagement always leads to another. If you have "the gift of gab," the word gets around quickly.

To expand her homebased stationery business, artist and former art instructor Darla Arni-Bublitz developed a "Kreative Kids" seminar for parents interested in helping their children develop creativity. This profitable idea was based on Darla's beliefs: "Creative thinking does more than produce artists," she said. "It produces individuals who can effectively handle life changes in a positive way."

To promote yourself as a speaker, design a brochure that includes your picture, some background information (your credentials), a description of your talk or workshop and its intended audience. Add testimonials as soon as you can get them. Subscribe to a variety of craft periodicals to learn about upcoming art or craft conferences that might offer speaking opportunities.

7. *Teach your art or craft*. Many creative people have found their niche by teaching their art or craft in adult education centers, at craft workshops or in classes held in their own home. For example, Linda Villa, who creates pressed flower artwork for sale, has expanded her business by teaching workshops on the Victorian art of pressed flowers. "The skills and information about your craft are very interesting to other people," she says. "The fine details and techniques that you perform can be developed into a basic workshop about your craft."

Offering a short one- or two-hour course on your art or craft may soon lead to conducting a series of classes or day-long workshops. Fees vary greatly for this type of work, from so much per student to so much per hour or per day. Contact local colleges and adult education centers for a catalog of programs to learn what's currently offered in your area. (See sidebar, "Teaching Crafts to the Mentally and Physically Challenged.")

Some craftspeople have expanded their businesses by teaching through how-to-do-it videos. After sewing crafts for four years and selling at area fairs and shops, Barbara Carpenter and a friend produced a two-hour *How to Tat* video comparable to a month's worth of classes. Except for organizational skills learned as a secretary, Barbara no skills related to this field. She was willing to learn, however, and she and her partner have produced many other videos since their humble start in 1988. Topics include needle tatting, crocheted tatting, Japanese tatting, quilling, macrame, chair weaving, crazy quilts and paper crafts. Barbara generously contributes to her community of Alton, Illinois, by giving half her video profits to a community center that helps abused women and their children.

8. *Demonstrate an old-time art or craft*. Such opportunities are limited, but they do exist. Large fairs and festivals often hire individuals who can dem-

Teaching Crafts to the Mentally and Physically Challenged

"Three years ago, my partner and I found a need for crafts that could be completed by the mentally and physically challenged," writes Kathy Walker. "With an increase of group homes in the community came an increased need for recreational activities. Simple yet functional projects that met these requirements were virtually unheard of."

In response to this need, Kathy teamed up with a friend, Jacki Widenor, to start Concord Country Workshop. Together, they designed several unique wood and ceramic projects that could be completed within a few hours—games, gifts and decorations. Then they began to teach classes throughout their area, working with various organizations. Before long they were serving nearly 125 clients.

"The classes have been extremely successful," says Kathy, "and the people we work with look forward to doing our projects." Many group homes in the area use our three-to-six-week classes, and we were recently hired as consultants to teach crafts to the handicapped."

onstrate old-time craft skills such as spinning, weaving, woodcarving, blacksmithing, candlemaking, pottery making, basketry, cornhusk crafts, tatting, lacemaking, folk painting, dollmaking and so on. Product sales may or may not be part of such arrangements. Subscribe to show-listing periodicals to learn about such events months in advance.

Mary Lou Highfill has built a business around the sale of sunbonnets made from old bonnet patterns in her collection and from drawings she has made of bonnets in museums and historical societies. Her growing reputation as an expert on sunbonnets has naturally led her into public speaking on her favorite topic. Her programs are popular at historical societies, museums, churches, heritage societies and reenactment events. (See sidebar, "Still Going at 85!")

9. *Become a desktop publisher.* Affordable computers and desktop-publishing software have made it easy for the average individual to become a publisher. Many artists and crafters now use their desktop publishing systems to produce calendars, notecards or greeting cards featuring photos or artist drawings of their original creations. Others elect to publish their own patterns and designs instead of offering them to a publisher.

Many self-publishers market their books by mail, aggressively pursuing publicity in craft and consumer magazines. Margaret Huber has been creating floral keepsakes since 1987. After customers showed an interest in creating their

Still Going at 85!

The nice thing about craft work is that age works to your advantage. Take Lyndall "Granny" Toothman, for example. At age 85, this West Virginia native is still spending four days most weeks demonstrating spinning and weaving at the Kentucky Highlands Museum in Ashland, Kentucky. She has made a fascinating life and a good living as a weaver, spinner and teacher. Her specialty is spinning dog hair and as she demonstrates her craft, she spins a few yarns on the side. "I've been able to spin the hair of all breeds of dogs except one," she jokes," and that's the Mexican Hairless."

In her last letter to me, Granny wrote, "I'm still doing fairly well, but I'm beginning to feel my age. I'm still doing festivals, however. In February, I made my seventeenth appearance at the Strawberry Festival in Florida, and in October, I will be driving to Tennessee to make my fourteenth appearance at the Appalachian Homecoming."

When Granny turned 80, she surprised a lot of people by buying a spiffy red-and-white sports van. Even more surprising to most is that she continues to travel alone, camping all the way. Once, after she had driven to Georgia to do the Foxfire Festival, Granny wrote, "An *old woman* of 70 asked me if I drove when I told her I had come alone. I told her no, the Lord was doing the driving, I was just holding the wheel."

own, she wrote and published a 36-page illustrated book titled *How to Preserve Your Bridal Bouquet*. (See sidebar, "Start Small, Keep Growing!")

Maybe you'd like to publish a collection of how-to tips on your favorite art or craft topic, or compile a directory of all the special supply sources you've spent years tracking down. (The more specialized, the better.) Such information is very easy to sell through classified ads and press releases to periodicals in the arts and crafts community. For example, Adele Patti of The Front Room Publishers in Clifton, New Jersey, has built a good homebased business around the publication of crafts marketing directories that she updates annually and advertises in craft periodicals.

Perhaps you've thought about doing a newsletter. Historically, small news-

Start Small, Keep Growing!

Mary Mulari has been helping women discover their creativity since 1983, when she first offered to share her ideas in a community education class. The overwhelming response she received encouraged her to develop many new designs and before long, she had enough for a book. Since she had no publisher connections, she took a chance and published *Designer Sweatshirts* herself, cautiously printing only 300 copies. It wasn't a fancy book—pages were hand-lettered and illustrated with designs and sewing directions—but all 300 copies sold within two months. Encouraged, Mary published a second book.

Now, with several book titles and thousands of copies in print, Mary has a large national following that enables her to print 5,000 books at a time. By helping others learn how to create designer sweatshirts, she has helped herself to financial success. A guest on several television shows, Mary presents seminars across the United States and has recently produced her own instructional videotape based on her first book. Although Mary now uses a computer in her publishing business, she continues to letter and illustrate her books by hand. "This has become my trademark," she says, "and the response to it has been very positive."

letter publishers do not make much money because there are just too many publishers vying for subscribers, but the promotional value of a newsletter cannot be denied. This is a good way to keep in touch with your customers and do some "soft selling" of new products or publications. If you're not interested in starting your own subscription-newsletter, consider offering your writing services and desktop publishing skills to local art, craft and needlework shops and other businesses that might like a newsletter for their customers.

10. *Offer marketing or business services.* Creative people often wish they had someone to do their selling for them. You might represent several artists or craftspeople at major trade shows, or act as a sales representative to present their work to retail outlets. A sales commission of from 15 to 20 percent is common.

Many crafters also need help in designing business stationery, cards, brochures and other promotional materials that could be done on a desktop publishing system. Others need bookkeeping or mail list services, photography, slide presentations, ads or logos designed, press releases written, etc.

As you continue your efforts to acquire the necessary skills and information needed for a profitable homebased business, remember to step back from time to time to give yourself and your ideas a critical analysis. Make sure you're building on an idea or concept others have already proven successful. If not, you may end up wasting valuable time and money pursuing a dream that can't be realized. Not every hobby can be turned into a profitable business, but this does not mean that you cannot profit from what you know by doing something else. All you have to do is have the courage and good sense to make necessary changes.

If you ultimately decide that your favorite art or craft activity is never going to be very profitable, consider getting interested and involved in something else related to it. Remember that you are capable of loving more than one thing, and with time and experimentation, you may find you have enormous talent for some other art or craft in which your moneymaking opportunities will be far greater.

Serendipity and Creativity

Now that you've seen how other people have accomplished their goals, I hope you feel more confident and adventurous, and are ready to capitalize on your creativity. As the creator of the Bartles & Jaymes commercials once said: "Creativity is just doing what other people don't do. We have two choices in life. We can dissolve into the mainstream, or we can be distinct. To be distinct, we must be different; we must strive to be what no one else but us can be."

If you make things with your hands, you are a creative person whether you can design original projects or not. In the book *Living Your Life Out Loud,* the authors state, "The difference between creative people and those who are not is purely a matter of self-perception. If you perceive yourself as creative, you are, and if you don't, you won't be." If you're striving to unlock your natural creativity, this book will help.

The one thing all creative people have in common, says PBS host Bill Moyers, is that they are infinitely curious. "They never take for granted what they're told. They take risks, take advantage of the unexpected and are not fearful of being wrong."

Moyers's research shows that, often, creative people have been touched and moved by another person at some point in their lives. "That person has communicated to them a sense of 'you matter' and made them aware of their own intrinsic worth as a human being."

The desire to do something special with your skills and talents and a positive "I can do it" attitude will take you in exciting new directions if you can only muster the courage to try something new. As a crafter once pointed out to me, "Some people weakly try positive thinking and when it doesn't work, they become discouraged, stop believing and quit. My favorite word is serendipity," she said. "To me, serendipity is the plan, idea or event that unfolds while making other plans, only to find the accidental happening better than the intended."

This word also means to "dip" into life with "serenity." I've learned that serendipity walks hand in hand with creativity, often playing a role in the creation of a new and original piece of craft work. Serendipitous things also happen where business is concerned. For example, you might set out to get publicity in one place, but through a chance meeting with someone, you will get it in another. Or you may try to market one way and in the process accidentally discover a new way that works better.

A serendipitous connection with one special person could literally change your life, so always stay open to the idea that life will naturally lead you in new directions when you least expect it. You will get involved in one thing, sometimes accidentally, and before you know it, you'll be off and running in a new direction, meeting new people, doing new things, achieving new goals. You will find yourself zigzagging here and there until one day—*voila!* You suddenly realize you've found work you want to do for the rest of your life. And how exciting it is when you also learn that you may be able to make a living doing what you love most.

In closing, I would like to share a success secret that took me far too many years to discover. Remember to thank God for the artistic and creative talents with which you have been blessed, and don't hesitate to lean on the Lord when you need support and encouragement in either your personal or home-business life. From experience I have learned that if we will simply put our faith in God and give Him an opportunity to work in our lives, He will lead us in the right direction and reveal wondrous things we never could have discovered on our own.

■ ■ ■

Well, I hate to say it, but it's time to say goodbye. It's hard for me to end a book because there is always so much more I want to include. Regrettably, publishers have limitations on the size of their books and I've already exceeded the limit for this one. By the time this book is published, however, I will be nearly finished with another book of interest to artists and crafters. If you would like to be notified of its publication, or if you want to write for any other reason, please use the coded address below. I am particularly interested in hearing from readers who have profited from specific ideas in this book as well as those who have developed creative marketing strategies not mentioned in this book. Meanwhile, I hope you will stay in touch with me by reading my monthly "Selling What You Make" column in *Crafts Magazine*.

Due to the large volume of mail I receive, I cannot correspond personally with all my readers, but I promise to read every letter I receive and I will immediately acknowledge all reader mail with an information package about my other home-business and crafts marketing books and reports.

Barbara Brabec
HFP Feedback
P.O. Box 2137
Naperville, IL 60567

 *Recommended Reading*

The Basic Guide to Selling Arts & Crafts by James Dillehay (Warm Snow Publishers). Includes a chapter on spin-off opportunities that discusses teaching workshops, selling supplies, opening a retail store, producing craft shows, writing and becoming a sales rep.

Crafting for Dollars—How to Establish & Profit from a Career in Crafts by Sylvia Landman (Prima). Includes chapters on designing, consulting, teaching, writing and self-publishing.

● *Creative Cash—How to Sell Your Crafts, Needlework, Designs & Know-how,* 5th edition, by Barbara Brabec (Barbara Brabec Productions). Includes chapters on needlework and design markets, marketing kits and related products, speaking, teaching, writing and self-publishing.

The Complete Guide to Writing Non-Fiction by the American Society of Journalists and Authors (Writer's Digest). One chapter, "Writing about Hobbies and Crafts," includes Barbara's advice and tips on how to write for hobby-craft markets.

Homemade Money—How to Select, Start, Manage, Market and Multiply the Profits of a Business at Home by Barbara Brabec (Betterway Books). Includes detailed information on copyrights and a chapter on how to diversify any business through writing, self-publishing, teaching, speaking and consulting.

How to Find Your Mission in Life by Richard N. Bolles (Ten Speed Press).

How to Write a Manual by Elizabeth Slatkin (Ten Speed Press).

Living Your Life Out Loud—How to Unlock Your Creativity and Unleash Your Joy by Salli Rasberry and Padi Selwyn (Pocket Books).

Newsletters from the Desktop: Designing Effective Publications with Your Computer by Robert C. Parker (Vantana Press).

Index